Dear Bar

Thanks for ... and all the rest of your support

[signature]

PURRS
& Promises

PURRS & Promises

by
Deanna Chesnut

PURRS & *Promises*

Copyright ©2016 by Deanna Chesnut

All rights reserved.

ISBN-13: 978-1539184997

ISBN-10: 1539184994

All rights reserved. No part of this book may be reproduced, stored in a retrieval system, or transmitted by any means without the written permission of the author.

All images, including cover photo of Mr. Bear, are copyrighted to the author, Deanna Chesnut, and may not be reproduced without permission.

DEAR READERS

This memoir has been a lifetime in the making and six years in the writing, interrupted by a recalcitrant computer and life in general, but it is here at last. Before you begin reading, here are some clarifications.

The incidents and characters recorded in *Purrs & Promises* are factual and as true as I could make them as filtered through time and memory, with one exception: all human character names are pseudonyms and some physical descriptions and details have been changed to protect identities. All the Animal Communicators named are actual persons who have reviewed and approved the sections that discussed their involvement.

The journey from that farm girl to the woman who now totally admires, respects, and loves cats was long and difficult, as you will read. I believe that the animal communications recorded herein did, and will, help lead the way to a mutual understanding and respect of those with whom we humans share the planet.

My hope and purpose in writing this work was to encourage humans to open-mindedly consider the *possibilities* and imagine the enormous potential in interspecies communication. Further, I encourage all caretakers to investigate animal communication and the use of flower essences to enhance their lives and that of any animals in their care.

My wish is twofold: first, that you enjoy reading about my wonderful cats and the magic, mystery, and mayhem we participated in; secondly, that you will be inspired, uplifted, and eager to share the information on the animal care suggestions and the possibilities of animal communication with your family and friends and especially with any of those working in animal rescue.

Sincerely,

Deanna Chesnut (a/k/a Purrfect Talker)

Disclaimer: I do not engage in animal communication for the public. I do not sell any products mentioned in Purrs & Promises.

I have worked peripherally in several areas of the medical field. I have a minor in Psychology, but no other degree in traditional medicine, human or animal. I have explored, taken classes, researched madly thanks to the Internet, and personally experienced many fields of study in alternative healing modalities, but I do not currently have a consulting practice.

All information in the book is based upon my personal experiences and knowledge and presented to the reader as subjects to pursue for further insight and clarification through their own personal research. Any opinions expressed herein should not be considered "authoritative" other than my sharing of personal experiences. I swear on Bear's soul that every word is true, as near as I can remember.

CONTENTS

Front Matter i
Chapter 1 FELINE RETROGRADE 1
Chapter 2 LOVE STRUCK 9
Chapter 3 HOME ON THE RANGE 15
Chapter 4 TREASURE HUNT 20
Chapter 5 BECOMING CAT MOM 26
Chapter 6 ONE BY ONE 34
Chapter 7 CURSE OR KARMA 39
Chapter 8 GOING BUGGY 43
Chapter 9 HAPPY HOLIDAYS 48
Chapter 10 LITTLE BROTHER 56
Chapter 11 NAMES GAMES AND FAMILY 63
Chapter 12 TRAGEDY 71
Chapter 13 CATAPULT 78
Chapter 14 MUST LOVE CATS 82
Chapter 15 GOOD ENERGY 89
Chapter 16 MULTIPLE OCCUPANCY 95
Chapter 17 PSYCHICALLY SPEAKING 100
Chapter 18 PROMISES 106
Chapter 19 THE AVOCADO TREE 112
Chapter 20 MAGIC FLOWERS 121
Chapter 21 ANIMAL TALK 130

Chapter 22 LIVING THE DREAM	136
Chapter 23 KING OF THE DOGS	144
Chapter 24 CRAWLIES & CREEPIES	149
Chapter 25 THE MYSTERY OF BELLA	154
Chapter 26 THE CROSS MY HEART PROMISE	163
Chapter 27 COMMUNION	168
Chapter 28 THANKSGIVING	175
Chapter 29 DEPARTURE	179
Chapter 30 KITTY GAMES	184
Chapter 31 THE BLUE BLANKIE	191
Chapter 32 THE HUMAN ZOO	197
Chapter 33 HOUSE OF STRAW	206
Chapter 34 CHAOS & CONFUSION	210
Chapter 35 LIFE CHANGES	218
Chapter 36 MAYHEM & A MIRACLE	223
Chapter 37 THE OLD BOY & THE GOOD GIRL	231
Chapter 38 BEAR'S MASTERPIECE	236
Chapter 39 LOVE YOU	241
Chapter 40 THE GREATEST GIFT	245
Chapter 41 CHILD OF MY HEART	251
Chapter 43 THE FOREVER PROMISE	254
Back Matter	*257*

MEOWS & PURRS

A huge thanks to those who encouraged me to write this memoir and to those who stood by me through my frustration of translating my life experiences into a readable manuscript. I include special gratitude to the following:

All four-legged, finned, and feathered souls who came forth as my teachers and guides,

My spirit and animal guides, psychic interpreters, and the angels who set up all those "coincidences" in spite of my stubbornness,

The amazing Animal Communicators, including, in order of appearance, Val Heart, Jeri Ryan, Ph.D., Leta Worthington, and Carla Meeske, who have taught, counseled, encouraged and supported the seekers in the field of Animal communication. These teachers bravely risk "coming out" in order to build bridges connecting humans and animals in love, compassion, and understanding in spite of "professional" naysayers who claim it's not possible,

A special thanks to Carol Wright, "our" communicator and figurative hand-holder. Had it not been for her, I would never have understood the responsibility that comes with being a caretaker/companion and cat-mom to my cats, who all accepted her without question and spoke their souls to her, as I did. She has been a light in our lives for over fifteen years,

The many amazing teachers who came into my life to lead me into new realms of knowledge, wonder, and healing, especially "Sunny," a graceful soul and a truly gifted healer. She yanked me off my conventional path, led me into holistic healing, and made me "feel the energy,"

To Jeb Seibel, Organizer of the Original Cedar Park Writers' Meet-Up Group, my first critique group, for his continued encouragement, friendship, and support,

To the members of my Ladies In Writing Meet-Up Group who gave up their Saturday afternoons for four years to support, to encourage, and to reveal their deepest selves through their writings and critiques,

And, not least but last in the publishing process, thanks to Barbara Hodge, the cover artist, and to Tory Abel for her help and support.

Most of all, my undying gratitude for all eternity to my wonderful, amazing, compassionate, loving cats—my teachers, who comprised my interspecies family—Sami, Bear, Bella, and later to Tucker, Birdie, and Gracie, without whom this book, and my life, would have been boring and characterless.

Kitty kisses and head bonks to you all from,

Deanna Chesnut (a/k/a Purrfect Talker)

Cat-Mom

For more information about the author: www.dchesnut.com
For the All-About-Cat Care Blog: www.purrfecttalker.com

Chapter 1
FELINE RETROGRADE

Southeastern Nebraska, 1950s. I didn't hate cats—I had never seen any—until I was six. Soon after that, I learned to fear, loathe, and despise them.

From birth, I had lived with my grandparents and my mother in a small Nebraska town, pop. 6,000 humans, quite a few dogs, and, as far as I knew, zero cats. My parents divorced when I was a baby; my father was career Navy and never an active part of my life. Mother worked a split shift as a telephone operator, usually gone before I woke up and, at my child-appropriate bedtime, still working.

Mother and I lived with her parents. Grandpa, a Prussian immigrant who became a US citizen in 1921, worked at blue-collar jobs six days a week. On the seventh day, in summer, he rested by growing beautiful flowers and the vegetables that Grandma preserved in Mason jars for our winter eating. In winter, he built things in his workshop. I helped by playing with the curly wood shavings, putting them in my hair and pretending they were real curls. I can't remember ever hearing my Grandfather's voice although Mother insists he spoke English.

Grandmother took care of me, taking on the role of mother. She seldom talked because of a neurological disease, tic douloureux, also called the "suicide disease" which causes excruciating jaw pain. Any slight breeze or loud sound could cause her jaw to visibly vibrate, and she would need to go to bed. She also had a weeping sore about the diameter of a pint jar above her ankle, an ugly varicose vein condition. When the pain got too bad, she used a kitchen chair to rest her knee on and hobbled around the kitchen, lifting the chair for each step.

My job was to play quietly in the house. I wasn't allowed to play with the neighbor kids when Grandma couldn't keep an eye on me. I do remember the singing/shrieking of her canary, the ticking of her grandfather clock, and listening to soap operas and her Sunday church services on the radio. Other than that, my memories of the house were of its silence and the plop, stop, plop, stop of her kitchen chair as she cooked dinner, did Saturday baking, or ironed other people's clothes for a small fee.

When I was five, I had my tonsils out. Mother was feeding me ice cream and reading me a story when a big man came into the hospital room and handed me a box of miniature books. Then they left.

The next time I saw him, he and Mother had just gotten married. If there was an explanation or a warning of the huge change about to occur in my life, I either had no understanding of it, or have forgotten it since. They took me to a very little house in the country, an hour away from Grandma and Grandpa. I was terribly lonely after the abrupt relocation. I had no siblings or cousins my age, and the only two other kids around were years younger. We lived there for a few months in that tiny house, a converted gas station, with no inside bathroom and only cold running water in the kitchen.

Then we moved to a two-story farmhouse, one of only four along a mile long gravel road connecting to a highway three miles from town. Temperatures varied in that region from +100°F to -20°F. This house, probably built before the turn of the century, was awful. We pumped our water from a well and hauled it to the house. Our toilet was down the hill—an outhouse with a hole in the wooden seat covered with hoarfrost, freezing in winter, and stinking and filled with creepy-crawlies in the summer. Both a small stove in the living room and a big old cook stove in the kitchen burned cobs and coal to furnish heat for the house. Any air-conditioning came in, along with the bugs, through the open windows. The two upstairs bedrooms had no heat. There was electricity for lighting, for cooking and for the small refrigerator.

One day I was wandering around getting acquainted with my new home. The landscape was depressing—flat, barren, with dried-up brown weeds wherever I looked, no color anywhere except for the red of my stepfather's tractor and the brownish-red paint on the big two-story barn. I noticed a white, black, and brown mound near the road, at the end of our long gravel driveway, too far away for me to really see what it was. I thought it might be an animal but it sat so still, if it was an animal, I thought it might be dead.

The man I was to call Daddy was standing next to his Allis-Chalmers tractor. I walked over to ask him my question. I had to look way up the legs of his blue denim overalls, past the bib, and up to his stern face. He looked even taller with the blue and white striped farm cap on, much taller than my round Grandpa who had a ring of silky white hair on his head that I got to comb.

"Daddy"—the word came out hard—"what is that animal out there?"

"It's a cat. Don't you know what a cat is?" His voice was as big as he was, and gruff. He didn't sound like he wanted to talk to me. He looked like that cowboy in the movies, that man named John Wayne. I already knew he didn't like me. I wasn't sure how I knew that, but I did. And if an adult didn't like a child, it must be the child's fault I reasoned, though I had tried to be very good.

"No. I've never seen a real cat before. There's a picture of one in my reader. But it's black and all bushy." I looked down at the ground, feeling embarrassed that I didn't know about this cat thing.

"That one over there's a calico. Calicos are girl cats. Stay away from her. She's wild and mean, and she'll bite you."

Disappointed, I returned to exploring this new place, looking for something to do. There were none of Grandpa's pretty flowers, no bushes, and no green trees. The few scrawny trees that were around stood dark and stark against layers of heavy gray clouds lining the uninterrupted flat horizon. They had no pretty leaves, no horizontal branches to climb or to hang a swing from, just skinny branches bristly with pine needles. This farm, my new home, was ugly. I hated it.

The cat stayed hunched down like a loaf of bread for most of that day, immobile, watching us. I watched it back for a while, then wandered away. Later, when I looked again, it had disappeared.

There wasn't much for a lone kid to do without any kids nearby except a lot of chores. Part of my job was to take the bugs off the potatoes and put them in smelly kerosene to kill them. And I played with the bright little orange lady bugs and sang to them to "fly away home."

We didn't have television, just a one-station radio with static that was clear or not depending on how bad the weather was. Mother couldn't drive, so the highlight of every week was Saturday evening when we all went to town. There I got to choose six books from the library and then go to the double feature movie, usually a Western. The highlight of every weekday happened when I could listen to *The Lone Ranger, Buster Brown,* or *Lassie* if I got my chores done in time. They always were.

Finally, my first spring on the farm came, and life got more interesting though there still were few trees, no flowers, just the green of weeds and the vegetable garden.

We had baby pigs but trying to make friends was scary because their mothers weighing four times what I did, were always on guard. The hens, too, were painfully protective, ready to peck or to claw me when I went to gather their eggs.

Occasionally, a cow would refuse to nurse her new-born calf. I would have to teach it to drink from a tin bucket with a rubber nipple extending from its side. I dipped my fingers into the milk, extended them to the calves that would latch on and enthusiastically tickle my fingers as they sucked off the milk. They would then follow my tasty digits to the bucket's teat where they could suck to get real cow's milk from the bucket. When they began sucking, I could have my fingers back

Once in awhile a stray dog would show up, usually dumped by people from town on Sunday drives. They would stay awhile and then disappear. They weren't allowed in the house, so they didn't make very good playmates. Mother had gotten a cocker spaniel puppy for me for that first Christmas after they married, but it became my stepfather's one-man dog, following him out into the fields every day. He didn't treat it well, rough-housing with it, even hitting or kicking at it, but for some reason the dog doted on him and had nothing to do with me or mother.

The only live things around small enough to play with were insects. Caterpillars, daddy longlegs, and worms became my friends, but my constant companion was loneliness that descended so heavily one day I disregarded Daddy's advice.

The calico cat had moved into our barn, and now, a couple of months later, I found her stretched out in the dirt, sunning, in front of the barn door. As I walked toward her, she suddenly bounded up and lunged toward me, ears flattened, teeth bared, spitting and growling out a hideous sound. Her back arched, and she went up on her tiptoes, her bushy tail fluffed out like the Halloween cats in my picture book. I had no doubt this creature wanted to kill me. Terrified, I turned and ran toward the house and safety. I never forgot how much she had scared me!

I had other outside chores—gathering eggs, hauling wood and coal to the house for heating and cooking, and carrying skimmed milk out to the pigs. Twice a day, Daddy milked the cows and then dumped the milk into a machine called a separator that sat in an enclosed porch attached to the house. This machine stood much taller than my head and had a big round stainless steel bowl on top of it. With the whole milk in the bowl, he turned the switch, and the liquid whirled around and around inside the container, centrifugal force separating the heavy cream from the rest of the milk. The cream poured out one spout, and the skimmed milk out the other. We stored the cream in ten-gallon metal milk cans before selling it as a "cash crop" to the Farmer's Union Co-op where it was bottled and sold to stores or turned into butter. The skimmed, no-fat milk was worthless—not considered fit for drinking by humans, nor for selling. After the evening milking, I was to carry the buckets of watery, bluish-colored liquid from the house to the pig pen and dump it into the troughs for the hogs. And for the cats to steal what they could. That's when my terror of cats really accelerated.

The wire handles of the buckets dug into my palms and pulled at my arms as I stepped out of the separator room onto the cement stoop. Two steps, four at most, and the cats would be on me like the locust plagues that the preacher had talked about on Grandma's radio and which had given me nightmares. With a cacophony of screams and growls, the feral cats swarmed onto their one provider of sustenance—me. They fought and shoved, growling, biting and clawing. As I stood there and looked down, all I could see were the furry bodies around my feet, like swirling floodwaters. I was unable to take a step through the churning mass, afraid I would fall over them and be attacked. The kittens leapt to the bucket rim, pulled themselves up and then fell down into the bucket, fighting to not drown. Cats hung from the pail trying to stretch their heads inside to lap at the milk. Most simply climbed me as the most direct route to food, dagger claws digging through my trousers to my legs, slashing at my hands, doing anything— *anything*—to get to the milk. Often, I would leave the buckets and escape, coming later to take what little was left out to the hogs. Every day was the same, varying only by the number of desperate felines so starved they would even approach a human. I was terrified every single day for the six years we lived on that farm.

There was one other incident that caused my loathing and hatred of felines to explode and coalesce into my vow to hate cats forever. A few years after we had moved there, I awoke in the stillness of a spring night to horrible shrieks and animal screams of agony, a not uncommon sound in the rural night. I had overheard my stepfather tell my mother several days before that the cats were mating. I didn't know what that meant, but from the sounds I had heard, I decided it must be quite a gruesome thing.

The next morning, Mother asked me to get a jar of tomato juice for breakfast from the root cellar under the house where we stored all our canned goods. To get there, I had to go out onto the front porch and lift the wooden trap door that was part of the floor, then climb down the uneven earthen steps into a cave-like space under the house. There was little light that penetrated the blackness until I crossed to the center of the room and flailed about in the darkness to find the switch on the dangling light bulb. I imagined there were many things lurking in the shadows that might jump out and get me. The smell of dank earth added to my fear as bugs scuttled away or crunched beneath my shoes while I slapped my way through countless spider webs. But I was dutiful, so I left the kitchen on my errand.

I went out the screen door and stopped abruptly, horrified. There, on the gray-painted porch floor, was the front half of a black and white, almost fully-grown cat, laid out like a sacrifice. The back half of the body from below the ribs was gone, as though it had been sliced in two, leaving only a bloody stump where the bottom half should have been. Even at my young age, I remember thinking that there should have been lots of blood as happened when Mom chopped the head off a chicken, but there wasn't any. Either the cat had been killed elsewhere or the blood that should have stained the boards had been licked away.

"Mama! There's a cat ..." I screamed, then bent over and tried to vomit off the porch, realizing what the wails and screams of the night before had meant.

"Arthur!" I heard her calling. "Come here!" My stepfather came, and the next time I had to go out that door, the half-a-cat had disappeared.

Later, I overheard him talking to my mother. We were at the supper table, and I was invisible, as usual, as a common saying at the time was "Children should be seen, not heard." It was preached at me regularly.

"Got too many cats. Shot 'bout thirty today, at least. Lost count after a while. That cat on the porch? Probably killed by another male, maybe its father. Males kill their own get sometimes so they can't take over their females and their territory. Course, he was prob'ly hungry, too."

"Well, it was really horrible to see that. But they've certainly kept the rats and mice away," Mother said.

"Yep, grain bins and barn all cleaned out. But there's just too many. When it gets so bad they're killing like that... gotta do somethin'."

"How did we get so many so fast?" asked Mother.

"Each cat whelps a litter two, three times a year starting once they get to be five or six months old. Litters can be four, even seen eight a couple of times. Wish my cows multiplied so fast. Ha."

My arithmetic skills weren't good enough to figure it out, but I knew that was *a lot* of cats. Their numbers had decimated the supply of any kind of cat food—mice, rats, snakes, birds, even the chicken eggs when they could get them. While the cows got the grain we didn't sell, the cats got only what they could catch, having to find anything, anywhere, with nothing but that thin-as-water, leftover skim milk from us.

"How many are still here?" Mother asked.

"Prob'ly more'n fifteen running around yet. That old queen is still out there, ran off before I could shoot her, belly swinging from side to side. She's ready to pop again. Did find a couple of new litters, put 'em in a gunny sack, and threw 'em in the pond. Pond's drying up, though, water wasn't very deep. Guess they drowned."

I heard and was glad he had killed them. I hated them. Mostly. There was one tiny part of me that felt bad for anything that was starving, but after the "cat-abolism" episode, I fiercely despised and hated all cats. I prayed every night, asking God to take me away from my stepfather, from the farm, back to Grandma and Grandpa's, to at least make the cats go away, or to give me some brothers and sisters. The only answer was silence.

My stepfather had never seemed to get over his initial dislike of me. His interaction with me was confined to making fun of me or telling me what else I had done wrong. "Hey, Little Beaver" he would say, laughing at my sticking-out front teeth, or, "Boys don't make passes at girls who wear glasses." Mostly though, and thankfully, he ignored me. Just like God.

Within a few years, the rains quit, and the prairie winds blew the good topsoil away. A great years-long drought made all the crops die. We saved and re-used everything until there was nothing left to reuse.

Eventually, the crops were so small we couldn't feed the pigs and cows, and we had to sell them as all the other farmers were doing—they were almost worthless; then we ate all the chickens. At the end of my sixth grade in school, we moved to town, leaving the farm, and the cats, behind. One thing I didn't leave on the farm was my hatred and loathing of all things feline.

Town life was a lot easier but not much more fun. I was stigmatized as a "farm kid" and poor. At age fourteen, I began working after school and on Saturdays at the city library, making twenty-five cents an hour while the carhops were making fifty cents an hour. After paying for school supplies and some of my clothes, there wasn't enough left for bus trips or Pep Club dues, so I didn't do those things.

The answer to my prayer for siblings was finally answered, a little late; I was sixteen when my half-sister was born. I adored her and spent all the time I could with her in between working, classes, homework, and housework. Grandfather had died, and Grandmother had come to live with us while we were still on the farm. Mother was working again. My stepfather, without his beloved farming, was seldom home, working temporary physical labor jobs or "hanging out" at the pool hall. By now, I was cautious, responsible, steady, negative, even old in my attitude that was mostly a reflection of my beloved grandmother's. I was runner-up for a college scholarship—almost good enough, but not quite. I gave up on my only dream—of going to college—at least for awhile.

Two weeks after graduation, I borrowed some money from my grandmother and boarded the train with all my worldly possessions in two suitcases. I had been serendipitously hired in the local station as a teletypist for the Rock Island Railroad's Chicago office. I had the name of a place to stay, but knew no one. I was scared, with only enough knowledge of social graces and manners to know I didn't have any. I didn't have much knowledge of the world in general and especially not the world of a big city.

Within two weeks, I had fallen in love—not with a man—but with the Windy City. Things I had never known existed—plays, museums, massive buildings, ethnic neighborhoods—all added color to that black and white world I had left behind. I was in awe at the intermixing of street sounds of foreign languages, and the smells of exotic foods, even the smell of the smog on my walks to work. I could spend all day in one department store—Marshall Fields, Carson Pirie Scott—each big enough to contain every store back in that town I had come from. I was busy learning and doing things every chance I had, exhilarated with public transportation that gave me an incredible feeling of empowerment, self-sufficiency, and freedom for the first time in my life. Every weekend was a new adventure—China Town, the Art Museum, the Planetarium. I was finding friends my age, though most were much more sophisticated than I was. Every day I felt like a kid at a circus, a county fair, and a party all rolled into one.

I still desperately wanted to go to college though. I wanted a home, a husband, kids—the stuff every woman was supposed to want. But I also wanted to travel, and to do something important. The Vietnam Conflict was raging, and the military promised training, college money, and travel. I joined the Air Force for those reasons and for adventure, but only got stationed in Montgomery, Alabama. After my discharge, I moved to Anchorage, Alaska, following a friend who raved about the beauty there.

After two years, I decided I wanted out of the frozen north; I had just become unengaged. I chose to move to Dallas, Texas, because it met my main priority by then—warm weather—and because I had friends there. I never could have imagined how that destination choice would lead me down a path that would change my heart and soul and alter the direction of the rest of my life.

Chapter 2
LOVE STRUCK

Dallas, Texas, 1972. After getting settled in an apartment in Dallas, I dug out my address book and called a friend. We hadn't seen each other since our Air Force days had ended three years prior, but we had kept in touch through those ubiquitous Christmas letters that told little but spread any good news.

"Hey, Betty, it's Deanna."

"*Deanna? Where are you? Oh, say are you—are you in Dallas?*"

"I'm in Dallas!"

"What are you doing here?" I heard the astonishment and genuine welcome in her voice.

"I just got unengaged and have moved here. At least temporarily. Can we get toge... "

"Oh, wait, wait. Too much! Come to supper. Friday. Matt and I will pick you up. Oh, I know, just plan on staying all night. We can catch up then."

On Friday, Betty and her husband arrived in a two-seater Karman Ghia sports coupe. They stood close together during the introductions, their shoulders almost touching. She was the taller of the two, a solid, farm-girl aura about her, with an infectious laugh, springy curls, and freckles everywhere. Matt wore dark-framed glasses and had an unremarkable but pleasant face.

I stuffed myself into the suitcase-sized back seat for the hour's ride to the south side of the city. I noted that her Matt was growing a bald spot. Even though this was my first time to meet him, the three-way conversation flowed easily as we caught up with each other's lives.

"Matt is a school teacher, sixth grade this year. I'm a secretary at a law firm. No kids yet, of the two-legged variety anyway, but we are hoping."

Later, I would remember that clue, but I was too excited for it to register just then. "I just had to get out of Alaska; I felt too isolated and our engagement was off. I've been here three weeks, interviewed once, and have a job at an attorneys' office, too! I'm hoping to take college classes next semester," I told her.

"Why Dallas?"

I laughed. "Mostly because it's warm! You guys are here, and I have another friend here who I went to school with. Seemed like as good a place as any."

The conversation didn't lag any time during the hour drive. When Matt drove their Karmann Ghia Volkswagen up to the curb at their house, the first thing I saw were two glowing orbs in the deep darkness of the gutter. As I was trying to unpack myself from the sardine seat, I watched the fiery gold circles moving toward us, getting closer, and bigger, and then a hated form materialized. Reaching Betty, it stopped and sat down. I felt panic rising and readied myself to jump over the car if the thing moved any closer to me. As I watched, Betty swooped down, picked it up, and cradled it in her arms.

"This is Princess," she pronounced, making it sound like the next words would be 'our first born.' "Do you know much about cats?" Betty kissed Princess on the head, waved a Princess paw at me, and put her back on the ground.

Boy, did I ever know about cats! But I couldn't tell her what I knew. Not yet, anyway. I kept my mouth shut, not explaining why, how, or what I had known when about those miserable animals.

Betty didn't wait for an answer but turned and headed for the house. Head and tail held high, Princess led her up the walk toward the front door of a small white clapboard house, very similar to my grandparent's home built fifty years before. Matt was holding the door open. Surely the cat wasn't going to go *into* the house? Oh, no, oh no! She was going *in* the house!

I was speechless, trying to accept the fact that my friends apparently liked these hideous animals. I took a deep breath and followed them inside, listening to Betty point out the cat's attributes in the same voice as my other friends did when they asked me if I had ever seen a prettier/smarter/more talented child than theirs.

"Princess is a Siamese, a Seal Point, which is why her markings are so dark. The legend is that they were worshiped in Thailand. When the princesses bathed, they slipped their rings on the cat's tail; the kink at the tip kept the royal rings from sliding off and getting lost."

I decided not to volunteer anything about my cat views, but her eagerness to explain the feline's wonderfulness was giving me concerns about the rest of the night. How was I going to keep my mouth shut and not say the wrong words that might end our friendship? It was obvious Princess was their holy grail.

When Betty switched on the inside lights, I didn't really notice the living room; I was focused on the cat. I could see the unusual pattern and strange coloring of Princess—dark taupe-colored coat with shiny black ears and legs, a black face mask, and, yes, a black tail with a slight kink near the end. Her coat glowed in the lamplight, the black as shiny as patent leather shoes. Even as I backed away on the pretext of looking for a chair, my fingers itched to stroke the silkiness of that incredibly luxurious-looking, mink-like coat.

"She's a great cat," Matt chimed in, the proud papa. "She might sleep with you tonight."

Oh, no, god NO! How was I supposed to respond to that offer? My brain was racing. Why had it never come up in our many conversations over the years that they thought felines were the cat's meow, or that I hated them? *Oh! Please, please, no! I would leave now. No, I couldn't, my car wasn't here, and theirs was too small to sleep in. I had some change with me, maybe there was a bus stop nearby. Maybe I could borrow cab fare? What am I going to do?* "Act natural, be calm, don't let them see you're upset," my inner voice instructed. I took a big breath and stayed put.

Matt got down on the floor and put on a workman's leather glove. Princess leaped onto Glove, grabbing it with teeth and claws, growling in her fury. She jumped away, turned, and pounced again, nails extended. Glove grabbed her and rolled her onto her back. Princess wiggled free, leapt, and clutched her prey tightly, hind legs kicking, teeth imbedded in the leather.

I had known this was coming! I scrunched myself into the cushy chair, bad memories surfacing, hoping she wouldn't attack me. What was Matt *doing*? How could he be like that with her? What if she attacked his face?

Meanwhile, Betty was talking; I tried to focus on the catching-up conversation while I continued to watch Matt across the room, Princess still trying to mutilate her prey. Finally, Glove came off. Princess immediately settled down, panting, but otherwise sitting quietly on the floor next to Matt. I let out the breath I had been holding.

"She knows when it's play time and to never grab us with her claws," Matt assured me, apparently noticing the panicky look on my face. Then he scooped that damn cat up into his arms, cradled her belly-up, kissed her on the forehead, and sat down with her on the lumpy, not-quite-vintage, green velvet sofa.

I was getting the idea that head-kissing must give a cat owner great satisfaction. Princess now rested in his arms, limp, totally relaxed. I felt the stirrings of envy at the look of mutual adoration on Matt's face and in her cat-like posture and rumbling purr. Never, not ever, could I have conceived of a human being looking at an animal as something that precious.

"Supper's ready," Betty called. "Come and get it, or I'll give it to the hogs." No one could know Betty for long and not envision her next to a milk cow in a field of daisies—she exuded earthiness, self-confidence, warmth, and cheerfulness.

Matt and I headed for the kitchen. Princess followed and sat primly and quietly on the floor near the table, tail encircling her feet, all very formal and proper. No growling, begging, or jumping into the food plates. I was impressed. It was beyond my wildest imaginings that a cat could behave so perfectly, like a well-trained kid.

"How do you keep her from jumping on the table or stealing food?" I asked.

"We just treat her respectfully and show her what we want," said Matt. "We don't hit or punish her. And we're consistent. Having Princess is good training for having kids, and this is the way we will raise them."

We lingered over the chicken and real-mashed potatoes meal, the conversation still flowing, then headed for the living room. The furniture was old, not quite worn out, and I couldn't see any claw-shredded fabric anywhere. Matt flopped down on the couch. The minute his butt hit the cushion, Princess made a flying leap and curled up in his lap. He stroked and petted her in a soothing fashion, a man with a small animal resting on his denim-clad lap, quiet under his gentle hand. The Irish quotation, "True strength lies in gentleness" went through my mind. Matt was twenty times her weight and could have crushed her any number of ways, but it was obvious she trusted him totally.

I watched in fascination and felt the stirrings of envy at the contentment on his face as he ran his hand down her back, again and again, in long fluid strokes, almost hypnotizing me. I also felt my heartstrings tremble; I didn't have designs on Matt, but I wouldn't have minded a cuddle from him after seeing him this way, so loving and calm. I felt a stab of envy toward Betty.

"How did you get Princess?" I asked.

That was all it took—the rest of the conversation focused on the cat. "She's wonderful. She's funny, sweet, smart. She's our practice child." Praise kept coming, and I kept nodding my head as they described how precocious she was. I tried to keep an amazed smile on my face even as I tried not to show how ridiculous I thought such affection for a stupid animal was. This was *our* reunion, and, instead, all they wanted to talk about was that darn cat. I tried to still my feelings of resentment.

Finally, it was bedtime. I left the door to my room open at Betty's request—something to do with the heating and ventilation. I pulled all the covers, including an honest-to-goodness patchwork quilt, up to my chin, put the pillow over my face, and laid there imagining the cat skulking about, waiting for a chance to attack. I was sure she was waiting, waiting and listening, and would soon...

The sun woke me. I felt all snuggly in the great bed, like being in a big down pillow. I just stayed there, lying on my side, peaceful, luxuriating, half asleep—until I heard a rumbling coming from my arm. I opened my eyes and there was Princess, tucked next to my side, facing me, purring gently, eyes almost closed, in total trust. I felt my heart thawing, a melting, a wanting-to-hug-and-hold-tight feeling creeping in. I'd only experienced something like that a few times in my life, usually connected with someone's baby, or a puppy, or a tiny chick.

Tentatively, I reached out to touch this cat, remembering the teeth and claws of those others on the farm but compelled to risk it. She opened her sky-blue eyes wider. I used a finger to scratch under her chin. She purred louder and faster, lifting her head, giving more access to her vulnerable throat. Last night when she was attacking Glove, she had seemed larger, but she now looked defenseless—everything about her small and soft. Ah, behind the ears was a good place to scratch; she showed me so by arching her head into my palm. She gazed at me for a moment, got up slowly, still purring, and moved upwards along my body to the location of my heart. Then she reached out with a paw, aiming toward my face. I held very still, sure she would scratch me if I moved. Instead, she gently, softly, patted my cheek. The movement was so deliberate, yet so gentle, I felt like crying.

She patted my hatred away and then sank down on my chest, heart to heart. I tried to match my breath to her purrs. I dozed off, the comfort of the morning sun shining in on us and her little furry body warming mine filled me with peace. I knew, just like that, that I loved this cat—was in love with her. It happened just as fast as when my first teenage crush had turned around and smiled at me. Now, at that moment, there in a Dallas bedroom, I realized I had been wrong to spend my life hating all cats.

I left Betty and Matt's a different person than when I had gone there, learning new lifetime lessons in only one intimate evening. After that transformation, I wanted a cat of my own, a nagging want that continued for years. But there was never a good time, never a good place, never the right circumstances. I also still wanted that elusive college degree, a husband, and a family, but my life was anything but stable. There was no place in it for a cat.

Perhaps the idea of a pet represented my dreams of a family and a stable home, a sense of belonging, or perhaps Princess had uncovered my motherly and nurturing instincts. Whatever had happened, I wanted that same expression on my face that Matt had had on his when he held his Princess. I wanted something to adore that adored me.

I tucked the cat-dream aside but knew someday it would come true. I wanted, I craved—*a cat,* craved it with the same passion that I had hated those others on that farm so long ago.

Chapter 3
HOME ON THE RANGE

Austin, Texas. 1986. Less than six months after I had arrived in Dallas, a boyfriend from Alaska showed up, proposed, and I returned to the Land of the Midnight Sun, expecting to live happily ever after.

Our tumultuous relationship ended in divorce ten years later. I was undone, feeling unattached to anything, unsupported by the universe, and unable to formulate a new life plan that made sense. The *only* thing I was sure of was that I wanted to get a college degree. I reluctantly moved back to Nebraska for the in-state tuition, thousands cheaper than anywhere else. In many instances I was older than the professors, and the other students seemed very immature. *Had I been that young at twenty? Had I ever been that young? It didn't feel like it.*

I rushed through my required courses. After challenging some classes, three years and two diplomas later I was ready for the next phase of my life. But it was a curious thing. Never before had I had difficulty getting a job. Several times in my life, employers had sought *me* out. But I had now completed a Bachelor of Arts and a Master's in Adult Education, in a recession, and my shiny sheepskin couldn't get me even an interview for anything in Nebraska.

I had freedom now, but few choices. Nebraska felt like a wet T-shirt, so tight I could hardly breathe—I wanted out; staying wasn't a consideration. I still had a love-hate affair with beautiful Alaska, but even in-town living was expensive and hard with cold and darkness for months on end. Dallas and Chicago were too big. When I had lived in Dallas I had once visited a charming, picturesque little college town. I wanted to go back there. The travel information I could find said

Austin was thriving with new businesses. Further, they confirmed the warm-to-hot climate with sun much of the year, and the reasonable driving distances to big-city shopping and entertainment in Houston, Dallas, and San Antonio. I packed the car and headed south, toward the quaint little town of my memory, Austin-on-the-river.

When I passed the sign that said Austin City Limits, I was confused. Nothing looked familiar. Austin was no longer a charming little town on the banks of the Colorado; it was a city with a double decker freeway, high-rise buildings, and lots of traffic. How had it grown so swiftly in only… *fifteen years*? I traveled straight through town, trying to orient myself, to find something I remembered. At the southern end of the city, I checked into a motel, scoured the Want Ads and found a "female to share condo." I interviewed by phone the next day, and then went to see the place. I looked up at the slim, long-legged woman who answered my knock. The first words out of my mouth, even before hello, were, "I don't know if I'm moving in, but I'm never going out in public with you."

She of the beautiful hair, Nordic-blue eyes, and tall figure stood in her high heels and laughed. "Of course you will! Don't mind the heels, I used to model and flats hurt my feet. Hi, I'm Rose," she said, holding out her manicured hand and pulling me into the condo. We were not a matched set—she with four-foot-long legs and three-foot-long blond locks, and me with short, dark hair, only five foot four in my Birkenstock's, and my once-Marilyn Monroe measurements looking a little matronly lately. We sat down and talked. Despite our different looks, we had many of the same likes, dislikes, and values. When we got down to food, and each of us swore the only thing we didn't eat was Brussels sprouts, I handed over a deposit.

She volunteered to help me unload my car that had now been sitting for an hour in 100°F of direct August sun, fully loaded with all my belongings. I reached for the driver's door, expecting a blast of hot air. Instead, the second I opened the door, Rose jerked me backward.

"Stop! Look!" she pointed to the bugs scurrying around everywhere inside my car, especially on the driver's seat that held the leftover crumbs from my two-day trip to Texas.

"See those? They're fire ants. You have just been officially welcomed to Texas by one of our nasty species of wildlife. Watch out for these things! There's a reason they call them *fire* ants. Their bites burn like crazy, and you can die if you're allergic to them," she warned. "They move fast, and have a vicious bite that can get infected. Let's go back into the house and let them finish eating your leftovers."

I was a little embarrassed by the messy car but more horrified at the rapidity with which the ants had found a way to invade the closed car, and at the overwhelming number of moving brown specs swarming over the seat, the floor, and the dashboard. While grateful for her warning, I wished it had come a few seconds earlier. The ants had swiftly left the crumbs and charged at me faster than I could see them. I was trying to brush them off my legs and my hands but small red welts were already rising on my fingers and toes, burning like... fire. She helped me swipe them off and took me back into the house for treatment.

Except for the cats, even with all the animals and insects on the farm, none had been quite that vicious. It wasn't feeling like an auspicious beginning. While Rose was applying ice to the already blistering bites on my feet, she warned me to beware of fire ants, rattlesnakes, scorpions, brown recluse spiders, and Texas cowboys in silk shirts. *What was I doing here?*

Following instructions in the how-to book on job hunting, I put out word of my availability. In less than two weeks, I had a job offer in the Patient Education Department at the Austin State Hospital. Finally! My degrees were paying off, even if I was now making considerably less than I had been in my Alaska paralegal job.

I settled into a routine. Rose, a long-time Austinite, proved to be a great roommate who was glad to share her knowledge of the area, including translations of Texan.

"Burnet isn't burNET, it's BURN-it, like DURN-it, and it's pronounced Manshak not Manchaca like it's spelled. Don't use I-35, traffic is murder, just use Loop 1, no transport trucks allowed. It's also Mo-Pac, for the Missouri-Pacific train tracks it parallels. You can't really go directly east or west across Austin—there aren't any through roads. And Anderson is only Anderson east of Mo-Pac; Anderson west of Mo-Pac is Spicewood Springs. Spicewood is a town west of Austin, too, and the other "Anderson" is Anderson Mill. Those are pretty much the main roads that you need to know. Oh, and if someone in a pick-up tailgates you, don't put on the brakes, just take your foot off the accelerator and coast."

I had learned to drive at the age of 29 in Anchorage where a road heading south, or north, or west, or east pretty much stayed in that direction until you got to the mountains or the sea. As Rose rapidly explained all these need-to-know driving instructions, I felt overwhelmed, my brain still back working on BURN-it and Manshak—*what the heck was a Manshak... or a Manchaca?*

There were a few glitches in the housemate relationship, though. I had told her I was a homebody and wouldn't be happy with a lot of company. She said she always went out. Except for special events. Which occurred only once in a while. She promised.

The first of those events would be the Thanksgiving dinner, the only time she cooked for the family. She'd take care of it, and I wouldn't need to do anything except enjoy. Of course, I knew I'd help. Rose bought food for ten. She planned the elaborate, complete-with-hors d'oeuvres, wine, and turkey-and-fixings dinner. The day before Thanksgiving, a gorgeous crisp fall day, she and a friend decided to play hacky sack. The leaves were wet, her foot slipped, and she broke her arm. The following day, she supervised, I cooked. And did the dishwashing in the only-one-person-at-a-time condo kitchen. I hadn't hated it as much as I usually hated that type of event, but I was glad it was over. I had never gotten over my shyness in social situations.

Just under two weeks later, I arrived home from work to hear her "yes," and then she hung up the phone. She turned to me, all chirpy and cheerful. "Guess what! We're having company Friday night."

"Oh? Who?" I asked, feeling myself tense up a bit.

"Well, you know my Dad and Mom are involved in a student exchange program that they helped set up with high schoolers from Japan."

I held my breath and stood very still, waiting for whatever was coming.

"There are twelve students scattered around Austin at host families, and they want to have sort of a reunion, so they asked if they could have a week-end together."

She paused. I could hear my heart pounding in my ears. I wasn't comfortable with kids or with teen-agers, *wasn't sure about the Japanese.*

"Mom asked if we could host them from Friday night to Sunday morning. She says they won't be any trouble. This week-end."

I genuinely liked her mom and dad, but... "I can go to a motel," I offered, inspired.

As usual, Rose talked me into her way of thinking, explaining that it would be fun, the kids would be great, and, the clincher, her folks would appreciate it.

Two nights later, a dozen black-haired, pale-skinned, small-by-American standards, Japanese boys and girls arrived en masse at our door. They took over the second floor—Rose's large master bedroom and my smaller room. Rose and I stayed on the first floor. Literally. And we did sleep. The visitors were quiet, respectful, and other than occasional bursts of laughter as they watched the Japanese videos they had brought with them, made little noise. I mentally compared their actions with the giggling girls, flexing-their-muscles boys, boy-girl flirtations, and always-pushing-the-boundaries attitudes of American teens that I was familiar with—a difference between house cats and our scarey old barn cat.

In early December, Rose went to California. When she came back and immediately got sick, she decided she could not endure another one of Austin's notorious cedar fever seasons which inflicted itself, from November to March, onto every age and gender of allergic residents and had-never-been-allergic newcomers in central Texas. The season came complete with nose-dripping, sneezing, fever, coughing, and eye-watering suffering caused by pollen from the junipers, also known as cedar trees. She moved to California.

I found a small house and signed mortgage papers, and—I had a home of my own for the very first time! I was thrilled. The house represented stability, a den I could shut myself into to keep out the world, and a financial advantage. I was also thrilled because I could have a cat without worrying about "No Pets Allowed" and exorbitant pet deposits. Finally, decades after falling in love with Princess, I was ready to make my cat-dream come true. I'd adopt my own Princess. *As soon as I could find her.*

Chapter 4
TREASURE HUNT

Austin, Texas. August 1987. In the years since succumbing to Princess's gentle paw, I had become more and more animal-oriented and even the thought of cages filled with death-row animals was more than I could face; I would have to find another way to locate my little girl.

I couldn't afford a purebred, but I was sure someone had a nice little girl-cat to give away. But week after week, no cat of any kind appeared, not at my door, not in the newspapers, not from the community bulletin boards, not from word-of-mouth advertising. My original wish list read: *"Wanted: Free, six-week-old, tame, affectionate, healthy, smart, purebred, female Siamese"* but had grown shorter each month I had impatiently waited. Six months later, it now consisted of *"Cheap female cat, preferably Siamese."* I tried to be optimistic, but that optimism was burning as low as an old light bulb.

As I headed home from a long Saturday of intensive new-house-furniture shopping, I wasn't thinking about my cat-shopping list, just about how tired my feet were. Then I saw the blinking signboard in front of Palmer Auditorium announcing *Cat Show Today!* I felt a spurt of energy kick in when I read the words. I'd never heard of a cat show—dog show, yes, but—cat show? Did they race them? Have them do tricks? *Maybe they sold cats at a cat show!* The car behind me honked as I stomped on the brakes and made a sharp right into the parking lot. I found a parking space in the sparsely occupied lot and rushed to the ticket office.

"Is there still time?" I asked the ticket taker. *Was my treasure inside this auditorium?*

"Another hour. They're still doing judging," she assured me. *Judging what and how?* I plunked down ticket money and trotted inside.

For most of my life, I had carried the idea in my head that felines were the most despicably evil creatures on earth, had hated their slinkiness, and their staring eyeballs with the snake-slits in the middle. And now, here I was, voluntarily paying to go into something called a cat show because of that long ago, one-night-stand with Princess. *Was I crazy? Or had I truly had a revelation?*

As I walked into the auditorium, I realized there were all kinds of people who loved, or at least liked, cats. They were sitting, strolling, and standing by cat cages displaying discrete *For Sale* signs followed by dollar signs with three, even four digit numbers before the decimal. These cats were expensive! Booths lined the perimeter of the cavernous auditorium, one next to another, all filled with cat toys, cat trees, cat clothes, cat food, and cat miscellany, all promising pampering for kitties and fun for their humans. I was getting excited as I meandered through the rows of tables, all topped by wire crates. *I might find myself a cat here. It might happen. Today! I could return the second-hand side table I'd just bought, and I'd maybe have enough money. Maybe.*

At one side of the arena, an audience sat on brown metal folding chairs, watching as a male judge in a red vest stood behind a table where purple, blue, red, gold, and white award ribbons covered the tablecloth. I sat down to watch. He snared a cat out of its cage and inspected it, opening its mouth, checking the teeth, stretching the tail out. *Brave man!*

I asked the woman with cat earrings sitting next to me what was happening. "The judge is assessing the cat's tolerance for being handled. He's checking the breed standards for the way its head is shaped, the body length, and general configuration."

"I never knew there were so many kinds of cats. What kind is that?" I whispered. I'd never seen one like it—all white, with long and silky-looking hair, and a smooched-up face.

"A Persian."

"Thanks for explaining. My first cat show." I smiled at her. She was already turning back to the stage and didn't respond. *I'd always heard that cats were standoffish; maybe their owners were also.*

The judge held the cat up horizontally at eye level—the way I've seen prize-winning fish measured—stretching it out to its fullest length. He pulled and turned and twisted the poor thing this way and that, turned it on its back in his arms, and finally set it down on the table. The official picked up a stick with a feather on it and shook it. The feline obligingly reached a paw out for it. The judge picked up a purple ribbon and handed it, along with the docile cat, to its grinning owner. The audience clapped.

I knew this was good, but had no idea why the cat won an award except, perhaps, because it hadn't scratched or bitten the judge. *Such passivity! Did they* dope them? These were more like stuffed animals than live cats. I mentally compared them to the screaming devils on the farm and wondered how all of them could be members of the same species. I watched awhile, then became bored and went back to wandering. The array of so many breeds, the ribbons on the cages, and the *prices!* left me stunned. No longer would I think of a cat as just a cat. I revisited some of the cages and studied the breed names, the exotic sounding names, and the lithe, graceful, calm, and beautiful animals. Had these cats been clothes, they would have hung in Saks Fifth Avenue with diamond collars attached. I needed something from the Salvation Army. *We had been selling the wrong thing on the farm—these cats were worth more than our cows had ever been.*

Disappointed from my impromptu and unfruitful shopping, I headed toward the exit. It was probably better that I hadn't found one. After all, really, what did I know about taking care of cats after only a few hours of exposure to Princess all those years ago? I had some learning to do before I actually became a caretaker. Maybe I wasn't supposed to have a cat. I could try getting a dog. I'd have to fence the yard—that would be expensive, though. I needed a reason to exercise, and I could walk a dog. I shuffled toward the exit, tired, let down, and now eager to take *my* aching dogs home.

As I neared the door, I glanced at the large wire cage sitting on the floor out of the way of the foot traffic. At first I thought it was empty, but then I saw a huddle of small white kittens piled up in a corner behind a hand-lettered sign, "Siamese Kittens $20." *Twenty dollars!* I had just passed cage after cage of cats with price tags of hundreds, even a few of them for thousands, of dollars for fuzzy, flat-faced cats, for cats with leopard spots, tail-less cats, no-hair cats that looked like little aliens, and now, here were kittens, Siamese kittens, for $20! I tried to tamp down my excitement. *Had the fates decided I was ready to be a cat mom after all?*

A jeans-clad woman sitting on a chair off to the side of the cage appeared involved in her novel. As I bent over to get a better look at these white kitties with faintly gray ears and tails, one of them—there were four in all—unraveled itself from the pile, stretched its front legs way out in front and pushed its butt into the air for a long stretch. Then it folded itself back into a cat again and strolled to the front of the crate. It stopped in front of me, sat down on its haunches and pushed a paw against the grating as though trying to touch me—or grab my swinging necklace. I straightened, and the cat again made pawing motions against the enclosure, now standing up on its hind legs. I stared at the blue eyes that seemed to be fixated on me.

I felt like this animal wanted my attention. It was choosing me, wasn't it? The sign said Siamese, but it didn't look at all like the beautiful Princess. *But it had come right toward me!* I watched as the tiny thing put all four feet on the floor again, then moved over a few inches to the food bowl. It nosed around, looking for just the right bite of kibble, like a woman choosing just the right pearl. I was hooked on this hungry kitten that wasn't trying to sink her claws into me.

Okay, so, maybe I was about to make a purchase, even if it wasn't a Siamese look-alike. I no longer had a list of demands, and the cat filled the cheap requirement.

"Excuse me," I directed at the woman who was still engrossed in her novel.

"Can I help you?" she inquired with disinterest, lowering the book but not getting off her chair. *Maybe she was just cat sitting and the owner would come back later?*

"Uh, what kind of cats are these? It says Siamese, but they aren't, are they?"

"Yes, Seal Point."

"Seal Point?" I could feel my face wrinkling into a frown. "Aren't Seal Points dark buff cats with black legs and tail? And a mask, a black mask?"

"Not as kittens. These are only eight weeks old. They don't turn their adult color until about six months and, eventually, the white body turns taupe, and the light gray points turn black, and you have a Seal Point Siamese."

"Why are these so cheap? What's wrong with them?" I asked suspiciously. I didn't want to start out with a sick cat, not on my budget, even if these were by far the cheapest things at the entire show—maybe cheaper than a bag of cat food, and available, and right here in front of me *now*.

Apparently sensing a way to get rid of one, the seller got up and moved over to stand beside me, brushing her bangs away from her forehead. "Nothing's wrong. They're purebred, but not show quality. I'm a breeder, and I can't keep cats I can't show."

"Why aren't they show cats?"

She shrugged. "The markings are wrong, the bone structure in the head a bit too round. They'll be fine as house cats, and they have the great Siamese personality. I'm going into breeding the traditional triangular-head Siamese instead of these Appleheads."

I stood silent, trying to make sense of what she was saying while simultaneously debating my next move. My feet hurt, I was stressed and ready to go home, with or without a kitten—the kitten that was now lapping delicately at a bowl of water, its little pink tongue flicking in and out, acting unconcerned about my decision. *I'd probably imagined it wanted me.*

"Is it female? Do you have a female? I want a female," I told her firmly remembering my shopping list. If she didn't have one, that would take care of it. I'd wait.

"These are all male."

I could feel my dream evaporating. I bit my lip, considering. "All of them?"

"Yes. Why do you want a female?"

"I've heard they're more affectionate."

"In my experience, it's just the opposite. The females are fiercer hunters, but the males are more likely to be lap cats."

I didn't want a male. I remembered those disgusting, humping male dogs on the farm. But suddenly, impatience and proximity overtook caution. I wanted a cat *now*. I'd been waiting a long time. My house needed a cat. I needed a cat. And here was one in front of me, I could afford it, it had put its paw out to me...

Suddenly, I flashed back to a special dress I had needed for a date. I'd visualized it clearly in my mind, but after checking every dress store in our little town, I admitted defeat. My perfect dress didn't exist. In desperation, I finally chose a second best. I bought it, and the dress turned out to be perfect, better than the one I'd originally envisioned. My date had loved the color, talked about it matching my eyes, and he kissed me that night. Hmmm. Maybe there was a lesson there.

I decided in an instant. "I'll take him."

After all, I just wanted the cat for company. And this one seemed OK so what did it matter if it was male or female, Siamese or barn cat? I'd get it taken care of, or whatever they did so it wouldn't hump anything or dispense babies. I had felt good when the cat had reached out its paw, like that time in fourth grade when the team captain had chosen me ahead of the other, bigger, kids for the first time. Being chosen "not as the leftover one" was good.

I pointed to the kitten that had finished eating and was now strolling back toward the nest. "How can I get him home? I didn't bring a cage."

"Oh, I have a cardboard carrier. He'll be fine in it."

The thought struck me that she was giving it away like an extra newspaper, of not much value and with no heart connection. *What was wrong with this cat? Why would she sell a $200 cat for $20 unless there was something wrong with it?*

"What's your return policy?"

"I guarantee all my cats to be healthy for a month."

"What if he doesn't like me?"

"Oh, he will. Siamese are very affectionate."

That made me feel a little better—it was good to have an edge. I watched as she snared the little rat-sized body and dumped it into the cardboard box with the air holes on the side. While I held the top flaps down, she put a couple of strips of packing tape across the top and then wound some twine around the box—up, down, around, and over—then tied it.

Buyer's remorse and a sense of inadequacy crept in as I watched her. *I didn't even know the questions to ask to get the answers I probably needed to care for him. He was so little, what if I stepped on him? How would I even know if he was sick? I really didn't want a male cat.*

I just needed to leave, just turn around and go and... The seller gestured that the cat was in the box, all wrapped up and ready for me, the gift to myself. I forked over the next to last bill in my purse, hoping that the cliché would be true, that I didn't realize how little I was paying for a lot.

With my purse hanging off my shoulder and my arms wrapped around the box, I headed for the parking lot. The box shuddered. I rebalanced the load and speeded up. The container dipped and shook again, and a cat yowl floated out from the air holes. That kitten couldn't have weighed two pounds. How could this box be so heavy, so noisy? I prayed I wouldn't soon be chasing a tiny animal around the huge parking lot.

I had a cat! Now what was I going to do? Before I could figure it out, the box gave another shudder and started tipping out of my arms. I righted it again with my knee and rushed the few yards to my car. I had a cat! I felt my heartbeat pick up speed. *Ohmigosh, what had I done? I was totally unprepared for this. Please let me learn to be a good mom, don't let me mess it up.* I felt my heart beating faster and felt the big smile on my face. It was the best shopping day of my life. I had just purchased my long-sought-after dream.

Chapter 5
BECOMING CAT MOM

Austin, Texas. August 1987. I balanced the box with its precious cargo on my hip, yanked the car door open, and shoved the cardboard box in before slamming the passenger door shut. And I inhaled. Then I ran around to the driver's side and peeked in. The disheveled box was still there, wobbling around, but the lid appeared to still be closed.

Driving was not one of my delights, especially on the Interstate that ran through Austin. Now I was getting sweaty palms when I had to merge with the flow of its four lanes of traffic just on my side. I'd heard this stretch of road toward home was one of the most congested highways in the nation. Whenever I had to use it, I'd clutch the steering wheel, clench my teeth, and relax only when I arrived at my destination. Now, I guided my car between the eighteen-wheelers pulling trailers loaded with double layers of new cars, vans filled with families, Ford F-150's hauling cattle, sightseeing buses, and a few midget cars like my Ford Falcon. Blessedly, the traffic was lighter today than usual since it was Saturday.

As I steered between the lines, a paw poked out of one of the side air holes of the box and flapped around, trying to find something to sink a claw into. That paw disappeared, and the other paw replaced it through the lid hole, slapping about. I wasn't given to much praying, but I did now—I had nothing else to fix the box with even if I pulled off the highway. If he got out, it could lead to disaster, but the only choice was onward. His howls had gone up several octaves as he strove to find an escape.

Remembering my first lessons in dealing with a cat by watching Matt and Betty, I acted like the kid could understand me as I talked to him. "Hey, kitty, kitty, hey sweetie, it's OK, you'll be out of there in no time." Kitty-kitty responded with another enraged howl. I sang Happy Birthday, out of tune and off-key, my usual singing voice. Apparently he didn't like that song. "Okay, kitty, I know I'm not a very good singer. But that's the best I can do. What should we name you? Huh? Do you want to be... Big Boy?" Silence. Ah! This was good. And then he started wailing again.

Silver ears, followed immediately by that little white hairy head, shot up through the middle hole in the box where the flaps had met but now separated. *He was getting out.* I took my right hand off the steering wheel and shoved his head down into the box again, then leaned on the flaps with my elbow while trying to steer the car between a bus and a semi.

"Dammit cat, get back in there!" I heard the rising panic in my voice. "Do you want me to wreck the car?"

I received an insistent and long drawn out *meeOOWW* in reply. The breeder had said he was only eight weeks old—*how* had he developed such an ability to cry so loudly and so ceaselessly? I checked my rear-view mirror and immediately tromped on the gas, trying to get out of the way of the big black pick-up that seemed to be wanting to hitch a ride in my trunk.

Oh god, here comes the head again! I shoved it back down, hard, eliciting another angry howling. Could I accidentally break his skinny little neck, pushing as hard as I was? I cursed again as I felt around for the back of the lemon-sized noggin while trying to keep between the lane lines and out of the underside of another adjacent semi that had appeared on the driver's side. Finally! I saw our exit and shot off the expressway, pulling up into a gas station parking lot, leaving the air conditioning on, my hands shaking. As high as the temperature was, I was pretty sure my anxiety temperature was higher than that—my hair and back were soaked. *Surely the car's air conditioning had stopped working?* Before I could check the vent, there was another squall from brat cat. *What kind of animal had I bought? This howling, yowling, madly meowing creature couldn't possibly be domesticated. This was not going well. Maybe I should just turn around and take him back to the seller. I could say he was sick in the head, and I was invoking the guarantee.*

I glanced at my watch. Darn, the cat show was over. I tried retying the string and re-sticking the tape, then pushed the now more or less circular box back into a semblance of its original square shape. Then I took off again, cursing that lying breeder who had assured me it was a sturdy box and that this little demon was only a few weeks old. *Nothing* that young could be this loud.

Finally! I swerved onto our street and into our driveway, and we were home. I looked at the mutilated box, the flaps ragged and torn, tape drooping down the sides, the mess looking like it had been run over by that semi.

Before I could relax, the whole of this determined cat shot up through the top opening like a Jack-out-of-the-Box and scrabbled out of the carrier. I made a wild grab and managed, before he disappeared under the seat, to get him by his ribs. He squirmed, and I clung. He fishtailed, and I clung harder until I realized I was probably breaking something. I got a grip on the fur at the back of the tiny neck with one hand and scooped the other under his butt. I rushed my new kid into the house, not even bothering to grab my purse. Six steps through the living room, two through the dinette, two into the hallway and one giant step into the bathroom, still clutching that neck fur, and I more or less dropped him to the floor. I exited and slammed the bathroom door on his loud protests, then I just stood there leaning against it, breathing hard, taking a few minutes to recover from my kamikaze drive home.

As I slowed my breathing, it sank in: *I had a cat!* The realization made me smile as I headed out the door to go to the store. My first duty as a mom was one of my favorite occupations—shopping. *This was going to work out well!* I actually didn't know what we needed. He'd need a carrier, that was for sure! A sturdy plastic box, litter, a scoop and, wow! I'd need my credit card on this one.

The nearest pet store was getting ready to close when I arrived, but my excitement was contagious and the clerk grabbed things, willy nilly. Food, nail clippers, a brush. Toy mice. Cat treats. A scratching post. I asked the clerk to take back two of the toys, but the cat carrier and litter box were both full of cat goodies as I struggled out the door. I shoved my contraband into the car, and, as I drove, visualized that little rascal running through the house playing and curled up on my lap while I read. I heard the crunch of him eating and felt a sense of satisfaction that I was a provider.

Shrugging aside any doubts, I assured myself that I could take care of him. He'd never want to leave me. I wouldn't sell him to put food on the table, or give him to someone so they could make money breeding him, or give him away if he was inconvenient. He'd be with me for a long time—my companion, my friend. I would learn to be the best cat-mom anywhere! And I would *never* ignore him, or hit him, or be mean to him. I would follow Matt's long ago advice; I would treat him with *respect*. I wouldn't seal him in a box ever again! I knew I would love him happily forever, because that's the only way dreams are supposed to end.

I carried my bounty back to the house, excited to show it to new kitty. I was greeted by the frantic screaming sounds of a very upset animal. The sound reminded me of those human babies screaming for a bottle, their faces screwed up into purple ugly, their fists slamming the air. I dropped the cat goodies and rushed toward the bathroom, wondering if he was trapped or drowning in the toilet. *Darn. I would have to make sure I always put the lid down.* The water was deep, and he was little—could he drown?

I threw open the door. There he was, sitting on his behind, his face about the level of my ankle, his big blue eyes looking up at me. *Waiting for me.* At a glance, he looked to be fine, though I would swear he had tears in his eyes. I bent down and scooped him up, so small most of him fit into my palm. He calmed immediately. I sat him on my left arm and used my right finger to pet the top of that little round head that was becoming a cliché. He fit. And he was blessedly quiet. My heart tripped about in my chest.

"Ah, little one, you were scared, weren't you? I'm *so* sorry. I had to get you some food, and we have to make you a bathroom," I crooned to him. "I wasn't expecting that you would come live with me today, so I wasn't quite ready for you." He cuddled into my arm, and I mentally gave myself a gold star for my amazing powers to calm him.

"Come on, let's go see your new home and your potty place, shall we?"

I took him and his virgin litter box into the garage and sat him on the floor. I wiggled my fingers in front of him, and let him chase them into the empty box, the same way I had enticed those calves to suck from a bucket. Then I dumped the litter in. My so itty-bitty kitty immediately jumped in, scratched and scratched, and scratched some more, and then showed me he was house trained. Just like that! Yes, this cat *might* be better than a dog that needed walking in the middle of a stormy night or a melting Texas day. And I deserved a purple ribbon as a cat trainer. I was *quite* impressed with us.

"C'mere, sweetie. Look. Here's your food and water." I walked back to the kitchen, and he followed. He sniffed at the water and then nibbled at the kibble. I left him to eat in peace and sat down on the couch in the living room. He immediately followed me, trying to jump up onto the couch that was about twice as high as his head, but fell backward. Then he moved over and tried climbing my bare legs but slid back down, those teeny-tiny claws leaving railroad tracks in my skin. I picked him up, put him in my lap, and petted him. He settled down for a minute or so, then jumped off and began exploring the living room.

Watching him was much more entertaining than watching TV. He sniffed, he scampered, he found a loose thread on the carpet and tasted, pawed, and jumped on it. He attacked a scrap of paper, sliding on it across the floor and into the kitchen. Then, apparently having an attack of separation anxiety, he ran back to me and again tried to climb my legs. In self-defense, I hauled him back into my lap. A minute later he crawled up my arm, then up higher to perch on my shoulder like the captain on the prow of a ship. Then he nibbled my ear. He was delightful and not at all afraid of me. I couldn't take my eyes off him. Whether kitty was bonding with me or not, the soft spot in my heart convinced me I was doing so with him.

The evening over, I tucked him under my arm, and we went to bed. Rather, I went to bed, and kitty went off to play, sliding off the bed and running around the room. I got up and put him into bed beside me. He struggled a bit and then went to sleep, apparently worn out from his first day away from his old home and his first day in his forever one.

I'd been divorced for over a decade and had forgotten how nice it was to have a warm body to cuddle next to, even if this one was very small and hairy instead of big and hairy. Instead of counting sheep, I fell asleep that first night thinking up cat names.

Some people have a knack for naming things—babies, animals, and businesses. I wasn't one of them. Over the course of the next week, I experimented—hollering, crooning, yelling all the names I could think of befitting a Siamese boy-cat. None felt right to me, nor to the kitten, apparently, as there was no response when I called the various names.

"Hey, Prince! C'mere Prince!" He continued investigating the dust bunnies under the bed. *Maybe that name was too doggie-like.*

"Simba. Simba! *Siiimmbaa.*" He disappeared totally under the bed, taking his tail with him.

Days later, getting desperate, I checked out a library book on baby names and found the Arab word, "Sami," defined as "exalted one." I knew it was right; it lilted off my tongue. I got him a blue collar and an ID tag with his name and my phone number. He was beautiful, and he was now officially mine.

Our house was only about eight hundred square feet, not much space for an active kitten to run, even with his little short legs. But the backyard was long and deep, with countless trees, saplings, bushes, and weeds, a perfect jungle for my young cat.

I empathized with Sami being cooped up alone all day and began taking him outside when I came home from work, staying close beside him. He was so busy he paid me no mind. He prowled through the weeds, nibbled the grass, and chased bugs until I got bored and took him inside. As the weeks passed, Sami grew, and I became more sure of myself and loosened the invisible reins. I let him stay out longer, until he came in voluntarily. But as I impatiently waited for him to finish his evening explorations, I'd remember the many lanes of traffic on one side of the subdivision just three blocks away, Interstate 35 in the other direction, and the dogs I could hear barking around us in the night.

I tried going to bed when he was outside, but I couldn't sleep. *Was this how moms with teenagers felt when their kids started driving?* I shuddered at the thought, remembering those many nights I'd waited anxiously in the early morning hours for my then-husband to get home after finishing his bartending shift and his last drink.

Finally, I'd get so anxious, I'd go outside in my slippers and nightgown, calling his name at a don't-disturb-the-neighbors level, my flashlight seeking out the reflection of glowing cat eyes in the dark.

"Sami! Come here. Come on, time to go to bed," I hissed. And I would keep calling, or hissing. When I was getting hoarse, he'd suddenly rush to my side and prance around my legs like he wanted a gold star for answering me so promptly.

One evening when Sami was outside, I was reading. Suddenly, the silence broke my concentration. I realized how quiet my home had been before Sami, like Grandmother's when she was sleeping. My hearing now was attuned to Sami's meows, his purrs, the thump of him jumping and running, the crunching of his food. At that moment, there were no sounds, and it felt as though a part of the house was missing some of its life force. Whenever I came home from work, I knew with surety that I had been missed because I could hear Sami meowing me a welcome all the way through the closed front door. Even just curled up sleeping, Sami added a presence, as though the house was breathing in synch with him. How could such a diminutive being add so much life to my home?

On the nights and rainy days that he stayed inside, Sami was great company; he reminded me how to laugh again at simple things. I'd had no idea paper sacks were so versatile—the crinkling sounds they made when he rolled on them, or the end crash after he ran, dipped, and slalomed all the way to smash against the bottom of one. I hadn't realized a half-used toilet paper roll still had enough paper on it to go from the bathroom through the hall and across the living room to the front door. Several times. He serenaded me by rhythmically playing the doorstop—a spring with a rubber end on it to keep the doorknob from poking a hole in the wall. After chewing on the rubber, he'd slam it with his paw. Boinggg. Boinggg. Boingboing! went his favorite toy, endlessly.

I considered renaming him Magpie. I had a bad habit of taking off my earrings as soon as I came in the door and ditching them on the coffee table. At least one would always be an orphan by morning when I remembered to retrieve them. The missing one seldom turned up, not even when I ransacked the couch or checked the litter box.

Little Sami was a great little helper and willing to be paid off in cat treats. "Making the bed, Sami!" He'd fly past me and burrow under the clean sheet while I tried to smooth the material over the cat lump. I'd start to dust, and he'd be there, chasing my dust cloth over the shiny surface with his black paw, and I wouldn't mind that he was leaving footprints on the shine. Sami was teaching me patience and tolerance, something I knew I had only in small measure.

When I put a new toy on the floor, Sami would come to a screeching halt, then bob forward and backward, finally getting brave and poking it with his right front foot, then his left, making sure this new thing was safe before sniffing it and claiming it as his.

He was always ready for me to pick him up and cart him around; the rest of the time he followed me everywhere. When we were in the house, he was rarely more than a few feet away, his head usually in my way—his version of helping. I was so enchanted with this little squirmy being, but at the same time, constantly scared to death I would squash him by stepping on him. One problem I now had with my enjoyment of Sami was that I hated to leave him to go to work. He was becoming an obsession. Now I understood why Betty and Matt had been sure there was no cat more beautiful, intelligent, funny, charming, or personable than Princess. But they were wrong. As amazing as she was, now I knew she was second to my Sami on all counts.

I was still working at the Austin State (Mental) Hospital, going through the motions of teaching Adult Education Classes on the locked wards. There was little interaction as the patients were usually either heavily sedated, in a world of their own, sleeping sitting up, designing tattoos on their arms, or otherwise non-functional and non-responsive. They would sit quietly, putting in their class time; then I'd give them a pass, and they'd claim a cigarette and go outside to smoke.

Sometimes, while I was trying to stir up some interest from the students, a shaft of sunlight would shine in a window, hitting the sill. And I'd think, *Oh! Sami would love to be here sitting in that piece of sunshine,* and I would want to show it to him.

I'd give out snacks to the patients, and reflexively bend down to give the not-there Sami a piece, too. I asked one of the other teachers one day if she thought I should be committed or just needed some meds to get over my obsessiveness. She assured me I was just a normal mom, that she often did the same things with her kids.

While I was learning how to be Cat-Mom, Sami, by six months of age, had grown into a long, slim Applehead Siamese. His ears, mask, feet and legs, and tail were now the deep dark black of a water-slick seal. When he walked, his slightly bowed front legs and undulating tail reminded me of a fashion model's runway strut. He stared out of only slightly crossed, sky-blue eyes onto a world he appeared to find always fascinating. Sleek, sinewy, healthy, smart, and beautiful. How *dare* that stupid breeder have said he wasn't perfect enough! He was *definitely* perfect for me.

Initially, I assumed Sami would be an indoor-outdoor cat; I'd never heard of an indoor-only one. But the more I began recognizing the outside dangers, the more fearful I became. I soon realized I had to make a choice. When I had first adopted him, I had recognized only death by car or his getting lost as possibilities. Then the awareness of the many loose dogs, and dogs behind fences that Sami could jump over, seeped into my consciousness—dogs willing to kill that little furry thing I was growing to love so much.

Now that I was animal-aware, I paid attention to the news report of a Chihuahua being carried off from a back porch by coyotes *in* Austin, just a couple of miles away. When I heard the TV broadcast about the dead, rabid bats found in the schoolyard, I shuddered at the thought of Sami finding one and taking a deadly lick. While in the vet's waiting room, I studied the posters about the spread of Feline Leukemia Virus, a potentially fatal, communicable disease.

I became aware of articles in the paper and on the evening news about how human serial-killer-crazies, when young, would precursor their murderous tendencies with small animal mutilation. With horror, I read about a Texas high school football team that thought it was "fun" to mutilate and vivisect a cat on their playing field before hanging it from the goal post to die. I learned about those individuals who grab stray cats and sell them to the science labs for use in "testing," and about the collectors/hoarders who "rescue" strays just to take them home to live with their other 98 cats. The articles popped up everywhere once I began paying attention. How was it that I had never known about all these dangers?

But cats were outside animals; what could I do about it? It would be unnatural to keep him inside all the time. Wouldn't it? What should, what would, a wise and loving cat-mom do?

What I did for the next several years was to live with growing apprehension, arguing with myself for and against restricting an animal to an inside existence.

And then there was The Surgery. Sami was almost seven months old when I noticed him doing a peculiar dance with his tail shaking like he was listening to a Rock-n-Roll band. By then I had a friend with a cat, and she explained the facts of cat life to me. I had a miserable day at work the day I left my little boy at the vets. I was scared to death he would associate me with the surgery and hate me forever. However, he seemed just as loving afterward as he had been before the neutering. I was unable to imagine the pain I would feel if something happened to him because of my decisions. Darn, this being a caretaker was emotionally hard work. How could I protect him from all the bad things that could happen? *How could I ever have been a real mom to human kids?*

Chapter 6
ONE BY ONE

Austin, Texas. Spring 1988. For months, I'd been seeing little holes scattered around the yard, holes about the diameter of a pencil eraser and rimmed in a wreath of tiny pebbly material similar to dark-gray coffee grounds. These wreaths stretched along the front and side of the house and even halfway along the back patio. *Maybe little snake holes? Or spiders?* I stood awhile and watched but nothing came out. The holes didn't seem to have gotten any bigger since I had first noticed them several days before; there were just more of them. Since they seemed harmless, I quit worrying about them.

Finally, though, the occupants appeared—not snake, spider, or wasp holes as I had suspicioned, but ant holes, so many ants, larger than the fire ants that had greeted me when I got to Texas. Although Rose had now deserted me, these insects had not, and once again I felt like I was under siege. *Were they following me?* The good part was that these did not seem so determined to bite me to death as the fire ant warriors had done. These were busy on a march, going into their holes with chunks of green leaves carried over their heads. Then they came back out again, leafless, and marched in a line from the back of the house to the front, one after another in an unbroken line, each less than an inch behind the one in front of it. Some veered off to chomp off hunks of leaves bigger than they were from bushes they were passing, then U-turned to form a line homeward, carrying the greenery over their head like women in Africa carrying goods to market. Alas, the ants were not off to sell their plunder, but instead managed to stuff themselves and their leaves back into those little pencil-size holes.

Thinking of my budget, as always, I decided to try a big bottle of powdered ant poison; I followed the instructions. The ants continued to march, the line seemingly growing much longer by the hour.

I bought a spray poison, guaranteed to kill all kinds of ants. And the ants continued to march. I discussed their possible demise with the neighbors.

"Hmm, don't know what kind of ants they could be," said the old-timer Texan neighbor from across the street, "but to get rid of most ants, you just pour gasoline down the hole, followed by a lit match."

"You do understand I want to destroy the ants' house, not mine?"

"Yup, that'd be a problem all right. Did you try flooding them out? That's the only other thing I know to use—gas or water. Kills 'em for sure."

I went home, turned on the hose full blast and aimed it down a hole. Nothing came back up—no ants, no water. After about ten minutes, I had visions of the house sweeping down to the nearby creek, riding a garden-hose-wave down to the sea. I turned the water off and waited. There still was no sign of any water, or ants, bubbling back up. Good. Maybe I had drowned all of them.

Feeling happy about the desecration I had hopefully caused to their homes, I went into the house and took a nap with the lack of conscience of a mass murderer. An hour later, I went back outside, and there they were, their leaf umbrellas in a waving but determined line.

Again I returned to the hardware store and paid an outrageous amount for a different poisonous spray that I couldn't allow on my skin, and a powder that I wasn't supposed to breathe. There were skull and crossbones on the labels. I used the stuff and survived. So did the ants—my bushes were *still* losing leaves nightly and some were almost naked.

I was realizing just how easy I'd had it in Alaska. I couldn't remember ever seeing ants there in 14 years. Yet, in barely two years in Austin, they had found me twice. I decided to quit harassing them and surrender, hoping they would run out of leaves. Since they weren't hurting anything else, I'd just live with them. For a while, all seemed calm.

A few weeks later it rained, a real Texas gully washer. I came running into the house after work, splashing through raindrops and puddles. There was no Sami at the door.

"Sami?" I yelled. No response. "Sami! Where are you?"

My heart began to beat too hard. Whether I came home after a day at work, or a ten-minute conversation with a neighbor, Sami was always, always—waiting for me at the front door. Then I heard a sound that sounded like someone sucking on a straw in an empty glass. "Slurp." *Slurp?* The sound was far away and faint, but it was a definite slurp.

What in the world? "Sami, what are you doing? Where are you?"

I followed the mystery sounds to the bathroom, pulled back the shower curtain and found Sami, all four black paws planted on the bottom of the bathtub, having the feast of his life. The white porcelain was covered in dark reddish-brown ants. The pencil hole ants had moved in. They were crawling on the walls, falling out of the faucet, swarming up out of the drain, and covering the tub walls, a veritable beehive of activity. Sami was licking them up like they were chocolate-covered. I'd heard that one kind of ant tastes like honey and one like bacon. Since cats don't have the taste buds for sweet, it must have been the bacon that was delighting my carnivore so much.

In places, the bathtub was almost dark with the tiny bodies piled on top of, and crawling over, each other. I pulled Sami out of the tub, brushed off his insects, closed the plug, and opened the taps full blast. Sami stretched up with his front paws on the side of the tub, head hanging over, watching the water—and the ants—rise. Soon the tub was half full with a layer of desperately floundering bodies floating on the water's surface, trying to escape the rising tide.

When I finally let the water out of the tub, corpses covered the bottom with barely any of the tub floor showing. I used a wet paper towel to wipe them up; when it was covered with the ants, I used another, and another. I lost count of how many towels, and it was impossible to count the ants, hundreds surely, probably thousands.

My four-legged exterminator might have been able to get rid of them eventually, but I felt the need for big guns and credentials after the name. I called one of the national bug companies. The young guy came, looked the ants over, and sprayed them, assuring me the yard and house would be ant-free in just a couple of days. What a feeling of relief!

And the ants continued to march. I called the company back. They sent another exterminator out. He sprayed; I prayed. And the ants just kept on ceaselessly. I could see them all the time now, spotlighted at night from the security light, marching in that endless parade all the way around the house, as though the poisons had energized them.

"My ants are still marching," I said when I got the manager on the phone. "I hired you, and paid you, to get rid of these ants. You *guaranteed* your work. I want the ants gone, or I want my money back," I told the company firmly, checking the calendar for my next free appointment time.

"Describe these ants again?" said the manager.

I could now describe them in detail and did so, including their leaf-carrying attributes. The supervisor said he'd call me back. Thirty minutes later the phone rang.

"Ma'am, this is the owner of the exterminating company. We're putting a check in the mail today to reimburse you for your fee."

I felt my jaw drop. "What do you mean?" I squeaked. "Are you not coming back?"

"No, ma'am. I'm sorry, but we can't help you." He hung up.

I sucked in air; when I could breathe again, I checked the Yellow Pages for "Entomologist." There were only three listed. Two didn't do private work.

When the third company answered my call, the man said he only did office buildings now after he stopped doing private homes a few months earlier. I did the best I could to sound helpless, putting a quaver in my voice, which wasn't at all hard to do. I whined out my story, my sentences coming out shorter and shorter as I fought real tears. Finally, he promised to come look, probably deciding it would be faster to do that than to keep listening to me. He arrived, took one quick look at the line of moving leaf pieces parading around the house, and pronounced, in a solemn voice and with a knowing nod of his head, "Yep, my old friends, Texas leaf cutter ants. Don't see them much in town," he continued, tugging on the bill of his maroon and white Texas A&M shop cap. "Maybe that's why the exterminating company didn't know what they were dealing with. They're usually down on the coast, though I've seen their mounds out on the ranches. They can strip a tree overnight and then make mounds as high as the small trees. They're hard to get rid of, partly because they have underground tunnels that can extend for acres."

That explained the disappearance of all that water I had dumped into their holes. "You *can* get rid of them, though, right?" I asked, hopefully and desperately.

"Let me take a look at the front of the house and see exactly what we've got here. When these get inside, the termites sometimes come with them. You better lock your cat up." I went in and coaxed Sami into the back bedroom, and then wondered why I needed to do that.

When I came back out, Mr. Entomologist had pulled off the front of my house, stripping everything away from what had been the bathroom wall that was also the front of the house. I was stunned at what I saw. All insulation, wallboard—everything—was gone, gone into a two-foot high mound of chewed-up debris piled against the side of the tub. He showed me the ants, the fungus that was the ants' food, and the termites that had trailed them in. Then he thrilled me with, "Only one thing gets rid of them, and the FDA outlawed it a few months ago from use around residences."

I could feel the tears welling despite my chin-up efforts, but I refused to cry. I was now a double-degreed State employee with a secretary's salary, part of that going to pay off my recent college degrees. Termite and ant damage was excluded from my insurance policy. I wondered how much I could get for a house with an open-air, spa-like bath. I also wondered what a half-grown, ant-eating Siamese would be worth if I tried to sell him since I'd now have to buy more cat food if the exterminator got rid of the ants.

The entomologist—he had cats—took pity on me and applied the illegal substance safely, or so he said. Finally, after months of dealing with them, the ants stopped marching. Handymen replaced the front of my house; I kept watch for signs of toxic poisoning in myself or my cat. Sami went back to debugging the back yard. But I had a dreadful premonition. First the rabid fire ants, now the defoliating leaf cutters. And termites. *Were the insect tribes seeking revenge on me for something I had done in another life?* Not that I believed in that karma stuff, but, still, this was strange. I'd talked to life-long Texans who swore they'd never had half this trouble with crawling critters.

Chapter 7
CURSE OR KARMA

Austin, Texas. 1988. While all of this ant turmoil had been happening, I had also been dealing with another traumatic event, an eye surgery. I'd worn glasses since the second grade and with every change of prescription the glasses got heavier, digging into my skull behind my ears and leaving red dents in the bridge of my nose even hours after I took them off.

I was ecstatic when I heard about hard contact lenses, and I promptly bought some. Unfortunately, I could only wear them for a few hours before my eyes became very irritated. Back to glasses. Then a Russian doctor developed a surgery known as radial-keratotomy. A few slits in the cornea with a diamond knife and near-sightedness disappeared, and the patient would have perfect 20/20 vision again.

After diligent research, I decided to have the surgery done, only on one eye first, by the Texan ophthalmologist who claimed he had introduced the technique to the U.S. He told me he had never had a failure. Alas, I didn't ask him what he meant by that. Apparently, as long as the patient lived, he considered his operation a success. My surgery was definitely not a success. Almost immediately after I left his facility, my eye started swelling and became painful. I diligently put in the two types of eye drops he had prescribed.

The next day, the swelling was worse and now the eye was weeping, bloodshot, and everything, including the lid, had turned black and blue; even my cheek was red, looking as though it had a chemical burn. I called the doctor and told him something was wrong. He told me to continue doing what he had instructed, he was at a party and couldn't come back to town until the next day.

On Saturday morning, I presented to his office. He determined that my appearance, reminiscent of actor Sly Stallone after Rocky's big fight, was because of an allergy to the antibiotic eye drops he had told me on the phone to increase and continue.

He had over-corrected the surgery, and I was left with visual havoc. Now one eye was near-sighted, the other far-sighted. Unfortunately, the vision didn't meet in the middle. As one doctor explained, the brain couldn't adjust to looking through a microscope and a telescope simultaneously. I now had zero depth perception and frequently fell off curbs and missed anything I was aiming at, like setting a cup on a counter.

On my last visit, the surgeon checked my vision, said to his assistant "release her to her primary doctor," and walked out of the room without even looking at me. He shirked all responsibility, without apology. I was consumed with anger against the injustice, felt a horrible sense of loss and regret at this betrayal by the M.D. who had promised but did not deliver. I was even consumed with guilt for having made a bad decision to have the surgery in the first place. I recognized by the twisting in my gut that my capacity to take care of myself had just greatly diminished. My inherent belief in myself and in my ability to handle anything life should hand me, and even my ability to make decisions, had been destroyed by one slice of the diamond knife. This was permanent damage. I would now have to wear contacts and/or reading glasses in multiple combinations to get through every phase of daily life, with one exception. I could read out of my left eye without any correction; that became my favorite pastime.

After the trauma of the ant episode, and then the trauma of the surgery and its aftermath, I had less and less energy and now often had a lot of aches and pains. I was always anxious, becoming very careful in my movements. I began a pattern of taking care of myself that affected everything I did, right down to the way I cared for my cat. All activities, even down to what kind of cat litter to buy, became big decisions—could I lift and carry the new litter that was on sale, or should I stick with the more expensive, but lighter one? Should I buy 10 cans of cat food, or 30 in case I got sick and couldn't go to the store? Should I paint the house or keep the money in the bank if I had to pay help? Could I see well enough to take that week-end trip? What should I do?

I had always been a Type A personality, multi-tasking long before anyone had a word for it as just a way of life. I was always working a full-time job and, simultaneously, at least one part-time job. I often took classes, I kept an immaculate, well-organized house, and, when I was married, managed to do all of that as well as picking up after my husband. The busier I was, the more I had liked it.

After the surgery everything changed. I was always exhausted but didn't sleep well. The idea of going out and having fun was slightly appealing until I realized that I needed to get dressed and put on make-up to go out; it was easier to stay home.

I went to several different kinds of doctors who all insisted the exhaustion and pains were just depression. I'd been depressed when I went through my divorce, and it wasn't what I was feeling now. Before, I didn't *want* to get out of bed; now I felt like I *couldn't* get out of bed. I lived with a night-before-coming-down-with-the-flu feeling, not engaging in even pleasant activities as the idea of making conversation seemed too overwhelming. No doctor would ever convince me that the only thing wrong with me was that I needed cheering up.

Then, a year or so after the eye surgery, I stumbled upon a newspaper ad about an informational meeting concerning symptoms that sounded just like mine. I went and listened and learned.

After that, I didn't need to go to a rheumatologist to know that I had the new diagnosis of an old disease with my exact symptoms, documented as far back as the 1800's when it was known as fibrositis or muscular rheumatism until 1976 when the name was changed to fibromyalgia. The diagnostic test was severe pain in sixteen places of the spine, hips, neck, legs, and shoulders when pressure was applied. However, there are good days and bad days, and some doctors pressed hard, and others pressed harder, so the diagnosis was considered subjective, and not a "real" disease.

The rheumatologist said it could be the result of the two whiplashes I'd had, or a traumatic emotional event (such as the eye surgery outcome), or a reaction to vaccinations (the military had used me for a pin cushion), maybe the result of a childhood disease or stress, or a thyroid issue. There were many theories, but no definitive answers—they didn't know the causation; they didn't know a cure. Despite the defined clinical signs and symptoms, medical dictionaries were slow to incorporate the new word. Because it could not be proven by X-rays or laboratory tests, many medical doctors, especially older ones, simply refused to use it as a diagnosis. In other words, the "scientific facts" were not available to support this "new" disease of fibromyalgia.

It was a conundrum for me. In my now-employment as a disability examiner, I was in consult with doctors on almost a daily basis. Upon seeing "fibromyalgia" listed as the reason for filing for disability, many doctors substituted their own judgment and gave a diagnosis of "malingering," defined as feigning an illness because the person was just too lazy to work. I didn't tell them, too embarrassed, that I had that diagnosis and was *not* malingering, simply working in a great deal of pain.

While it was a relief to have a word for my aches and pains, it was disappointing to not be offered a cure or even an alleviation. Pain pills weren't an option as I needed to stay awake to work, and most over-the-counter drugs did nothing. The good news was that I didn't have a terminal disease but, alas, recovery was unlikely.

As far as emotional trauma went, after the eye surgery my reaction to chemicals such as perfumes and room deodorizers had become intense, leading to instant asthma attacks and bronchitis upon exposure. I had to curtail many activities: church was agony with all the various colognes and the hard pews, I left meals partially eaten when a perfume-wearing patron was seated too close, and I no longer went to movies because I often couldn't stay for the ending. Even grocery shopping could send me into an asthma attack if I forgot and went down an aisle with soaps or cleaning products. I felt like the parameters of my life were slowly closing in, making my world smaller and smaller.

My best stress reliever was Sami. I had occasional fits of grief and anger at my situation; cuddling helped. Simply having another living being I was responsible for was a good panacea, and the slow stroking he enjoyed also calmed me down. He kept me centered, and the responsibility of keeping him happy and cared for forced me to find the energy to get off the couch. He was my lifeline, a furry little clown who made me laugh and kept me entertained with his antics, asking nothing of me but my presence. *He was one of the best things I had ever done for myself.*

Chapter 8
GOING BUGGY

Austin, Texas. Summer 1988. A few months after the great ant extermination, I was relaxing on the couch, reading—the one thing I could do without corrective lenses. It was after midnight on what would have been a lovely summer night except for the mosquitoes. Sami was still out, periodically rushing in through the open patio door to check on me, then rushing back to his great outdoors.

Suddenly, I snapped alert when I heard the sounds of water sloshing, sounds coming from the kitchen. I didn't have a dishwasher; there shouldn't have been any sounds of water sloshing in my kitchen.

I threw the book on the floor and barreled out toward the sound. There, I stood dumbfounded, staring at the circular puddle of water in the middle of the floor stretching from the cabinets on one side of the galley-style kitchen to the refrigerator on the other side. Sami was darting in and out of the water, which action seemed to have something to do with a something in the middle of the puddle. What was in there? Squinting hard and leaning forward, I finally figured out what the dark, skinny thing was. The sight of a snake had always caused me extreme agitation, and it made no difference what kind or how big—watching any snake practically paralyzed me. I was pretty sure no limb could be moving that fast and that left me with only one conclusion. Sami was playing with, bathing, or trying to capture a snake.

I began jumping up and down, trying to keep my bare feet off the floor and away from the reptile that was writhing in large "S" motions in the kitchen pond. Sami was trying to grab the thirty inches or so of a pencil-thin black body looking for any escape away from the water, the cat, and the screeching human. With each swirl, the snake was moving closer to the dark void under the refrigerator—a possible source of the puddle. If he got under there, the snake could stay until he decided to investigate the rest of the house. I got a quick vision of rolling over in bed and finding him tucked against me.

Grabbing the broom and a long-handled dustpan, I did a superlative job of scooping the snake into the pan and rushing the whole thing outside. Sami, upset at seeing his snake disappearing without him, followed, trying to retrieve it from the dustpan that I was keeping covered with the broom. I just threw everything out into the yard, captured Sami and carted him inside, then slammed the patio door closed. That took care of the snake.

The puddle was centered in front of the refrigerator, which probably meant the leak was coming from behind or underneath it. I'd never be able to move the appliance by myself. Since none of our three houses in Alaska had ever had any kind of plumbing (or termite or ant) problem, and I'd had a husband if that had happened, I hadn't thought to look for the water shut-off valve before an emergency. I was sure there was a handle or knob of some kind in the yard, but where? And hunting for some mysterious thing out there, barely able to see anyway, with a flashlight, in a snake-infested yard, was not going to happen. I looked at the clock, then called the first Yellow Pages listing under Plumbers anyway, willing to pay an obscene amount of money for a rescue.

"Hello?" A raspy voice answered the phone.

"I'm sorry to bother you, but I think my refrigerator is leaking. A lot. I know it's late, but can you come make it stop before it floods my kitchen?"

My Texas white knight agreed and made me a deal on a service call. Within an hour, the leak from the icemaker had been fixed, the puddle cleaned up, the plumber paid. I presumed the snake had escaped into the night, getting as far away as possible from the snake-napping cat.

Sami and I went to bed. I laid there reflecting on gifts. Boyfriends had brought me flowers, my husband had given me jewelry—easy things to buy. But Sami had hunted, captured, and then tried to share his snake with me. I was pretty sure he had been bringing the thing to me when he lost it in the kitchen. As I had always heard, it wasn't the gift itself, it was the thought that counts. I pulled Sami close. I kissed him on the top of his so-round head for his loving thought, and fell sound asleep, not even dreaming about snakes because now I was sure Sami would protect me from them.

A month or so later, as Sami cuddled close on the couch while using his hind foot to scratch enthusiastically behind his ear, something bit me! Just then, he changed positions so he could scratch under his chin. The word jumped into my head the way the speck jumped onto my arm. Fleas! I couldn't remember ever knowing I was seeing a flea, but instinct told me that's what this was. We were sitting on the couch with the tightly woven, rosewood-colored material with little black dots on it, but, unless my eyes were deceiving me, some of those pepper-flake-sized dots were moving.

I remembered seeing a flea comb at the pet store, but hadn't had any idea that I might need one. Now, I scrounged around and found a small-toothed comb in a drawer. I ran the teeth through Sami's coat, seeing the fleas flee back into his fur. He was *covered* with the little critters. *How had I never noticed them before?* So tiny, with hard shells, almost invisible against Sami's seal-dark patches, they were totally camouflaged. I started combing faster but didn't know what to do with those tiny bodies that clung to the comb. Then I got inspired and filled a glass with water and stuck the comb, after each stroke, into the glass. The black specks floated off into the water and then, very slowly, floated to the bottom. I wanted to vomit at the idea of these things feeding on us. I went to bed but dsidn't sleep much, scratching at possibly imaginary, possibly real blood-suckers crawling around on me all night. I had a flash back to the farm where animals were never allowed inside, and it was next to heresy to suggest that one could sleep in the house, never mind on a bed. Now I knew one reason why it had been so.

The next day, I went to the pet store. They recommended a powder. I sprinkled it on Sami, the couch, and the carpet. We sneezed. I vacuumed. I had no idea how lethal what I was spreading around was. I found out later it had been banned and could have killed us, but it didn't have much effect on the fleas.

The pet store then recommended bathing him with flea soap. If I ever had any doubt about how much Sami loved me, the fact that he allowed me to bathe him without hurting me, albeit amid much howling and yowling and attempts to climb my head, left me with no doubt. I was overjoyed to notice the number of dead fleas, but also noted that the fleas apparently loved him even more than he loved me. They still stuck to him despite the bath. Back to the pet store.

"Bomb the house!" I was told.

I pulled all items out of all the cupboards, cabinets, and drawers and put them in sealed boxes and plastic bags. I washed all the bedding in the hottest possible water. I shut and sealed the doors and all windows. I put Sami in his carrier and stuck him in the car while I set off the bombs, pouring more poison into the house.

When we returned several hours later, I wiped everything down and in and out, vacuumed everything, and finally felt my shoulders relax as I admired my spotlessly, probably poisonously, clean house. I was positive I had triumphed again against the insect kingdom.

Less than a week later, Sami was again on my lap, I was combing him, and—I combed off another flea.

"What are we going to do, Sami boy?" I wept. Sami leaned against me and licked my arm.

The next day I arose like the phoenix and again began searching for things to kill with. During the next month, I got a flea collar and watched Sami continue to scratch frantically. I dipped him in vet-prescribed flea dip and watched him froth at the mouth when he tried to clean himself. I combed like crazy, and watched more black specks drown as they fell off the comb. The next day, I repeated that gratifying experience. And the next. It was like the leaf cutter ants all over again. They just kept *coming*.

Eventually, I won a few battles and the fleas disappeared from where I could see them, but it was obvious they were still on Sami. I itched just watching the poor cat scratch. I noticed I was worrying more about him than I was about the probability that I was sleeping with the darn things. I hated those little specks; I wanted them gone, but I didn't know what else to do. I'd done everything anyone had suggested. And once again, life had shown me I couldn't control anything, not even little bitty fleas.

I was so distraught I engaged in my best stress-coping tactic—I went shopping. I browsed awhile in the mall, then stumbled into a vitamin store. I found a few items to fill my medicine cabinet. At check out, I began talking with the owner. I told him the long story of my flea eradication efforts, then sighed. "Don't happen to know anything that might help, do you?"

"This is what helped my cat," he said, presenting me with a bottle of pet vitamins. "She licked all the hair off her fluffy tail because of fleas. When we gave her some of these, the fleas left and never came back." He flipped open his billfold and pulled out a picture. "This is her, and you can see how good she looks now." The all-white cat with the long, lush coat and plume-like tail was indeed beautiful.

"What's in the vitamins?"

"They're just a multi for pets, but apparently the fleas don't like the taste of the copper or the brewer's yeast in them, we're not sure which. We've been flea-free for two years."

"Is it hard to give them to her?"

"No, she loves them." I instantly pulled out my billfold even before he finished.

I hurried home with my copper-laced yummies, excited to share them with Sami. The cat gods were benevolent—he loved them. Within days, the fleas disappeared, and with them the possibility of typhus or bubonic plague; I felt the flea boulder roll off my shoulders. Thereafter, I made it my mission to spread my anti-flea knowledge to everyone, whether friend or stranger. If they had a cat hair on them, or a cat pin, or wore material with cats or dogs on them, I told them how I had won the flea war—with vitamins.

The side benefit was that Sami *loved* those little wafers so much, all I had to do was holler his name, shake the bottle, and he would come charging at me from wherever he had been. I had accidentally found the way to teach a cat to respond to his name. That was the one positive I could come up with from of all this turmoil—Sami, my exalted one, had learned his name.

Chapter 9
HAPPY HOLIDAYS

Texas to Nebraska. December 1989. Sami had grown up so fast from that little kitten I could hold in my palm. He was now over two years old, always enthusiastic, ready to be in the thick of things supervising, and happiest when we were busy together. If I was having a crabby day, it seemed that he deliberately tried to cheer me up. If I felt miserable and achy, Sami, my non-electric heating pad, snuggled close. And by now he had learned that when Momma slept, Sami slept, always on the bed, making me feel as though I had a personal bodyguard.

Never before had I felt like I was someone's whole world as I did now with Sami. He brought out my latent nurturing side. I found it very ironical that one of those hated felines of my childhood was transforming me. I wished there was a human male as perfect as Sami in my life—one who arrived on time for all meals, ate with great gusto, snuggled upon request, and didn't leave his whiskers in the sink. Sami even tried to help with expenses, still bringing me various food offerings, often wiggling ones but smaller than the kitchen snake, and laying them at my feet.

Life was quiet, a welcome change for me after the unsettled decades that had followed my graduation from high school with multiple cross-country relocations, marriage, divorce, college, and, finally, settling in Texas. I had a stable job I disliked but which paid the bills—barely. And I now owned a house, small but serviceable, and a car that ran well enough. I felt that my life was *finally* on the right track.

All I was missing was closeness with a human family. Christmas was coming, and the nonstop carols promoting love, celebration, and joy suckered me in.

Nostalgia for all those good holiday times that should have been but never were as I was growing up set in. But maybe, maybe this year it could happen. True, Mom had never *invited* me home in all those years, but she had never said no, or seemed upset when I invited myself. I had visited a few times during the summers, but it had been a long time since I had been home at the holidays.

For years, my Christmas shopping for that year began in January. I loved those clearance sales and drew great satisfaction from finding bargains even if I didn't need the item. Bargain shopping was my entertainment, my distractor, my empowerment—my addiction. When I bought something, it was always destined for a specific person—to my mind, my way of saying, *"Hey, I love you, and am thinking about you even if I'm not there."*

I opened my gift closet with the refrain of *Jingle Bells* in my head. Surveying all the twelve months of loot, I realized it would be easier and probably cheaper to drive the gifts to Nebraska than to mail them. The more I thought about it, the more enthused I became—maybe we *could* have a "God bless us every one" Christmas this year.

The next day I ran into the first glitch in my newly formulated plan. After multiple calls, I found I was too late to find a boarding place or a cat sitter for my loud-mouthed Siamese. How could I make this work?

I called Mom. After a few minutes of her latest gossip about people I had never known or had forgotten, I took a deep breath and plunged in.

"Mom, I'd like to come home for Christmas."

"Oh." Silence. Then, "Well, how long will you be staying?"

"Five days. I could leave here Friday since we're off work, then leave there on Tuesday."

"Well. That's fine. I guess," she finally said. "Are you driving?"

"Yes. I'll need to bring Sami, but he won't be a problem. If he hurts anything, which I know he won't, I'll take care of it."

I knew this was a big request—she liked dogs but was unfamiliar with cats. I rushed to explain. "I can keep him in the spare bedroom with me. He'll probably stay under the bed the whole time."

"Oh."

I again listened to the silence before offering, "We can stay in a motel if you don't want him there."

"I guess it's OK. He'll use a box? What else should I do to keep the furniture safe?"

"He won't hurt anything! I know you don't much like cats, but Sami is really well-behaved."

"Well, if you think it would be all right. It's an awfully long way for you to drive, isn't it? Are you sure you should be driving that way all alone?"

"About thirteen hours, more or less, same as last time I came up."

"You're sure the weather will be OK?"

"No, I'm not sure." I felt the irritation seeping into my voice. I already felt disappointed with her attitude. I was never sure when she started with excuses for me if she was just expressing concern or if she was trying to say no to something. Whatever it was, I always felt deflated during these encounters. "If it gets bad, we'll stop somewhere and check into a motel."

Finally, she acquiesced, and I hung up. *Damn those Christmas songs.* I was tempted to call back and say I'd changed my mind, but I didn't, still holding out a bit of hope that maybe *this* time things *would* work out, that we would make some good memories, and, if wishing could make it so, maybe the angels would get their wings.

"I don't think she wants us to come, Sami. But you and I will have fun, won't we?"

Sami responded with a couple of meows and twined around my legs.

Two weeks later, I was barely able to squeeze the gifts into the trunk, and my luggage into the back seat. Then I went to find Sami—the last thing to pack. Earlier I had given him the motion sickness pill I'd gotten from the vet, but I hadn't been paying much attention to him while running in and out of the house packing the car, fascinated to see my breath coming out in little white puffs, an unusual occurrence in Texas.

I found Sami leaning against the living room wall, a facsimile of Lee Marvin's very drunk horse, cross-legged, supported only by a weather-beaten shed in that classic movie, *Cat Ballou*. Sami could have doubled for the horse. Obviously over-medicated, the only thing holding his floppy body upright was that wall.

At least he won't be hollering, I thought as I tried to load him into the carrier. He was like a rag doll, but I couldn't seem to line up all four of those floppy legs, his tail *and* his head to insert him into the carrier. Finally, I grabbed him and carried him out to the car, sans carrier, and laid him on a towel on the front passenger seat. Unfortunately, not everything was relaxed; his vocal protests and cries of distress began undulating in volume from a moan to a shriek, in pathetic waves of distress.

As we headed north on I-35, I flipped on the radio. I had not checked the weather forecast, willing to believe this trip would be blessed with good weather, dry roads, and sunshine all the way. *We'll have a perfect trip.* If wishing could make it happen, it would, I vowed. Still trying to find a new music station, I got the tail end of a weather report.

"...fast-moving snowstorm hitting Waco by noon, bringing up to five inches of snow as it moves north to Canada. Expect a white Christmas folks."

Oops. I felt my hands getting sweaty as I pushed harder on the pedal. I would be traveling just ahead of that front for eight hundred miles. "Sami, we could be in trouble here," I worried out loud. "This is not good."

I noticed that the sunshine we had started out in was still in front of us, but the rearview mirror now reflected dark and threatening clouds. Surely I'd remember how to do ice driving even though I hadn't used snow tires or chains since leaving Alaska. Wouldn't I? My stomach gave a flip-flop of anxiety.

We sped forward throughout the day, trying to outdistance those blackening clouds as the red dust of Oklahoma, frosted with leftovers of a past snowstorm, and then the stark and barren fields of Kansas flew by. Everything was as I remembered it from my days on the farm—endless space above the undulating fields. My glass of holiday anticipation was almost empty. I felt like crying. Should I turn around? I was left with the isolation of this road and the stress of outdistancing the storm. Mom and I had always had a distant relationship, even when we were in the same house. *So why was I doing this?*

Finally, we arrived. I wrestled Sami into his carrier, carried him up the walk, and knocked on the door. Mom answered, even though it was almost 11:00 p.m., way past her bedtime. She was dressed for bed, neat as always, even her short, more pepper than salt hair well-groomed. I had always felt messy and mussed around her. I reached over and pecked her cheek, surprised once again that the extra two inches of height she had always had on me was now gone. She didn't kiss me back but smiled. Another ambivalent hello.

"Where do you want me to put Sami?" I asked. "I'll get him settled and then unload the car."

"He can stay down in the basement."

I felt the blood drain from my face in instant fury. The basement was an unheated area dug out under the house when it was built in the 1920's, with earthen walls, wooden shelves holding canned goods, and a sump pump that got rid of most of the water that had leaked in every rainy-weather period for decades. Through some kind of timing device, once or twice a day, poison for cockroaches, spiders, and other six-legged inhabitants was unleashed into the air.

I felt utterly betrayed. She would never have put one of her dogs down there. I stood and stared at her, waiting to see if she had anything else to say. After a minute of silence, it appeared she did not.

Without a word, I turned around, grabbed the cat carrier, and stormed out to the car. I knew if I opened my mouth, the dam on my bitterness would break. I would not challenge her for myself, but I would protect Sami with every cell and muscle in my body.

I walked into the old motel at the outskirts of town just as big fat flakes began flying into my face. We had run the race and won. I checked in, not mentioning anything about cats. I set up the litter box, opened a can of cat food, changed to my p.j.'s, plopped into bed hungry, and instantly fell asleep.

When I awoke, I looked outside at a world of bright light. The snow was deep enough to provide a pristine blanket sparkling in the morning sunshine, covering the uglies. Glistening icicles decorated the metal fence and lampposts. I considered what to do next. Go back to Mom's, unload the gifts, and get on the road? Stay at the hotel until after Christmas, by which time the roads should be cleared? Or should I just...

My thoughts were interrupted by a knock. I clutched the spare blanket around me and stuck my head in the door crack far enough to talk.

Charles, my mother's significant other, was there. He was a nice man, one I would have loved to have had as a father. I had met him only a few times in the five years he had been with her. On one of my trips home, Mother had commented that my old, but favorite, shoes were looking worn out. The next morning, they were sitting, shiny and with new soles, on a newspaper in the middle of the kitchen table after a visit to a little old shoemaker. I knew I'd remember Charles's surprise act of kindness forever.

"I told your Mom your car was still here. She thought you'd left. She'd like you to come back to the house," he said, looking down at the floor, bashfully turning his red shop cap in his hands as he delivered his message.

"I was getting ready to leave." I looked at him. He met my eyes and nodded, a silent communication of understanding.

"Charles, I won't go to the house and toss Sami into that basement. *I asked*, I *told* her he was coming, I *told* her he wouldn't hurt anything, and if he did I would pay for it," I justified myself.

He nodded again. "She says you can put Sami in the bedroom with you." He stood patiently.

Christmas was now just another chore, the excitement and anticipation gone. "Let me get dressed. I'll be at the house in about an hour."

Mother and I offered mutual apologies. Sami crawled out of the carrier and scooted under the bed where he stayed for the rest of the visit, quite unlike his usual social self. I helped decorate the tree and wrapped her gifts for her. Mother relayed all the hometown gossip as Charles sat in a rocking chair, watching TV.

My half-sister Jean, the one I mothered for almost two years before graduating, brought her kids to the house and then left to do some last minute shopping. My nephew and nieces, ages four, seven, and eight, found smearing frosting on their faces more interesting than decorating our slice'n'bake cookies, but they seemed to have fun with an aunt they couldn't have remembered very well. Mom hovered around, cleaning up as soon as anything dropped on the floor.

The next day, Christmas Eve supper was ready at 6 p.m., as scheduled. I looked at everyone gathered around the table: my mother, looking much younger than her seventy years; Charles, with his beautiful white hair shining above his shirt and tie; and Jean's good-natured husband, in a flannel shirt, relaxed after a couple of beers at home and seemingly unaware of any tension. And Jean, pretty, looking nothing like me or Mother, sitting with her arms crossed, a frown on her face, as usual. I never knew whether this was her reaction to life, or to my presence, but this was her pose every time I had been home since she had become an adult. The three kids were on their best behavior but uncomfortable, like most kids, more used to McDonald's than stuffed turkey dinners.

Conversation at the table was sketchy. I felt like an interrogator. "How's the job going, Jean?" "Mom, have the nasty neighbors moved yet?" "What books are you reading in school Judy?" They answered, and I squeezed my brain for yet another topic of conversation that was never picked up or returned, a game of tennis with only a server. We ate the usual Christmas fare, stuffing ourselves because chewing was easier than talking.

Then we opened presents, resulting in a few moments of triumph and distraction for the kids as they ripped through the wrappings, sometimes finding things they obviously liked, tossing aside others. I loved to fill up stockings for each person, each with a dozen gifts, little funny things, or, I hoped, thoughtful ones. The unwrapping of seventy gifts took awhile. With the gifts unwrapped, Jean said she needed to take her headache home. After they left, Mom and I cleaned up. By 8:30 p.m., Christmas was over. We spent Christmas Day talking a bit, sleeping a lot, eating leftovers, and playing board games.

I left two days later, a day early because of the forecast of another storm on the way. I packed, put my gifts in a sack, Sami in his carrier, hugged Mom a quick goodbye—for some reason goodbye hugs were acceptable, but hello hugs weren't—and we were on the road again. The sky was a leaden bluish-gray reminding me of one of many reasons why I had always found Nebraska winters depressing, knowing there would be few days of sunshine until around April when the tornadoes would start.

The two-lane highway to home was almost devoid of traffic again except for 18-wheelers on their way to or from Canada or Mexico. Sami had resumed his winter's discontent though now he was a cat again, not a rag doll. I felt an urgent need to outdistance this entire fiasco as speedily as possible. I floored the accelerator and flew by a rattletrap truck, loaded with turkeys, doing 45 mph. And I looked into the startled face of a State Trooper coming straight toward me out of a dip in the highway. I eased off the accelerator and waited for the law to catch up with me. Sami was blessedly quiet. The cop ripped off his ticket and handed it to me. "Drive slow now, hear?"

I put the tribute to this trip in my purse and my car into gear, cursing country cops, Christmas songs, and the turkey of a truck driver who had cruised past as the cop was ticketing me. As we pulled away, Sami roused and began screaming again, at me or the cop, I wasn't sure who.

Eight hundred miles later, my butt and my nerves were numb from winter driving, constantly scanning for black ice, deer, and bad-mood-holiday cops. Sami kept up his protests, interfering with the fascinating farm-to-market reports about hog bellies. I'd never had such an urge to strangle an animal. Or a radio. Or Bing Crosby.

The next year, I ignored Bing and put the checks and gifts in the mail. I stayed home for the holidays, spending my time keeping Sami from eating the tinsel off our little tree. The days were restful, quiet, lazy, and all spent within an hour's *blessedly quiet* drives to and from friends' celebrations.

Two years passed before I had to leave home again, this time for a retreat. I pulled the suitcase out from the back of the closet and opened it flat on the bed, then went back to dig out appropriate clothes. When I turned around, Sami had already packed himself and was sitting squarely in the bottom half of the suitcase. As I started toward him, he gave a menacing growl. Startled, I backed off and looked at him, clothes clutched against my chest, not sure I had heard correctly.

"Sami? What are you doing? What's the matter?"

He sat staring at me, slapping his tail angrily against the bottom of the suitcase. This was cat language, but I clearly understood the message—"I'm one *mad* cat!"

"What in the world is the matter with you? Are you *threatening* me?" I moved a bit closer, totally astounded. Sweet Sami, growling *at me*?

"Ggrrrrr... hhisssss..." Speech delivered with ears flat, pupils dilated, tail slamming even more authoritatively against the suitcase. I backed off, feeling a twinge of fear of this twelve-pound, clawed and fanged cat for the first time ever.

"Sami! Get out of the suitcase! Now!"

His tail slammed down... Slap... Slap... SLAP!

"Honey, you aren't going anywhere, you're going to stay home. Penny will bring you treats and will play with you," I wheedled, placating him by reminding him how much he liked my neighbor. "You don't have to go," I promised, moving toward the suitcase again. My advance was met with another set of deep-throated, guttural, seriously-about-to-attack-growls.

In four years of companionship, I had never seen him anything but happy and enthusiastic, except for the Christmas trip. I hadn't known Sami *could* growl. Unlike some of my friends, I never had scratches on my hands, arms, or legs—just an occasional leg puncture if I was wearing shorts when he used my lap as a launching pad. He had never hissed or growled at me, not during a flea bath, vet trips, taking medicine. Now, everything about his behavior warned me that he was ready to attack if I put *anything* into that piece of luggage. I truly felt afraid of him.

I surrendered, threw the clothes on the floor, and went downstairs to watch TV. Eventually, Sami came downstairs, jumped on my lap, snuggled in, and went trustingly to sleep. I later snuck upstairs and finished packing, still baffled at his odd behavior. Did he remember that turkey of a trip? Was he upset that I might be taking him with me? Or perhaps that I'd be leaving him home? I'd read that cats had only very short memories. *Was three years short?*

Whatever had had him in a tizzy, he'd given me another clue to cat behavior contradictory to what the experts said in the books and articles I had read about a feline's inability to think, remember, or associate events. Sami had communicated his feelings about that suitcase *very well*, and he certainly did connect them to the trip. But who would believe *me*—a person with no significant credentials pertaining to cat behavior except as adoptive Cat-Mom.

When I later told my vet about Sami's reaction, he assured me that there was some leftover smell in the suitcase that bothered him because cats can't remember that long. My respect for that vet went into the litter box. The better I knew my cats, the more I was growing in the conviction that vets had no concept of what cats could understand, feel, and remember.

I was left with a belief I was unable to prove—that Sami didn't just decide to jump in a suitcase and spontaneously growl at me for the first time in his life because of a scent from years before. I knew as well as I had ever known anything in my life that he remembered and associated that suitcase with that trip as vividly as I did, and he wasn't going to let me go through that again. Thank you, Sami. *Christmas. Bah humbug.*

Chapter 10
LITTLE BROTHER

Austin, Texas. Spring 1991. During the four years we had lived in the ant house, the area around it had deteriorated, with daily news reports of arrests of gang members, prostitutes, and drug dealers just a few streets away. I was growing more and more concerned about our safety, especially since I was still letting Sami go outside. It was time to move.

I found a recently remodeled, two-story townhouse. I hoped the stairs would give Sami lots of exercise, and I could make him an inside-only cat. The move went smoothly. I loved the new place. Sami hated it! Even with twice the room to play inside, all he wanted was *ooOUTTT! OOOUttt!* His main exercise was trotting from door to door complaining endlessly that his exit was blocked. Apparently thinking I hadn't understood when he asked in a quieter scream, he practiced turning up the volume as he ran up and down the stairs looking for an opening to the great outdoors.

No matter what toy I bought, he wasn't pacified. I installed a cat tree, played with him with interactive toys, and spent long minutes brushing and combing him. It wasn't enough to keep him happy. How could that compare with pouncing on bugs, chomping on grass and grasshoppers, and finding snakes to carry to mom? Six months into the move, I was at my wit's end about what to do with him.

Then Penny, the cat-person neighbor from the next building, called me at work. "Do you remember you said you thought Sami was lonely?"

"Yeesss," I admitted, slowly and reluctantly, right away having a suspicion of where this was leading.

"And do you remember when you talked about how you would like a gray cat like a neighbor had? And you said you might keep a female grey kitten—if one ever showed up?"

"Hmm... yes." It *had* been a really cute kitten.

"Well, there's a grey kitten, about six weeks old, that's been in our yard for a few days. Some guy took it, and then it was back here today. I can't find where it belongs. Would you...?"

"No!" I responded quickly.

She waited quietly, and I started caving.

"Male or female?" I asked, looking for reasons to say no.

"Oh, I'm sure she's female, though you can't really tell when they're this young," she said. "She's got blue eyes, and Mom says she'll have longish hair."

My mind was busy scrambling for reasons why not, but mostly I just didn't want another cat. I loved Sami dearly but didn't need any more food and vet bills, and I didn't want to clean another cat box. Still, I thought about it. Maybe it *would* keep Sami occupied and inside. And quiet.

"OK, let's try it," I said, succumbing to the silence. "Some conditions though. You baby-sit her during the next two days until the weekend when I can be home all day. I'll take her home at night in the meantime. Also, we continue looking for her real owner. If Sami doesn't like her, you take her back." I gave her half a second to object. Nothing happened. I hung up and went back to typing.

On my way home, I stopped to pick up the lost girl. I wasn't impressed; though she was friendly, I didn't see her as pretty. As I was carrying her out of their condo, Penny hollered, "Call me if you have any problems with him."

Stopping abruptly, I turned around. Surely I hadn't heard her right. "Him! I thought you said it was a she!"

"Oh, I couldn't tell when I called you, but I'm sure now that it's a him—that's what my mom says."

I was sure I had just been had. Her mom had rescued many cats before. Nevertheless, I carried the little thing home to keep my part of the bargain. And the poor baby was ugly, at least in my view, if any bright-eyed kitten could be called ugly. His head was crowned by big bat ears and his white bib looked like a spill of milk, with a drop still on his chin. Dark stripes going every which way decorated the medium gray coat. His hair stood up, the top layer making him look like his fuzzy tail had been plugged into a light socket. On top of that, he wouldn't match Sami at all; they would look ugly together. I'd take him back in the morning, but I'd go ahead and feed him tonight.

For all his unattractiveness, he seemed to have a sweet nature, not crying or hissing, just contentedly staying in my arms like he belonged there as I carried him home. I shut him in the bathroom, locked Sami into the bedroom, and then let the kitten out to explore while I fixed supper.

He wasn't much bigger than a good-sized spot on the rug, smaller even than Sami had been when I brought him home. It took him awhile to explore the house. He never once tried to find a hiding place, though he periodically rushed back into the kitchen, I presumed wanting to see if I was still there. I got a wobbly feeling in my heart region when I realized that's exactly what he was doing. Once he could see me again, he went back to exploring every cubbyhole and corner. And I heard him introducing himself to the cat box.

After supper, I let Sami out, hanging onto the disciplinary spray bottle of water I had used with him when he was doing something that put him in danger, and he refused to cooperate.

"Look, Sami. We have a visitor tonight. Be nice to him!" I held the kitten out toward Sami who sniffed, his lip curling in response to the stranger's unique smell. There. Introductions were done, and no one was upset.

Surely, the angels on duty had been sent to us as chastisement for their lousy performance at Christmas; they were making sure they didn't mess up again, now watching out for my cats, keeping them safe from each other and my naivety. I hadn't thought to get any advice about introductions; in retrospect, I had done everything wrong. I put the kitten down on the floor, then settled into the recliner next to him to read while he and Sami got acquainted. Instead, Sami turned his back and went to the kitchen; the kitten scrambled over beside the chair where I had settled in and crouched down, bread-loaf fashion, head lowered in subservience.

For several hours, as I read, the kitten stayed right beside my recliner, making himself as small as possible, paws and tail scrunched up under himself. The inhospitable Sami finished eating and stomped past us on a route from one side of the living room to the other, then turned back again and stomped the other way. On each trip, he slowed down as he neared us, glanced toward the visitor, then gave a threatening, long drawn out "ha-aissss" as he went by. The kitten never moved, just sat as still as a dead mouse, eyes lowered. Sami finally got tired and disappeared upstairs.

Later, I put the new kid in the spare bedroom and went to bed. Sami settled down right outside the visitor's bedroom door, apparently intending to stand guard through the night to make sure the intruder didn't come out and attack me.

The next morning, I dropped the bitty thing off at Penny's on my way to work. As I stood just inside her condo giving her my schedule for the day, my bitty kitty made straight for the kitchen and the food bowl, chomping through the kibble as though he hadn't eaten for weeks instead of a few minutes earlier. He was still eating as I closed their front door and left. Halfway down the driveway, I heard Penny hollering.

"Oooh. Look at this!"

I turned around. Above two white paws hooked over the rim of the bottom panel of the screen door, the top half of a little gray face with huge eyes and bat ears peered out at me. *He had quit eating to run after me!* My heart melted. No one, nothing, had every tried to follow me as I walked away. I finally knew what a mom felt like on that first day of school. For better or worse, I was keeping her-him.

Two evenings later, while still going through the same "mom in recliner, kitty in bread-loaf position, Sami stomping and hissing" routine, I was terrified when kitty suddenly unwound and went tearing after Sami. The No Name kitty raced up from behind and appeared to take a bite out of Sami's butt, or maybe he goosed him. Whatever happened, Sami took off running like all the jungle tigers were after him instead of that bitty kitty.

My adrenaline kicked in as I struggled to scramble out of the chair in time to prevent a tragedy—to grab the kitten from Sami's potential jaws of death. Before I could take a step, they had both disappeared into the hallway and were thundering up the stairs.

By the time I could get going, the kitten came scrambling back down, Sami in hot pursuit. *Would my sweet Sami chew up the kitty? What should I do?* I was in such a panic, I couldn't think straight. Reaching the wall at the end of the dining room, with nowhere else to go, the kitten stopped abruptly, turned around, and faced Sami. Sami screeched to a halt, wheeled around, and went racing back across the floor, four little white paws pumping after him.

I was still trying to decide who to grab first and how to do it when they came racing past me again in reverse order. *The game was on.* This brave little cat had engaged Sami in a game of chase, and Sami was loving it! Just that quickly, they bonded. From that moment on, they were the Siamese and his twin. When I needed one, I knew I would find them both, curled up head to head, or cuddled back to back. I was thrilled. I was sure the kitten would settle Sami down, and he would be too busy to pace and scream to be let outside.

Unfortunately, the newcomer didn't make everything well in our paradise. Sami seemed ill, almost stopped eating and refused my attempts to interact, to cuddle, even to feed him. He no longer sat on my lap. Most cruel to my heart, he slept at the bottom of the bed, far out of my reach, for the first time in our four years together.

He didn't appear ill exactly, just very lethargic. After a couple of weeks, it was evident that he was losing weight. I worried that perhaps the kitten was a carrier of some dread disease without exhibiting any symptoms himself. After another attempt at trying to coax Sami to eat by finger-feeding him baby food—the last resort for appetite enticement—I called for reinforcements.

"Penny, help. Sami seems to be sick. He's not eating at all. He acts really confused, and he doesn't want me to touch him. Can you come see him?"

She came over. Sami, uncharacteristically, ignored her.

"Here, Sami, want a treat?" She extended a bit of cheese, then tried a few flakes of canned tuna. Sami acted as though he wasn't even aware of her. It was obvious something was terribly wrong.

The next day, the vet was unable to diagnose anything and needed to charge me for that verdict. For the next month, Sami continued to eat only enough to keep himself alive, getting very thin, his eyes dull and uninterested, his once glossy coat now ragged-looking. He was either sleeping, sitting in a daze, or, which was quite puzzling, he was playing enthusiastically with the kitten. How could he go from such an extreme of lethargy to enjoying his play? It didn't make sense. A friend highly recommended another vet.

This vet was probably in his mid 40's, walked with two canes, and was massive. He listened to my complaints, but asked no questions. He sat on a stool throughout the exam, instructing me to put Sami on the floor, call to him, hold him in my arms, and interact. He observed Sami *not* walk, *not* respond when I called him. I put him on the exam table, and the vet felt him all over, listened to his heart, pressed his stomach. Then he held Sami up and out at arms' length, like that cat judge had done, looked long into his eyes, then brought him in close and rubbed cheeks with him. Finally, he asked me one question.

"Do you have a new animal in the house, new husband, baby?"

"Yes, a new kitten, but that was weeks ago," I said. "Sami adores him."

He spoke authoritatively. "There's nothing wrong with this cat except he's depressed because of sharing you with a new cat."

"But he *loves* the kitten. I don't understand. I didn't change anything in the way I treat him. How long will this last?"

"You have betrayed him, it's that simple. Could be another day, could be a year before he comes out of it, could be never."

"What can we do?" I asked in dismay, unable to imagine that Sami could go on like this for long with no more than he was eating.

"We can give him an appetite stimulant, might get him eating again, might not. Not much else you can do, except wait it out and give him lots of attention."

Grumbling to myself about yet another vet bill with no real solution, I left the office with a very low opinion of another vet who obviously didn't know what he was doing—giving a human diagnosis to my cat! I was devastated. My wonderful Happy Cat Sami was depressed. *Really?* By now I had come to love No Name kitty. Would I have to give him up?

I gave Sami the appetite pills. He started eating a little, but with no interest. He shied away when I tried to pet him, breaking my heart each time. He went back to not eating when the pills ran out. I tried to give him extra attention—he walked away. I gave him extra of his beloved vitamins—he reacted slowly, dazedly, looked at them, and then ignored them. He had an eerie, vacant look in his eyes most of the time, as though he wasn't really there. He slept about twenty hours a day; when I looked for him he was usually hiding under the bed. He came out to play with the kitten, but sought no interaction or enjoyment in anything else, especially me. I didn't know what else to do after two different vet visits. When I gathered him into my arms and cried into his fur, he was unresponsive and limp.

At work one day, I borrowed the *Physician's Desk Reference Manual* from our medical library and looked up "major depression." There they were, all of Sami's symptoms in print: decreased appetite, lack of interest in activities, reclusive, avoiding interaction, sleeping all the time.

I berated myself because it had never occurred to me that a feline and a human could have the exact same *emotional* diagnosis. I owed that vet an apology for the way I had casually dismissed his theory. How had he known?

Here it was again; my learned information, gleaned from higher authorities—doctors, vets, preachers, farmers—not agreeing with what I was now seeing in my animals.

For Sami to react so radically just because I got a companion for him was incomprehensible—a *cat* being so loyal to me that he went into clinical major depression because he thought I had betrayed him? Depression, betrayal? These are the most complex of *human* emotions. Sami was certainly teaching me that we intelligent humans had not gotten it right. Of course, Sami was exceptional, so perhaps, by some genetic fluke, he was different from the rest of his species?

My new knowledge didn't help much, however. The kitten had now been with us over three months with no sign of improvement in Sami. As I stood in the kitchen one day, again reading the ingredients in a new nutritional supplement a friend had recommended for me, I noted it had a milk base. Maybe not great for a cat, but then again, nothing else had helped, so why not? I was feeling better, aching less, with a definite increase in energy. I looked down at Sami standing motionless in the middle of the kitchen, seemingly confused about what he was supposed to be doing and why he was there.

"Sami? Do you want some good stuff?"

He slowly raised his head and looked up at me with those vacant eyes.

I licked my finger, stuck it into the can of powder, and offered it to him. He looked at it, but didn't move. I plopped my finger on his nose, sprinkling the powder on him. He licked it off. I stood and watched. After a few seconds he looked up at me, actually making eye contact, seeming to ask for more. I sprinkled some on his food. He moved slowly to the bowl, then licked the powder off the kibble.

At last, and just that fast, Sami was eating! I gave him a half-teaspoon of powder that day, a little more the following two days. Within three days, he was again eating like he was enjoying it. I called the manufacturer to ask if it was OK for animals; they said they wouldn't recommend continuing it as it was processed and calibrated for humans, but a little probably wouldn't hurt him.

But the powder had done enough. Sami was eating again and quickly gained back some of his weight. He seemed to have aged years in those few months, though, moving more slowly and deliberately now. But his eyes shone again with the light of life, and he allowed me to pick him up, even choosing to climb into my lap. *My Sami was back.*

My view of animals was changed forever. I had now experienced what I felt was irrefutable evidence disputing the "common knowledge" that animals are animals and have no "higher" emotions, "like ours." They weren't sentient beings, didn't have emotions, so I had been told. I thought back to the farm animals and felt a wave of grief so strong that I was almost physically ill. Up and down weren't in the same place anymore, the bad was now good and vice versa, and the rules of a lifetime didn't make sense. I didn't know what to hang on to, who to believe about what. My life had been a puzzle with all the pieces that I had made for it fitting where they were supposed to, but now, there was no border and the pieces wouldn't, couldn't, fit. *What had Sami done to me?*

Chapter 11
NAMES GAMES AND FAMILY

Austin, Texas. Summer 1991. While Sami had been in his blue funk, little No Name kitty had been growing. And growing. I'd had him three months, and his lack of a name was embarrassing. Penny, the super-namer, suggested Bugsy. Certainly, he looked like a Bugs Bunny, right down to the big white feet and big ears, but he didn't act anything like a know-it-all rabbit. Despite his mischievous nature, I felt a dignity about him that didn't fit an ornery bunny. I was frustrated that I couldn't settle on something as simple as a cat name. *What if I had had human twins?*

Then, on a shopping trip, I found it on a children's book. *Little Bear,* a grizzly cub with silver tips on his coat, sharp claws, long teeth, big feet, who moved with a shaggy walk, was just like my kitty—probably even about the same size.

As soon as I got home, I called Penny. "He has a name! Come over for a christening party."

When she got there and I explained, she agreed it was a good name. We opened a bottle of sparkling apple juice, wiped some on his head, and dubbed him Little Bear. He was not happy with his anointing and took off. But I felt a big relief; now when I took him to the vet's, after admitting to months of ownership, I wouldn't have to write *None* in the name blank. And a vet trip was coming up fast. Penny reminded me that a six-month deadline to get Bear fixed was approaching. "Fixed"—such a polite term for one way to stop a male's spraying his pungent realty sign warning other cats to "Stay Out, this is *my* place!"

"Thanks for the reminder. I'll make an appointment soon."

Little Bear, though, was in his usual hurry and *soon* wasn't soon enough. He greeted me at the door two weeks later, turned around, and sprayed the front door as I stood there, not believing what I was seeing. And smelling. Three days after that, I was picking him up from the vet's, post-surgery. I pulled out my charge card and handed it to the receptionist, asking for a report.

"He's ready to go," said the receptionist in a lackluster manner while printing out the bill. Then the vet came out.

"How did he do?" I asked. He was my Little Bear. Surely he had done perfectly?

"He's fine," replied the vet in a blasé voice. How could he be so calm! This was a new vet. The wonderful one who had diagnosed Sami's depression had closed his practice. I wasn't sure I liked this one at all. He had just done painful surgery on my little man—my little non-man. And all he could say was "He's fine?"

"You're sure? *What weren't they telling me? Why wasn't he telling me how perfectly the surgery had gone, how fast he would heal, faster than any other cat?* When will he wake up?"

"Oh, he's been awake for an hour or so, still a bit groggy, so keep him in a dark and quiet spot and leave him alone. He'll probably sleep all evening. Just keep him isolated so he doesn't play too hard and hurt himself." I could feel the tension easing in my shoulders, only then realizing how eager I had been for a good report.

"So, when can I feed him?" I asked, knowing Little Bear would want to know.

"He probably won't want to eat, but you can give him a little food and water."

The vet tech handed me the carrier; I peeked in. My little boy was crumpled up all the way at the back, looking pathetic and at least five pounds smaller than he had that morning. His eyes were completely dilated, with only the barest blue outline around them, telling me he was in pain.

Once home, I took my little one upstairs to the master bedroom closet. He promptly curled up all the way at the back on the towels I had readied as his nest. I left to get his water bowl and some food, walking the few steps across the bedroom to the top of the stairs. Before I could put my foot on the first step, Little Bear went hurtling past, "ass over tea kettle," as grandma used to say. His back parts were still asleep, and when he tried to follow me down the stairs, his hind end passed his head, he turned a somersault, and then went into an uncontrolled slalom to the bottom. He landed in a heap at the foot of the stairs.

I hurried down, cursing myself, knowing that I should have known he would follow me! Didn't he always? Why hadn't I shut the closet door? I picked him up gingerly, checking him over as best I could. He seemed to be fine, just confused or maybe still too numb to feel pain. Carrying him on my arm, I grabbed water and food bowls and took him back upstairs to the closet, closing the door this time.

Carefully, I put him back on the towels and then sat down beside him, talking soothingly, apologizing for putting him through the trauma. Even as I petted him, he dozed off. I decided to let him sleep off the surgery and the subsequent Olympic-qualifying Cat Slalom event. I opened the door, tripping over Sami who was parked right in front of it. I tried to shoo him down the stairs. He objected, dancing around, meowing and crying, refusing to move away. Then I heard Bear on the other side of the door, crying, wanting out. Or wanting Sami.

Giving up on the vet's advice, I picked up Little Bear, called to Sami, and we all trooped downstairs. The cats melded together on the couch, I sat down in the recliner, and we all took naps. By the next day, Little Bear was hopping around like always, seeming to be in total recovery and having passed a milestone on his way to adulthood almost two months sooner than Sami had.

For some reason, I had naively assumed that all kitties had to read a Cat Manual and then pass a test before they could be born, and thereafter they would all be much alike—a cat is a cat is a cat—doing the same sorts of things at the same approximate times. However, after Little Bear's arrival, it was apparent that my assumption was very misguided. Obviously, there were very different versions of that Manual.

Until Little Bear showed up, I hadn't realized what an easy cat Sami had been. Besides their physical differences—Sami was a thoroughbred race horse, Little Bear a Clydesdale. Sami had a languidness about him, sauntering when he walked while Little Bear charged from place to place on sturdy legs and fat paws, thundering through the house, seeming to vibrate with energy even when he stood still.

Sami loved a few of his toys, but mostly played with milk bottle rings, long and ropey things like my earrings, my shoestrings, and gift ribbons. And when Sami was upset or wanting something, he told me so, clearly, loudly, and when he wasn't upset, he "talked" to me, quietly.

Bear, the usually silent kitty, made the world his toy; he was into everything. If something moved, he chased; if it sat there, he pounced; if it had a hole, he was in it, and if he could get it in his mouth, he needed to taste, chew, or carry it around for a few hours. I was constantly rescuing him from dangerous things and places—under the rocking recliner, off the rim of the full bathtub, out of the clothes dryer as I was throwing wash in. Now I could empathize with mothers having to deal with their toddlers' curiosity and fearlessness.

Even their sleep was different. Sami slept soundly. I had once lifted him and slid a newspaper out from under him. He never woke up. Bear could appear to be sleeping, but when I was within six feet of him, his eyes would pop open, and he would search until he saw me.

As soon as I, or any of my guests, abandoned their shoes, Bear was into them, rubbing on them, sticking his head in, fighting them until they were soaked with slobber. I warned guests, but they just watched in fascination. He also had the curious hobby of shredding paper of any kind. He'd clasp a piece of paper between his front paws, chomp down, and pull with his teeth, spitting out the confetti-sized spit ball, then going for another chew until there was almost nothing left of the original paper. As I vacuumed, I wondered if any teacher would have believed me if I told them "the *cat* ate my homework." Thank goodness, I was done with school.

One day, a Best Thing came into Bear's life as a piece of hard plastic in the form of a funnel. I was pondering where and how I had come by the small apparatus I found when cleaning out the drawer. Before I figured it out, I dropped it. Little Bear glommed on to it in an instant, as though it was his lost child. The diameter of a silver dollar at its wide end, the funnel tapered into a long, skinny tip that would release one small drop of perfume at a time. Bear grabbed it, making the point stick straight out from his mouth like a cigarette. Funnel instantly became his most-prized possession. I wasn't so fond of Bear's Best Thing. Stepping out of bed onto the sharp end of a piece of hard plastic hurt, as did rolling over in bed onto the point. Bear had discovered his toy made a lovely noise when he slammed it across the tile floor in the kitchen—clackety-clack, clack, clack each time he whacked it. It sounded the same after he had run it down and slammed it back to the other end of the kitchen. Repeatedly. Daily. Nightly. The activity kept him occupied for ten or even twenty minutes at a time and kept me awake for the same amount of minutes.

Alas, months later there came the day I noticed Bear crouching to look under the sofa, looking under a chair, squeezing behind furniture. I soon realized the tragedy; Funnel had disappeared. We simply couldn't find it, and I was unable to find a replacement. Bear refused to accept any substitute out of the big toy box and continued to look everywhere for his plastic blankie.

Many months later, I went to a home organizing store on an errand. There, sitting on the bottom shelf in the cooking aisle, was a stack of *ten* small funnels. I bought them all and started spreading the news as soon as I came in the front door.

"Bear, Sami! I've got presents!" Little Bear caught my enthusiasm and started dancing around; Sami stood and waited.

"Look! Look, what Mommy brought you!"

I pulled Funnel II out of the bag and dropped it in front of Bear. He grabbed it and didn't let go of it all evening except to eat, and even then he placed it by the food bowl and picked it up again as soon as the bowl was empty. When he later took a nap, Funnel II was right in front of his nose.

"Look, Sami. I got you a present, too! See, it's all silvery and snaky." Sami immediately started pawing at it, then grabbed the long, silver twist-tie in his mouth and ran off, apparently not the least bit jealous of Bear's Funnel.

Another of Little Bear's fun things was water. Any time I turned the faucet on in the bathroom sink, he came thundering through the house from wherever he had been. Leaping up to the counter, he'd shove his paw repeatedly under the stream and then lick the drops off. Enthused, he'd hunker down and drink and drink, his head almost under the flow. But, if a drop of water hit him, it was a horrible thing to watch. It was obvious he understood the crisis: he was going to dissolve like Oz's wicked witch. The shaking and flicking of paw and running in circles were pathetic to see, my brave boy reduced to a wild-eyed crazy cat until he got all the water licked off. The next day he'd repeat the histrionics all over again. Sami, however, just wanted his water in a glass, period.

I'd rarely had to use any discipline with Sami who was much more compliant than my headstrong Little Bear. With younger son, I wheedled, bribed, and cajoled, but sometimes even that just wasn't enough. From clapping my hands, yelling his name, and stomping my foot, we graduated to the squirt bottle. At first, one spritz of water would get his attention. Alas, it was not always to be.

For health and safety reasons, the kitchen counters and table were off limits to my cats. I amazed myself at my patience in trying to train them to my way of thinking, but I persevered—I was afraid they would get scorched on a hot pan, or eat a human food that was poisonous, or leave cat-box germs on the counter.

Then the day of the Great War happened. I found Bear sitting on the kitchen table; I told him to get off. He dropped down onto his stomach and looked at me as I pointed at the floor. And he refused to move. I told him again, swearing to myself that he would get off the table without my having to use the squirt bottle, the most dreaded form of coercion. When he didn't move, I picked him up and put him on the floor. He walked to the other side of the table and jumped back up. I walked over and lifted him down. Over and over and over. Finally, defeated, I got the water bottle. And sprayed him. He just sat there, letting me do it, again and again. He won. I stopped but not before he was saturated. There is nothing more pathetic-looking than a wet cat; it diminishes them somehow, making them small and taking away their dignity. I put him down on the floor again, and this time he started to walk to the other side of the table, hesitated, then turned and stumbled toward the living room, throwing a look at me over his shoulder.

A few weeks later I again found him on the table. As soon as he saw me, he jumped down, and leisurely left the kitchen with a backward glance that was clearly a communication. I wasn't sure, but I felt he was tossing me the finger—"see, you can't stop me, but I just don't want to lie there anymore." I never caught him on there again. But I felt ashamed, using my power to force him. This was not what I had promised myself—that I would always treat my cats with respect. I put the water bottle away and never used it for discipline again.

Bear's caring and compassionate side showed up when I found India. One dark and stormy evening, I stopped by the grocery store. When I came out, a little bitty kitty was sitting in a puddle by my car door.

"Are you lost?" She looked up at me, not making any attempt to get away. "Is your mommy here? Where did you come from?"

She didn't seem to have anything to say, and offered no protest when I scooped her up. I waited a few minutes, but no one claimed her. Since I'd been told parking lots were favorite places for people to dump animals, I took her home and called Penny to tell her I had a kitten needing an owner and asked if she could come meet her.

"You're a lucky kitty, India," she said as she picked her up.

Yes! Just like that, Penny had named her. India—a perfect name for this cat that looked like an exotic rug, with black and brown swirls on a gold background. During the next week, we fruitlessly looked for India's owner, past or future.

Meanwhile, Bear adopted her like he had just found the woman he was going to marry, even abandoning much of his cuddle time with Sami, who didn't seem very impressed with her. Little Bear showed her around the house, where the food bowls and the cat boxes were, and generally took her under his whiskers. She was willing to follow wherever he led, which got them both into trouble one evening.

I was in the recliner reading, facing the dining room where my first-ever new, shiny-topped dining room table sat. To the right of the table stood a half wall, separating the dining area from the kitchen, and on the opposite side of the table was the sliding glass door. Over the tops of my reading glasses, I caught sight of something flying through the air from the kitchen divider toward the table. Followed closely by a second something. I registered that the flying objects were cats, the first large and gray, the second small and brownish.

Bear had apparently felt an obligation to entertain India. He had jumped onto the forbidden kitchen counter and launched himself down onto the shiny and slick surface of the table, slid across it, then jumped down to the floor. India was right behind. Then they ran back to the kitchen to start the cycle all over again. With visions of long cat scratches on my prized furniture, I reluctantly stopped the action, even though charmed at watching the delight they had had in their game.

A few days later, while sitting in my office at the top of the stairs, I glimpsed something red out of the corner of my eye. I turned my head toward the hall. At the top of the stairwell, I saw a red *Open House* helium balloon I had brought home the night before "for the kids." It wasn't just rising straight up, it was *coming* up the stairs. The red ribbon attached to the balloon then came into view, followed by the tips of two grey ears, then the mouth that was tenderly holding the ribbon. Then all of Little Bear appeared, followed by India a step behind. Bear looked like he would burst his buttons he was so obviously proud to be the standard bearer of the red balloon parade.

I was *so* impressed with my big-hearted Little Bear and his sweetness and compassion with India. Sami allowed them their time, coming to me for companionship when they played. So quickly India had adopted us, but I just could not see myself with another cat. I called Penny.

"Have you found anyone interested in adopting India yet?" I waited for her response.

"I thought you might want to keep her."

"She's so sweet, I'd love to, but I just can't handle the expense, and three cat boxes in the condo are just too much. I'm also concerned what might happen with Sami if India and Little Bear get too close. I couldn't stand to see Sami so depressed again, and right now, Little Bear is spending more time with India than with Sami."

A few days later, a couple came and fell in love with the sweet girl. Sami, Bear, and I watched as she was carried away. Little Bear returned to the couch, and Sami went over and snuggled next to him. Sami had finally forgiven me for my gift of Little Bear, and he and the "intruder" were best buddies, chasing and wrestling each other, sleeping crammed together, eating together—always together. Even with me, if one was on my lap, the other pressed close against my side.

One day, I looked at them, and the thought came to me once again that we were family. I was amazed to say it, but I loved them, and I believed they loved me for more than the food I fed them, even though I had been assured in the cat books I read that animals could not know such an emotion. If family is defined as protecting and seeing to each other's welfare, showing affection—that was us. My cats welcomed me enthusiastically when I came home, as though all they had been doing since I left was waiting for me. They didn't carry a grudge. They ate their cat food with an attitude of gratitude and seemed to find the cat boxes acceptable even if I forgot to clean them. They asked for praise when delivering a toy catch of the day, offered companionship by snuggling at night, and awoke me in the morning by purring in my ear. If family is defined as individuals loving, nurturing, and caring for each other, then, yes, we were a family, even if we were an unconventional and interspecies one. I knew, beyond the shadow of a doubt, that they wanted to please me as much as I wanted to please them. *Wasn't that what loving families did?*

Chapter 12
TRAGEDY

Austin, Texas. December 1992. I led the plumber up to the bathroom, showed him the leak, left for the kitchen, and then heard a yell from above, something that sounded like, "What the...!"

I raced back upstairs. "What's wrong?"

"Wasn't expecting to find this in my bag is all, a surprise when I grabbed him, think it belongs to you," he said, holding out a ball of gray fur. "I wouldn't mind taking him home."

"You're not the first to offer, but no—no, I'll keep him. Thanks anyway!"

After he left, I considered his words. So often, I had read of or overheard people making fun of cats and their owners' relationships with them—that they were standoffish, independent, and had bad attitudes. I could not see those things with my cats. Further, I realized there was no way I could even contemplate the idea of being parted from either of my furry kids. I had loved Sami for over seven years, and Bear for almost four already, yet it seemed that every day I found something new about them, something else to love. They were as much a part of daily life as my arms and legs. I felt my anxiety rise as I again tried to figure out how to keep them both safe *and* happy, a seemingly opposing impossibility.

Shortly after getting Little Bear, I had made an attempt to let them outside. Sami's tenacious cries at the door grated on my ears like a dentist's drill. Finally, worn down, I succumbed to his demands just to get him to shut up, letting him out into our postage-stamp-sized patio surrounded by a privacy fence. I walked outside with him, and he seemed satisfied eating grass and chasing bugs while

Little Bear stood inside the door and cried to come out. That practice run only lasted a few minutes, but it was enough. The change in Sami that evening was a huge relief—he was content, almost silent.

A few days later, I risked it again, even letting Little Bear out into the beautiful autumn day where flowers still bloomed and monarch butterflies stopped on their southward migration. I was pulling Bear out of the vine covering the fence when Sami high-tailed it over the top to freedom. Little Bear ran after but his legs were short and one giant leap took him only about half way up the fence before he crashed backward into the rose bushes. I rushed to pick him up, imagining him bleeding and blind, but relaxed when I didn't see any broken bones. He had learned his lesson and thereafter seemed to be content to catch the bugs in our little patch of grass.

I caught up with Sami at the side of the condo. He came when I called him, so we began going out every day, making sure Bear stayed inside the fence. In the meantime, I swore I could see Bear growing bigger daily. Then, a couple of months later, it happened. I opened the patio door and Sami flew out and jumped the fence, Bear running right behind him. The last I saw of them was Bear's bushy tail waving good-bye.

When I caught up, they were ambling around, inspecting the grass and shrubs along the side of the pool. They didn't try to run—too busy sniffing, very content, and happy. After that, fifteen minutes of out-time became a part of our daily routine as they explored, and I followed closely behind, and so it had been for two years.

Ironically, the day of The Tragedy, I had not let them out. I never let them out in the mornings, afraid I might be late for work if they decided not to come back in. Both Sami and Bear were lounging in their respective wicker chairs on the far side of the living room, watching me. I struggled to hold the front door open with my butt while pushing the storm door wide open, all the while juggling several large packages destined for Christmas mailing.

Suddenly, Sami shot between my legs, almost upsetting me. I was shocked—he had never done such a thing. I watched, powerless to stop him, as he raced to the end of the driveway. I could barely breathe as my heart jumped into my throat, and the adrenaline poured into me as I envisioned the immediate future.

I let the storm door slam, dropped the packages on the ground, and started to run, hearing the sound of a heavy motor. I felt sick to my stomach, sure this was going to end in disaster. Then I remembered to slow down; whenever I tried to catch Sami, he would tease and run away, a game we played in the house sometimes. By now, he was investigating the leaves in the gutter across the street, obviously feeling frisky in the crisp winter sunshine, and very obviously proud of himself for accomplishing this escape, prancing and tossing his head like a young colt.

I'd seen movies where everything went into slow motion; now I experienced it. I heard the sound of that big engine revving two driveways away. I saw Sami hear the sound. Sami didn't like noise. I was torn between calling him or praying that he would stay put. I knew, just knew, that he was going to run back across the street to home and safety. He tried. The black SUV accelerated, on a collision course. Its rear tire hit Sami. It didn't stop, just slid into a right turn at the stop sign half a block away and then raced onto the main road and away.

Sami was flopping down the middle of the street after the SUV, his body rolling over and over. I was screaming. I was *trying* to *move*. To run after Sami. My feet seemed stuck to the street. Sami staggered up. By the time I could start moving, he was turning in disoriented circles. Then he chose a direction and ran, heading for the across-the-street neighbor's woodpile. A trail of blood followed him.

I followed as fast as I could. Too slowly. I got to him as he was trying to find a place to hide between the stacked fireplace logs. I grabbed, barely got a grip around his ribs. It was enough so I could pull him out. I couldn't hold him. He was twisting wildly. I dropped him. He ran back across the street into Penny's driveway and dove under her car. I followed, hollering for help. By then Penny had heard and was rushing out her door.

"What happened? What's wrong?"

"Sami. Under your car. He's been hit! He's bleeding, and his eye is out and... it's... *it's awful.* I have to get him to the vet. Can you get the carrier? Door's open."

"I'll take care of it."

"I'll stay here to be sure he doesn't run away again. Hurry! *Please hurry.*"

Sami stayed crouched where he was, under the exact middle of her car, way beyond my reach. I could see the blood dripping from his head mixing with the slobbers from his mouth. I waited, trying to stay calm but failing, frantically trying to figure out if I could get him to a vet... or, should I get my gun? Could I? Had to stop his pain! But...

"Here's the carrier!"

"He's not moving. We have to move your car," I told her.

"We can't! He'll run again if I start it. Let me see if I can crawl under and grab him." She dropped her much younger, more limber body to the ground on the other side and started crawling, getting part way under the car. She made a grab for him. He ran. *Thank god, he ran straight to me!*

"I've got him! Hold the carrier open."

As we struggled to get him in, my beloved Sami turned and bit deeply into my hand, bringing blood, screaming in outraged pain. I held on to him for his dear life. I was *not* letting go again. Between us, we got all his parts into the carrier at once, and I locked the wire door shut.

"Call the vet." I was yelling instructions to Penny even as I ran to my car and shoved the carrier onto the front seat and made a dash into the condo for my purse. I took off, speeding the few blocks to the Interstate, arriving at prime time morning rush hour. In-bound traffic was its normal—a parking lot. I slammed on the emergency blinkers and plunged through the vehicles. The car swerved in and out. I hit the horn over and over, forcing my way into any possible opening. I know anyone looking could see how upset and determined I was, and many obligingly, amazingly, moved over to let me squeeze between the lanes. Sami howled in pain and moaned non-stop; I silently echoed him.

The vet was waiting and took him right in. I paced the waiting room for fifteen very long minutes before she returned.

"It's not as bad as it looks. I've given him a sedative, and I think he'll be OK. The chin bone on a cat is like the chicken wishbone; his is broken, snapped in two, so I'll wire his jaw shut, and that bone should heal OK. This is a common injury. He has some swelling on his brain. The worst problem is the eye. His vision may never be good in that eye, but other than that I think he'll be fine."

I felt dumb and dazed and just gave permission for all of it, not asking a single question. Then I went to work only because I knew I would need that job for the vet bill. I watched the clock until two, then couldn't stand it. I called for a report.

"This is Sami's mom." I stopped, unable to get another word out. I was having trouble making my throat work.

"Yes. Sami will be ready to go after four o'clock today." She was efficient, business-like.

I hung up, spent a few minutes deep breathing and shedding a few tears in relief, then tried to accomplish something called work until quitting time, and snuck out a few minutes early.

The vet came into the reception area just as I arrived.

"I think Sami's going to be fine. He's just coming out of the anesthesia. His jaw is wired shut so he won't be able to eat kibble for a while. Just feed him water with a syringe for a day, then he can have anything he wants. All-meat baby food is good. He's had a pain shot and should sleep until morning. The swelling in his face and brain should start going down by tomorrow."

"What about his eye?" I knew I would have nightmares about the way I had last seen it, an audition for a horror film.

"It's back in the socket. I don't know how useable his vision will be, but I think he's going to look all right."

Once again we got on that familiar expressway, now full of out-bound rush hour traffic. A whole day had gone by at the same slug speed the traffic was going now, but at least we were going home. *Sami was alive!* I should have felt better, but I was still tense, unable to relax.

Within minutes, Sami woke up. And then went totally insane. He howled and screamed, he clawed at the plastic carrier sides, he had somehow gotten a tooth hooked on one of the metal bars on the cage door, and his head was turned completely upside down while his feet remained on the floor of the carrier, *somehow* doing this all with his mouth wired shut! He turned somersaults, tried to claw me through the bars. And screamed. And screamed. I was frantic.

"Sami! Sami, stop!" He continued to twist and writhe. *Why wasn't the pain medication working?*

What could I do, so many lanes of bumper-to-bumper traffic? I just wanted to get him home, as I had when I first took on the role of cat caretaker. I had never experienced a more helpless feeling than I did now, knowing there was nothing I could do to lessen his pain, at least not in the car. He was suffering terribly, and I felt torn apart watching him.

Once we made it home, I opened the carrier door. He crawled out and crouched in front of it, refusing to go any further. I gingerly picked him up and sat on the couch with him, not sure where to touch him without hurting him. Tears and snot were running down my face as I tried to figure out what to do for him, how to comfort him, how to ease his pain.

"Sami, I'm so sorry you feel bad. You are such a brave, brave, silly kitty."

Little Bear paced nearby, trying to get up to lick his buddy; I kept pushing him back down on the floor.

"Sami, I don't know what to do! Please go to sleep. I'll be right here beside you, all night. I won't leave. I promise. Little Bear and I will stay right here." I moved him over, then curled around him and invited Bear up into the space behind me against the couch pillows. Sami settled down a bit and then, finally, passed out. Bear watched over us, and I kept my hand on Sami's body all night to reassure myself that he was breathing.

At the end of six weeks, Sami seemed recovered except for his eye which was very *not* OK and never would be. It was in place, but vacant and not tracking. His coat had become dry and spiky and his bones angled out of his now-loose skin. Otherwise, he was doing well. He was apparently finally satisfied that I still loved him, and the little bit of leftover depression he'd had since Bear's arrival now disappeared. How could he not know how loved he was with all the attention and babying he was getting from me and from Little Bear? Life, and Sami, returned almost to normal. I thought.

A few months later, my mother came to visit. She brought along some crystal glassware she had been storing for me for years. We sat in the middle of the living room floor, pulling out each piece from the box, unwrapping it from the newspaper, and throwing the paper into a pile on the carpet.

Sami came over to see what we were doing. Then, as I watched in horror, he placed himself over the paper pile, spread his hind legs, squatted tentatively, rocked back and forth a few times, and, before my disbelieving eyes, he peed. Sami had been perfectly litter box trained, never missing once in all these years, not from the first hour I brought him home. If a cat is going to "be naughty" about their bathroom habits, I knew they usually did it in secret, not right in front of their person. The exception would be if they were really "pissed off" about something, or were sick. I knew Sami wasn't angry, but I thought he must be very confused. And he was definitely not all right as the vet had assured me he would be. The pee on the newspapers was the first clue that things might never be right again.

Periodically he repeated that performance, but the periodic became more frequent and more inappropriate as time went on, extending to places far beyond the newspaper, but always preceded by that strange rocking squat. There were other instances when he appeared confused—walking to a wall and standing there meowing angrily at it, or bending his head to eat from his bowl with his mouth ending up several inches outside the bowl. Most of the time, though, he was fine—my old Sami. He was safe and loved and able to function well enough. I was just grateful that I still had him, even if he was displaying signs of confusion and having problems with depth perception, which I understood perfectly with my eye issues.

I vowed that I would never let the cats outside again unless I could guarantee their safety. The problem with that vow was Little Bear's zoom-zoom energy. He was wearing me out trying to keep him occupied, always into something, the attention-deficit kid.

Then I read a newspaper article about a woman who walked her cat, just like people walk a dog. That would *so* simplify my life. With no clear idea of how to do such a thing, I bought a turquoise harness made for a Chihuahua and a pink lead that I attached to it. I put everything in the middle of the living room, sprinkled catnip on and around it, and left it there. They sniffed. Sami played with the lead. Little Bear ate the catnip, then rolled around on the carpet. I let them get used to it.

Several days later, I slipped the harness contraption over Sami's head, hooked it quickly around his skinny torso, and stepped back. There was a brief stillness, then an explosion comparable to a mad bull emerging from a rodeo chute. Even as I watched, he fought the straps, his short-haired but sleek body shooting backwards and sliding out of the back of the harness like a kid pulling off a T-shirt. My wonderful idea was crushed.

With only a little hope, I buckled the harness straps under Bear's square body while he stood stoically. I did a test pull, tugging on the lead. He plopped down. I pulled again, dragging him a few inches. No go. I got a treat, headed for the door, and Bear followed me. It was just that easy. Bear and I practiced in the patio, more for me to get the hang of guiding him than for Bear to get used to walking in tow.

Finally, I felt ready. "OK, Bear, let's go for a walk." I hooked him into the harness, picked him up, and carried him outside, watching him sniff the breezes and look at the trees until he stiffened to indicate he wanted down. I obliged, making sure he wasn't tangled in the leash. As he investigated the grasses, the bushes, and the bug on the cement, I practiced with the lead, learning how to keep *him* from backing out of the harness. He was too engrossed in his findings to object.

"Bear, you are just such a good little guy! This is so good, now we can go for walks." Bear loved it—a whole new world of smells and textures under his feet and sunshine on his fur. He showed no hesitation or fear and seemed oblivious to the harness as more than a guide. We stayed out for about fifteen minutes. When we finally went inside, Bear flopped down, leash and all, temporarily satiated, and, for the first time I could remember, out of energy.

At first, I found it amusing to watch drivers do double takes and swerve back into their lanes when they realized it was a cat, not a dog, on the end of the leash. I felt pride that I was able to teach him, and that he was able to learn to walk that way, though I quashed the feelings, somewhat ashamed that I would use my cat for stroking my own ego. But still, I thought of him as a little ambassador, a living example of a cooperative cat, one who could be outside with some degree of safety.

Sami didn't seem to mind staying indoors now. Since the accident, he no longer clamored to go outside. It was obvious that he sometimes didn't know where he was. To make up for my guilt at his enforced captivity, when Bear and I took our walks I collected blades of grass for Sami to nibble and leaves from bushes for him to smell. I bought him more snaky toys and gave him extra treats and cuddles.

There wasn't much I wouldn't do to make my kids happy. Just like a real mom, I thought with satisfaction, which helped somewhat alleviate the guilt I knew I would always feel about Sami's accident. If I had never let him know the joys of being outside, he would never have been hurt. My fault. Bad Cat-Mom.

Chapter 13
CATAPULT

A*ustin, Texas. November, 1995.* The cold rain poured down out of the gray autumn sky as I dashed into the condo, ready for a cozy Friday evening. I was immediately assaulted by silence. Where were my welcome home sounds, the excited meows of my kitties? And... why was the sound of the pounding rain inside as loud as outside? Why were my neck hairs standing up? I tried to put it together but only knew *something* wasn't right. I finally saw that the picture window that looked out onto the patio appeared to be open. Except this was not a window that opened. As I got closer, I saw that sharp points of broken glass still remained in the opening and shattered glass was scattered all over the carpet.

"Sami! Bear! Come here!" I called loudly, hearing the tension in my voice. I began breathing again when both cats immediately hopped through the opening of the window back into the house. Both were completely dry.

"Oh, my babies, what have you done? Did you break the window? What happened?" I demanded answers, but they realized I was now home and began circling around me, crying out their stories, probably explaining why they hadn't met me at the door. I checked them carefully but didn't find any signs of blood. Then I realized the window hadn't been broken *out*, it had been broken *in* which meant the cats weren't the culprits.

As I hurried through the house trying to find the answer to what had happened since I couldn't decode what the cats were telling me, I saw empty spaces where my favorite videos had been, and my stereo and TV were missing.

Upstairs, my few bits of mostly-fake jewelry and a few dollars and change were gone from my nightstand.

As soon as I got back downstairs to the kitchen, I knew what had happened. The tip-off that this was no big-time robbery was the two missing bottles of $.99 Boone's Farm Strawberry Wine that had been on the kitchen counter. I relaxed as the suspicion solidified that teenagers from the high school a block away had been here.

When the police arrived and concurred with my assessment, they did point out that, next time, I should call them *before* I made my own investigation of a house that could still be harboring a criminal. I didn't bother explaining that I knew it was safe because if there had been a burglar in the house, Bear would have been entertaining him, not wrapping himself around me.

I called a co-worker who did man-kind of things; fortunately, he was still at work and answered his phone. He promised to stop by on his way to the airport and his Mexican vacation to put up boards over the opening before leaving town so we weren't camping out.

After he left, I gave thanks that everything had been so easily taken care of, and that we were all safe. But I felt very vulnerable, my expectation of security having vanished with the TV. Now I *knew* we needed to move. I had already been looking at "home for sale" ads, but I just couldn't see my way financially to make it. I kept racking my brain for a way to change things for the better—a safer environment certainly, less financial stress, and a way to get out of the work-home-work-home rut I had fallen into lately.

A few nights later, I woke up out of a sound sleep with a very clear, complete, and viable plan of how to make my life work better. I would buy—not just another house, but a bigger house—which would please the cats. To pay for it, I would get a renter to help with payments, and give a discount for house and yard work—I still battled fibromyalgia. The next weekend, I was still pondering the details of a move when I saw an ad for a psychic fair. Just for kicks, I decided to go—my first ever. I was a bit scared; my only other venture into the psychic world was in high school with a Ouija board with a planchette that had gone crazy when I tried to use it, moving frantically, then throwing itself off the board seemingly in a tantrum.

The instructions on the signs at the door of the auditorium were simple. "Walk around until you find a psychic that feels comfortable to you. Sign up for an appointment."

Instead, impatient, I simply stopped at the first booth where there was a vacancy. "Shuffle them and choose seven," said the normal-looking woman, with not a shawl, a dangling earring, nor a bejeweled ring in sight as she handed me a deck of brightly-decorated cards.

I shuffled, chose, and gave them back to her and waited, curious about this game. She asked if I had any questions. I told her about my finance-job-house dilemma. She spread the cards on the table and stared silently at them.

"Your plan is a good one. This is the right thing to do, and now is the time. Everything is in your favor."

"I'm not sure that I can handle things financially. Should I look for an additional job?"

"No. No need to do that, things are in place and will work out. You need to relax more. You also need to expand your horizons, to open yourself up to new things, new ideas, and trust more."

"Oh, OK." I didn't care about that. I went on to what *was* important. "Will my cats like the move?"

"It will be very good for them. But," she seemed to have an amused look on her face as she peered over the top of her reading glasses at me and added a cryptic warning, "you're in for a wild ride."

"What do you mean?"

"It will be a good thing for you, all of you," she said simply, without explaining.

I was willing to suspend my disbelief and immediately start the house hunting if it was going to be good for my kids. It was lovely to imagine things working out for a change. I liked this psychic!

With no more hesitation, I started searching for our next home. The first house I looked at, a large four bedroom, mother-in-law plan on a third of an acre lot filled with islands of trees in Oak Hill, a southern suburb of Austin, was perfect. It had been on the market for months, but their realtor hadn't put it in the MLS listings for some reason. *The owners must have been waiting for me.* Now they were very eager to sell quickly to meet the husband's new job deadline in Dallas, so anxious they were willing to negotiate considerably on the price. I was amazed and excited—I couldn't ever remember anything so complicated being so easy.

With incredible faith, for me, I signed a contract to buy our new home and then immediately put the condo on the market and waited with growing concern for an offer. My realtor held an open house, a bank-approved buyer appeared, and, suddenly, I was free of that mortgage. So easy! Too easy? Always, when things were going right, I would become anxious, waiting for the glitch I was sure would happen.

My new house was far more splendid than anything I had ever imagined myself living in, and I kept comparing it to that wretched two-story, bathroom-free, heat-free, water-free, uninsulated home I had grown up in; I felt I had moved from poverty to princess. I found myself very anxious though, wanting this to work but doubting. Yet, within a few weeks, the castle was ours—mine, the cats, and the bank's.

I might have reconsidered signing on the mortgager's dotted line had I known what magic, mysteries, and mayhem would occur in that house. Oblivious to forthcoming events, I finally relaxed and enjoyed my most beautiful new home. This home was over 2200 sq. ft on one floor. There were three bedrooms—two I would rent out and the other would be my office— and a bath on one end, and a master bedroom with a bathroom suite on the other end. I put only the sheerest of curtains in the bay windows in the bedroom that looked out on the large lot with three islands of trees scattered around. Even though I had not been thrilled with my home in Nebraska, some part of its wild must have rubbed off because I loved feeling like I was cocooned in nature. And the nature was visible everywhere, all of the rooms have wide and tall windows on multiple walls, except the one wall with a fireplace. Daniel Boone would feel comfortable here—there was definitely plenty of open "elbow room."

With all that open space, the cats developed a new game. At least, I think it was a game. I was still free feeding them kibble at that time, so this could not have had anything to do with when they ate as they ate, or nibbled, all the time. But shortly after my supper, around 7:00 p.m. the crazies would start. As though injected with adrenaline, they would begin charging through the house, chasing each other in every direction, letting out occasional yowls, but mostly just running head long throughout the house. After about fifteen minutes, they would stop and go back to life in general. What set off these Seven O'clock Crazies I never found out, but they were faithful to the schedule almost every night for years.

For a few months, the cats and I luxuriated in all that open-design interior; then, regretfully, I faced financial reality and knew it was time to get serious about a renter. The first step was to advertise, but I was concerned about posting in the newspaper. Who, or what, would I get in response? This would be my property, and I wasn't a 20-year old sharing a two-bedroom apartment. A friend had told me about the movie with the woman who had placed a for-rent ad and ended up with a psychotic killer roommate. *Oh dear. How was I supposed to accept the psychic's advice to relax?*

Chapter 14
MUST LOVE CATS

Oak Hill, Texas. January 1996. I made a list of the qualities I wanted in a prospective renter. It would be a bonus to have a congenial person who had time to do things together, who was mentally challenging, with a good sense of humor, and who would be interested in sharing cooking and sometimes going to a movie. I didn't want anyone who was messy, an alcoholic, or on drugs, who had boyfriends over every night, or made judgments about my affection for my cats. And someone who wasn't home much. And who paid the rent on time. I was reminded of my cat-shopping list. Well, that had worked out OK after taking out just a few words, but I could show some optimism and see what happened.

Looking at the list, I envisioned grad students, airline personnel, contract workers, maybe a night worker. Then I had an inspiration. A few months earlier, I had gone to a massage school that offered cut-rate student massages. I had treated myself to one and had felt like a pile of pudding when I got off the table. The atmosphere of the school, quiet, almost reverent, was very relaxing, and the personalities of the students were nurturing and calming. It would be great to have a masseuse as a renter! I immediately sent letters to two of the schools in town, asking them to post my "Renter Wanted" ad:

Seeking quiet, responsible female for two bedroom and bath private suite in lovely large home in quiet area. Must like cats. NO smoking/drinking/drugs/partying. No pets. Month-to-month rental with discount for house and yard help. Must love cats. Deposit and references required.

There, that summed it up quite well. I'd see if there was anything to this psychic stuff. I waited by the phone, and waited, and tried to remember to relax—this was going to work, the psychic had said so. The sell and buy could not have gone this easily if it wasn't supposed to be.

Finally, the phone rang. "I saw your ad about the house to share. Is it still available?"

"*Yeah!*" I rejoiced silently, keeping my fingers crossed and hoping to find out good things about this pleasant voice. "Yes, it is. Can you tell me about yourself?"

"My name is Sunny, and actually, there are two of us. We're ministers and healers, and we've been traveling around the country doing work on the reservations."

Two of them? Ministers? On a reservation? I felt my hopes drop. "This is... you and your husband?"

"No, it's just me and Amy, one of my students. We're here in Austin temporarily to do some spiritual and healing work. Since you have two bedrooms, this sounds like it would be ideal. We're both in our thirties, and we want something homier than a hotel room. We'll only be here three to six months, then we will be relocating."

I thought about it. For two seconds. I wanted *one* quiet person. Long term. And a preacher? *No way* was I going to be preached to in my own home, and I didn't figure God had much to say to me anyway.

"I'm sorry," I said. "I just wouldn't be comfortable with that." I had my doubts about their financial ability to pay rent anyway. In my experience, preachers were always just above poverty level, and ministering, healing, constantly moving—they could not have been earning much money, if any at all. Then, too, they would probably want *free* rent if they were ministers, like those in my hometown who got free rent and a small salary. For me, this deal was a straight financial necessity, no charity work involved. My ability to pay the mortgage depended on a steady income, and I didn't want to be adjusting to a new roommate every few months. I wanted a long-term, dependable renter.

"Well, in case you change your mind, we're at this number, and my name is Sunny Walker."

I wrote down her info, hung up, looked the note over, and threw it in the trash. I went back into the living room to watch TV. During the commercial, voices in my head started chattering—stern words and certainly not *my* words. "*Don't be so afraid to take chances. You need to call these women back and at least meet them. Don't be so pessimistic and judgmental. Call them back!*"

I ransacked the wastebasket for that little piece of paper and called. Two hours later, I watched a little Toyota pull into the driveway. That was good, my favorite car. I went outside, and we made introductions.

"Hello, I'm Sunny Walker," said the tall, slim one. "And I'm Amy Bell," said the shorter, not so slim one.

"Hi. Come in and let's get acquainted."

I did my usual meeting-new-person once-over. They didn't look like my idea of missionaries, nor did they look like they had been living in a tent.

Amy wore her long, light-brown hair hanging straight down her back and an in-style maxi dress of dusty blue that brought out her light blue eyes. She had a pleasant, round face, spoke with a soft voice, and seemed friendly enough.

Sunny was dressed in a red knit T-shirt, and a long, wildly-colored, tiered skirt that had been politically incorrectly called a "squaw skirt," in fashion in the 1950's. She also wore what appeared to me to be a silver and turquoise Navaho squash blossom necklace that could have paid their first month's rent. Her short red hair was naturally curly, framing a beautiful peaches-and-cream complexion. She wore the brightest red lipstick I had ever seen on anyone except Betty Boop in the comic strips. I offered them chairs, but they said they preferred to sit on the floor.

"Tell me about yourselves," I invited after they had accepted glasses of tea, and I had settled on the couch.

"We've been traveling around, going where we are called as healers. I've been studying herbs and other healing with a Cherokee medicine man," said Sunny.

Hmm, fascinating though a bit unusual. "So, why did you decide to come to Austin?"

"We were told by our spirit guides that we had work to do here. There's so much healing going on in this area, and I wanted to check out the Chinese School of Medicine," said Amy. "Unless the school works out, we'll be moving on in about three months; if we stay and I get into their two-year program, we'll get an apartment."

"And I've been asked to teach a class at one of the massage schools which is where we saw your ad. I graduated from the school a number of years ago," offered Sunny.

"And you like cats? As you can see, there are two," I pointed out as Sami pranced back and forth in front of Sunny, and Bear, usually in the forefront of the action, laid near me and surveyed them, apparently as fascinated as I was.

"Yes. In fact, I have two," Sunny said.

"Oh! They must miss you."

"Oh, no. They've been all over with us, and they won't cause any problem. Amy has a bird. That won't be a problem, will it?"

I was trying to digest this. Her cats were *with* her? She expected me to rent to two women, two cats *and a bird?*

I don't remember actually answering. One part of my brain was still trying to unscramble this information when the other part asked, "What kind of work are you looking for?" *In other words, how are you going to pay the rent, ladies?*

"We've only been here three days, but we have some leads. We're checking out the alternative medicine community, but we are open to other things. I also do psychic readings," said Sunny. "Is it OK if I have a few clients in the house?"

"Do you mean, clients in for…?" I was having a great deal of difficulty following all this.

"I'm a seventh generation psychic on my Irish mother's side, third generation on my American Indian father's side, and I do readings."

What did they mean they had *two* cats? *To move in with?* My ad had said *no* pets. And a bird? And there were *two* women, not *a* woman? And one was Indian and Irish and the other's ancestors must have come from Northern Europe with those glacier-blue eyes, and she was going to a Chinese school? And one was a massaging psychic. On top of that, both were, when you got right down to it, jobless transients. I felt like my brain had split in two, one part trying to put the pieces together to see the whole picture and one part working on interview questions I was supposed to ask but couldn't seem to formulate.

One thing they *had* said finally penetrated, and I addressed this minor point as I was too overcome to look at the rest of what was going on.

"I guess a bird would be OK," I said, envisioning my mother's sweet little blue parakeet that rode on her shoulder for the couple of months we had had it on the farm before it flew away. It would be in a cage. I could handle that. I wasn't sure that Bear wouldn't eat it, though.

I tuned in again as Sunny continued. "My cats are used to being around other cats. Your cats can get along with other cats OK, yes?"

In retrospect, I don't remember saying yes or agreeing to anything *except* the bird, I don't remember agreeing to let these two unemployed itinerants *and* two cats move in. I also don't remember agreeing to be a housemate with a psychic who was going to set up a business in my home. *To do massage? To tell fortunes? Wait, they said they were preachers, and they were looking for jobs.* I just couldn't seem to grasp one single piece of information to hang on to, like opening an over-stuffed kitchen drawer and then trying to figure out which of the web of silver utensils would be the one I needed.

I do remember mumbling something about zoning and revealing that they would be living next door to a cop couple, and I didn't think it would work for them to be doing much business from home. *The police—yes, that was important for me to let them know that I was not just some unprotected woman. Just in case.* I had seen America's Most Wanted. And there had been that movie.

"How much traffic do you think the neighbors might be willing to ignore?" asked Sunny. I grabbed at a small number, and she agreed there wouldn't be any more than that.

Somehow, they were forking over a cash security deposit and a slightly increased first month's rent for the extra utilities for two, and I was writing a receipt to my new renters. Then they asked if I would mind if they started moving in that evening, and they quickly left when I agreed; then I started panicking, my survival instincts kicking in. *What* was I thinking?

After graduation, I had moved to Chicago, knowing no one, with a job on swing shift at a train station in the downtown Loop. For six months, every midnight, I walked six blocks along skid row where the sidewalks, alleys, and store entrances were littered with derelicts and addicts of every kind. I was an example of the cliché, "Fools rush in where angels fear to tread." Surely, after all of that, I could handle some preaching and healing by massaging psychics and their feathered pet. And two cats. *Couldn't I?*

I tried to reassure myself, reviewing everything positive I could remember, trying to calm the bubble of panic along with that feeling of being in a runaway car. I was a plodder when it came to making plans, checking and rechecking, matching all the pieces before making a decision. Usually. Why was I not reacting in my normal fashion now? *Maybe that psychic had put a spell on me?*

I liked these women, Bear had seemed OK with them, though it had been a bit odd the way he didn't try to impress them as he usually did, as well as the way they ignored him. And Sami had plopped down in Sunny's lap, also odd. Besides, my protectors—my guardian angels, alluded to by the psychic who had started all this—would be on guard. Wouldn't they? They approved of this plan, she had said. *Was* this even part of the plan she had foreseen? *My head hurt.*

Within the hour, while still discussing my decisions with myself, I heard the noise of an old engine chugging into the cul-de-sac. I stood in the doorway watching as Sunny and Amy began to unload the 1960s-hippie era Volkswagen van, complete with a peace sign on the side; I knew the uppity cops were going to be mortified. The small Toyota the ladies had originally arrived in had been towed behind. In short and efficient order, blankets, suitcases, baskets, boxes, cat carriers—and a bird cage—all marched into the house.

I instantly felt buyer's remorse, or more correctly, landlord's panic. Oh god, *what* had *I done?* I excused myself and took my fear to bed to let them finish moving in without my suspicions watching over them.

The next morning, my lovely house contained three humans—though before long I was beginning to suspect there were more than that—plus four cats, and one damn bird. That cage had held a Conure parakeet—the size of a small parrot and allegedly the noisiest bird on the planet as I was to learn. Sami acted as though it was invisible, but Bear watched her closely, waiting for his chance at those beautiful green feathers. Within a couple of days and hundreds of piercing screams later, I was mentally encouraging him to go for her throat.

Much to my surprise, everything else in the household went smoothly, even the cat introductions, but I grew to detest that bird. She screamed at night, at all hours of the day, and rode around on Amy's shoulder, then climbed under her shirt and roamed around. I found the sight both fascinating and repulsive, closest in real life to something from a *Star Trek* show featuring aliens with slithering internal body parts. If I was in the same room as the bird, my ears rang for several minutes after she shrieked, and she shrieked for no reason that I could comprehend, over and over.

Because of the conflict over her pet, Amy and I started butting heads over everything. At one point, I made some angry comment after she left the room while Sunny was still there.

"Why does she have to be so bull-headed!"

"You two just aren't made to work together. It's a clear case of Chinese astrology. You are Monkey, Amy is Tiger, and they don't mix. I can see sparks shooting off the closer you get to each other when you come into a room from opposite ends. On the other hand, you can both get along with me because I'm a Dragon. It's too bad, you are both amazing women, kind, generous, intelligent, but you will never be friends."

"I don't even know what sets me off around her," I admitted. "She's nice, she's not bossy, she's always calm and kind, but it's like I'm an Alka-Seltzer, and her presence pours water on me!"

For the next three months, we rocked along, Sunny and Amy in pursuit of healing and knowledge, me thankfully paying the mortgage each month with enough left over to buy cat toys. Despite the conflicts between Amy and myself, all four cats were calm, never fighting, or even hissing. For some reason, my cats seemed to find Sunny's very round, crotchety, black and white girl, BB, invisible, which was a good thing. Sunny's Precious, a medium-haired tortoiseshell with an attitude that didn't live up to her name, started following Bear around in obvious adoration, though he paid no attention to her. Sami ignored all the newcomers except Sunny, giving her almost as much attention as he gave me.

I had started letting Sami outside when I could watch him. He often went out to an island of several trees by the fence where he slept for hours. Sunny's two cats were allowed out whenever they wanted to go out, and they never left the yard. I was still letting Bear out only in a harness since moving to this house with its fully-fenced, third of an acre lot. When I could watch him from the kitchen, I clipped two leads together, then to the clothesline, giving him a thirty foot diameter circle to explore, long enough to play in the bushes, scratch the trees, and lay in the sun. Life was good.

Sunny kept her promise of scheduling clients only when I was at work. Both renters were frequently out on their various job-hunting endeavors, attending classes, and doing whatever other activities they were pursuing. When they were home, they were usually in their rooms. I had my necessary alone time that kept me balanced, or as balanced as I could be with all these bodies in the house.

Alas, the bird let out one shriek too many. Normally, I did everything possible to avoid conflict, but that day, after the bird screamed again so sharply it felt like an arrow pierced my brain through my ear, I screamed from the pain. That was the end.

When my tenants came home that day, I gave them little choice. "The minimum three months we agreed to is up. I don't care who leaves or who stays, either or both of you, but *that bird* is officially under eviction notice. Get it out of here, or I'll let Bear play with her!" I knew I wouldn't really do that, but there were always "To Give Away" ads in the newspaper.

With that pronouncement, I stomped into my bedroom, slamming the door to make sure they knew I was serious. The bird, and Amy, left a week later. Sunny and her two cats stayed behind. I was both surprised and pleased that I had stood up for myself, but also appalled at the way I had handled the situation. Mostly though, I was just totally relieved to see the last of those tail feathers.

Chapter 15
GOOD ENERGY

Oak Hill, Texas. March 1996. I was sure the reported high temperatures of Mars were benign compared to what was going on inside my body when the hot flashes came roaring through. I hadn't been around to learn from my mother's change of life. I had done a good job of avoiding doctors until the disastrous eye surgery, and I had doubled my efforts to avoid them since then until now. I tried their pills; they didn't help much, plus I found out that the hormonal chemicals were under scrutiny by the FDA. I wanted more options to control my symptoms than that offered by modern medicine, so I was open to the sometimes seemingly outlandish cures offered by Sunny and by Amy, who now visited often, without the bird.

Sunny and Amy had talked about, suggested, or introduced me to alternative health therapies right from the night they had moved in. Both women amazed me with the knowledge, methods, and practices they used to make themselves, their friends, clients, and even the cats feel better. I watched in fascination but was not easily seduced into their beliefs. However, I now felt bad enough that I allowed myself to be persuaded to at least try some of them. When I did, I was surprised to find I got as much relief from herbals as I had from the pharmaceuticals. There was one cure, however, that almost brought my receptivity to a screeching halt.

Amy was visiting when I went out onto the back patio and noticed the large crock that had mysteriously appeared. I peeked in and saw some glutinous tan material, vaguely resembling a flat, mushroomy-looking something covering the underlying liquid. The spongy glob was floating, revolting, and obviously spoiled.

"Hey, guys," I yelled into the house, "there's something horribly ugly out here! It's either a brain from an alien or some kind of rubbery jellyfish. I'm going to throw it out."

Loud shrieks of "no, no" preceded their hurried arrival outside.

"It's kombucha tea, it's a health tonic! It's fermenting—that's what's making the bubble over the top. The tea detoxes the liver, and it's healthy, and anticancer and lots of other things. You don't want to throw it out!" said Sunny.

"Are you sure it's not a jellyfish?" *It really looked repulsive and alive.*

"No! Kombucha. It's a type of yeast that has been used in China for a thousand years, and in Germany and Russia. It will make you feel better if you want to drink some when it's done. It tastes really good! It's fizzy and sweet and different. It helps with PMS and arthritis and—just all kinds of things."

I looked over at it again and decided I preferred to let the train roar through.

Most of Sunny's and Amy's health practices were beyond my understanding, including herbs, energy-based therapies, foot reflexology, and incorporation of spiritual practices and beliefs that I was unfamiliar with. I found them all quite intriguing but viewed most as maybe "reality-based fiction" at best.

One day, I unsuspectingly turned into the cul-de-sac and saw a boulder sitting in our front yard. I parked and surveyed the very large, gray, caliche rock. I studied it from all angles, trying to figure out how this oversized piece of gravel—far too large to lift into a car—had wandered onto my little patch of a front yard. When I couldn't come up with anything but Sunny as the reason, I went inside the house, hollering all the way in.

"Sunny! Why is there a... a big... a *boulder* in the front yard?" I yelled, not even bothering to say hello.

She came out of the kitchen with a dishtowel over her shoulder. "Isn't it beautiful? It's a *bear* rock. The man at the construction site said I could have it." Her eyes were sparkling.

"Would you mind coming outside and showing me why we want it?"

She pointed out the bear lurking in the stone. Ah, yes! From a certain angle, it *did* hold a resemblance to a modern sculpture of a grazing bear. Especially if I squinted really hard. And the texture was rough, resembling a furry bear hide.

"OK, now I see that it is a bear boulder. But why is it here?"

"Oh, he's not staying *here*. I got him for that place of dead energy in back by the fence," she enthused.

"What dead energy spot?"

"Oh, you can't *feel* it? It's in the empty part, by the trees where Sami likes to sleep."

"And how is a rock going to change anything?" I asked.

"Oh, it's a *good* rock, it has good energy, and bear totem is for strength and grounding. Its spirit supports physical and emotional healing and transformation. And, you know what else?" She nodded her head vigorously, bouncing her curls like a small child. "It also offers strength and power when things are going badly."

Fascinating. I certainly felt the same way about Bear energy, but in a totally different concept, not in a *rock*.

"But I just want to be able to take him with me when I move. Is that OK?"

"I promise you can have Bear Rock any time you need him. He's yours."

Made stronger by her enthusiasm, we somehow rolled the boulder across the patch of yard, squeezed it through the gate, and rolled it about an acre into its spot in the backyard. The top of the bear was up to my knees in height and almost twice as wide as it was tall. Further, he had obviously been eating well to form his bulging stomach.

"How... I need a moment to breathe... how did you get this animal home? It's more like a pig than a bear. In fact, where *did* you get it?" I gave one final shove that positioned it nicely about three feet in front of the privacy fence.

"I went for a walk, and it was just there waiting for me where they're building that new house." She waved toward the undeveloped part of the subdivision. "The man with the big piece of machinery, he told me he'd put it in the basket and follow me home, but he couldn't get it into our yard so he had to leave it out front, and you know what? He only charged twenty dollars!"

I moved back and took a more long-distance view of the grazing bear, noting the hole right where his eye would be. I found this piece of garden art quite to my liking actually, and he did seem to fill in the open space nicely, like he wanted to be there.

Sunny walked over and bowed to him in gratitude as I watched. This was the first time I had ever considered thanking a rock for something. But the more I thought about it, the more it seemed like a right thing to do, sort of spiritual somehow. Not that the rock was spiritual, of course, but it did represent something that made my life "better," so why shouldn't I be thanking it?

Shortly after Bear Rock's arrival, I had a remembrance of a movie I'd seen with a Native American shaman offering thanks to Mother Earth. Sunny was convinced the rock, and by extension—all rocks, and everything else that we know as living or that we think of as "dead," had energy. I decided I needed to pay attention and honor the things that contributed to my well-being. And this was central Texas—there were *plenty* of rocks to practice on.

I came up against Sunny's concept of "energy fields" quite often, though after months, I still couldn't feel or sense what she was trying to tell me.

Then Sunny added to her belief system. She discovered another kind of energy. I walked into the house after work, and she was waiting for me in the living room, an anxious look on her face.

"We have an appointment at 7:00 for the Feng shui man," she announced rapidly while wringing her hands, a sure sign she was uncertain about a request.

"What? The... *who*? Could you repeat that please?"

"Yes, at 7:00, to get the house Feng shui-ed."

I waited a minute to see if this was going to register in the correct part of my brain. It didn't. Instead, I just felt a bit exasperated by yet another crazy scheme of hers.

"Sunny, I think I've been very generous in letting you "redecorate," but there is a limit. I've never heard of this thing you are talking about. What are you going to do to the house?"

"Oh, it's magic! Feng shui creates good energy, and brings money, and boy friends, and everything. It will make our house safe."

"How?"

"I told you, it's magic."

"Are we *paying* for this magic?"

"I'm trading a psychic reading."

I sighed and took a deep breath. "I still don't know what you're talking about, but let's get supper. He isn't going to, uh... *paint* anything is he? Or do anything we can't change back?"

"Oh, we won't want to change it." She gave a beatific smile before she turned and led the way to supper.

When Feng shui Man showed up, *he* was magic—standard American issue, no hint of Chinese genes, tall, good-looking, and definitely boyfriend material if I didn't mind robbing the cradle. Or he didn't mind robbing the geriatric home. He introduced himself as "John," and we shook hands; I hated to let go of him, not in a sexual way—he just had a comforting feel about him, like Matt with Princess on his lap. Oh, my! Was this, I suddenly wondered, what Sunny meant about *good energy*?

John explained what he was going to be doing. "Sunny asked me to come and find any energy in the house that is stuck and could cause discord, or not be to the benefit of all who live here. Feng shui is a very ancient Chinese practice—some call it science, or art, philosophy, superstition, or magic—which focuses on the flow of energy around everything. When energy gets stuck for some reason, it can cause discord in the house in any area, even financial and health issues. I'm here to find that stuck energy and get it moving again."

His explanation struck a chord. I had recently had an acupuncture treatment and the practitioner had talked about the needles removing the energy block that caused my back discomfort. The other dozen or so needles had been painless, but when the practitioner added one on my wrist, I felt as though I had been zapped with an electrical charge that sparked down and off my arm. It had definitely hurt, but the pain, both in my wrist and in my back, *had* disappeared almost instantly, like magic.

John took very little time to tour the house, inside and out, with Sunny and I trailing after him like eager puppy dogs. He pointed out our energy deficiencies, offered remedies for some rules that we had inadvertently broken. We needed water at the front door, and something that moved—like a wind chime—also. We rearranged a few pieces of furniture. Then he pronounced, to Sunny's relief, that our house had very good energy. He made a few other recommendations, then took his beautiful self and departed. I wondered how much the absence of that darned bird which I had evicted months before had contributed to our good energy.

Thereafter, a new remedy of some kind or another appeared in the house on a daily basis—a red whistle protecting the entry, animal totems reproducing on a shelf, the "most auspicious color (red)" ribbons hanging by the back door to protect us from... something. Plants, real and fake, grew overnight, filling empty spaces of the rooms and softening corners. When Sunny brought her two good luck *gold*fish home, I finally understood the reason for all those fish tanks in Chinese restaurants. Now that I thought about it, mostly the very nice, expensive, restaurants had fish tanks.

One night Sunny placed a new, round-leafed plant on the end of her desk and explained it was a money plant, helpful in bringing wealth to the desk owner. Approximately thirty minutes later, I heard her phone ring. A few minutes later, she came out of her area with a little hop and skip and announced that she had just gotten a new client, totally justifying her belief in magical Feng shui financial remedies.

I did notice that a room that had been Feng shuied had a feeling of calmness that most rooms didn't. Maybe there *was* something to this "feel the energy" Sunny was trying to teach me. I felt a softness in our house that I had not noticed before, like sharp edges of air had disappeared. Inexplicably, it was similar to that night I had noticed how different the house felt after I had adopted Sami.

Then I had an odd experience. I was visiting a new friend's house. She went off to another room to take a phone call, and I was left sitting in the living room. But the longer I sat, the more anxious I felt. I soon focused on a floor plant that seemed in the wrong place, as did a chair and an end table. I couldn't stand it! I felt like I was suffocating. Suddenly I got up and moved the items to where they seemed to want to go. Then I sat down and drew a deep breath and felt myself relaxing. At the same time, I was appalled—never, not ever in my life had I done such a thing—I *never* crossed anyone's boundaries without asking first.

When the friend returned, I started to apologize, but she immediately said, "Hey, you moved that plant! I like where you put it." Indeed, the room seemed lighter, not as heavy. I got an inkling that maybe that was what Feng shui was really about, and the suffocating feeling was from the stuck energy. It was the first, but would not be the last time I changed the "feel" of a place with a simple Feng shui remedy. Before, I had just felt it was part of furnishing a room to make things look good. Now I realized the association between the Chinese art, or science—whichever it was, and plain old decorating was mostly common sense.

When I got home, I gazed around. After the scarcity I grew up with, and the uncertainty of being poor, I treasured my home and its English-cottage motif, very feminine, a few antiques mixed with comfy chairs and couches, a fireplace. And two inside toilets. And not to forget The Beatles' requisite "cats in the yard." I had loved this house since I first entered the front door, and I had bought it, and had made it mine. I loved it more than any place I had ever lived. But now, while the basics were still the same, Sunny had made her mark also, spicing it up with objects I considered to be "in fashion" only in a teepee or a restaurant. I was amazed that I felt comfortable with it all, and not just comfortable, but special for having made it happen, for creating a calm space for myself, the animals, and even Sunny, so far away from that poverty stricken house on the prairie.

The parameters of my world had been structured, organized, *rational*—until Sunny. Now, my neat squares of beliefs and understanding were gelatinous and shifting, like the inside of a lava lamp. I wasn't the same, and I had changed in a very short time, a matter of months. Life had more color, and I felt more confident, more open to trying new things with the expectation that it would be a positive change. *My energy was very good.*

Chapter 16
MULTIPLE OCCUPANCY

Oak Hill, Texas. April 1997. Sunny and I behaved like a family, celebrating holidays, helping each other out, and having movie nights with popcorn, though we didn't actually spend much time together. We still had four cats living mostly in peace and calm. Her cats and mine weren't friends, though they tolerated each other. BB stayed outdoors or in Sunny's area and didn't associate with the rest of us. Precious stayed outside or wandered around in the house trying to find Bear, stopping at the invisible line to my area. For the most part, Bear ignored everyone except Sami, who now loved Sunny; she returned the favor. She catered to his every suggestion of need or want, letting him in and out of the house every ten minutes when he couldn't settle down, and sneaking forbidden treats to him.

She spent a lot of time at the kitchen table, writing. Sami liked to get behind her, squeezed between her back and the chair back, and go to sleep. They had been like that for a while one day when I heard Sunny give a yelp. I ran to the rescue for whatever had happened. She was getting out of the chair, and the back of her skirt was soaked.

"What happened?"

"Sami peed on me!"

I gasped, disbelieving, horrified. *My* Sami? "Oh no, I'm *so* sorry. How can I help?"

"It's OK. I'll take care of it. He must have been sleeping or something, he was just laying there."

She changed clothes while I mopped up and apologized profusely. I checked Sami; he appeared fine, though he needed mopping up also. I blessed Sunny for being so calm about it, but my ongoing worries about his head injury made *my* head hurt. He just wasn't acting right, but I didn't know what to do.

I was glad Sunny had been so helpful—lately I never knew what to expect from her and was becoming increasingly puzzled by her personality shifts. I'd come home from work one day to find her stern-faced, glaring at me for something I had done that offended her, though I was never sure what. Then she would slam into her room. A few hours later, she'd come out all excited and ready to watch a movie or go for a walk, all with child-like enthusiasm. *How could she change moods so quickly?*

By this time, I had also come to understand that Sunny lived with a great deal of fear, evidenced by the number of things she kept dragging into her rooms from garage sales, bargain stores, and flea markets, always explaining the purchases by saying that they would "keep us safe." Her rooms were so filled that, when I poked my head in to say something, I could see almost no visible wall space. Her bed was a small trough, the vacant spot surrounded by blankets, stuffed animals, feather boas, and pillows.

I didn't know why she didn't feel safe, but I had seen the fear on more than one occasion, brought on by something simple, such as a smell, a sound; I never knew what the trigger had been. She would seem to physically shrink right in front of me, and her face would look panic-stricken. Other times she would sit and rock, or get up and go into her room and shut the door. Later, she would return in the guise of "Sunny normal" as though nothing unusual had happened. Occasionally, there would be some odd forgetfulness. She would agree to do something or to meet me somewhere, then wouldn't show up. When I reminded her, she would swear she had not made those plans. She was far too young for Alzheimer's, but she appeared so honest in her denial that I had to believe she believed it. On the other hand, with her business, she was the ultimate professional. I found it very confusing. Sunny did tell me that she had received a head injury twenty years before in a car accident and had almost died. I accepted that as the explanation for the oddness. Still, it was a puzzle.

One Saturday, we were in the kitchen discussing plans for the day. Sunny was in another of her cantankerous moods, not pleased with any suggestion I made. I had been to the farmer's market earlier, and was now simultaneously cracking fresh brown eggs to scramble and playing with a chicken feather the farmer had generously included with my purchase.

Sunny was on the other side of the kitchen island, staring at a couple of little chicken figurines I had put out in honor of the upcoming Easter. She looked up and saw the floating feather. As I looked at her, her entire face changed, becoming slack, her features less pronounced. Her haughty Mother Superior vestige of a few minutes earlier disappeared, replaced by a child-like softness, as though her cheekbones weren't fully developed yet. Her eyes took on a sparkle, and she became animated, clapping her hands and exuding enthusiasm, talking little-girl talk as she often did when she was happy about something.

"Oh! Oh! Look at the chickies. I *love* little yellow chickies."

Comprehension hit me like a peck from a hen. I *finally* understood the little oddities I had dismissed all along. I knew now why there had always seemed to be more people than just Sunny in the house with me—there *were* more. I remembered reading *Sybil* back in the 1970's about the woman with multiple identities. I was shocked at my obtuseness at not recognizing the signs sooner, but I finally understood completely. I now asked her, "Who are you?"

Sunny obligingly introduced herself. "Don't you know me? I'm Rosie, and I'm…" She frowned and held up her hand, counting out her fingers—"This many old!" She triumphantly held up five fingers. My suspicion was now as solid as Bear Rock.

Sunny had Dissociative Identity Disorder, more commonly called Multiple Personality Disorder. The identities of Sunny and of little Rosie were so obvious—I should have figured it out long before: the little girl, always ready to play, who believed in magic, and collected animal totems to keep her safe. Then there was the harridan who was never pleased, who frowned most of the time, and who had a way of throwing back her head, shoulders straight, and talking in a very deep and authoritative voice. And that shy, quiet person who appeared when something needed fixing. Then there was the real Sunny, little Rosie grown up to a woman: gentle, strong, caring, and smart. And psychic.

I took a mental step back as I finished dishing up the eggs, hoping my face wasn't reflecting my shock as I continued to work through the puzzle.

"Breakfast is ready. Come and sit down. I need to talk to you."

"OK. What are we going to talk about?" she asked, always eager to cooperate as Rosie. She bounced into her seat and picked up a fork.

"Sunny, I know sometimes you forget things. Do you know why?"

I could tell from her face that she understood immediately what I was asking. I was honored that she felt safe enough to tell me everything. Rosie had sat down at the table, and Sunny appeared. Sunny confessed she knew there were others; she'd been in therapy several times. Sunny was the dominant personality. She was able to function well most of the time, so well that I had not caught on for over a year of living with her. She told me about her uncle and the chicken coop, about a rape in the military, about a beating, and the terrible car accident when she almost died.

I suggested she find a psychiatrist again. She agreed it was time. She told me later that other personalities kept popping out during the sessions, and her counselor suspected there were at least ten, probably more, that had developed to protect her from facing the after-effects of trauma and abuse. The counselors began working on re-integrating her.

Now her fears made sense—the burrowing in the bed, the constant search for things that would protect her. Unfortunately, the therapy didn't seen to have much immediate effect as far as I could tell.

One fine day, we drove to Fredericksburg, a tourist destination about fifty miles from Austin, filled with antique shops, German restaurants, and historical landmarks. At the end of the day, Sunny asked to drive my car home; since she had been a careful driver when I was with her in her van, I agreed. She was cruising slowly and carefully through the old town when she switched personalities. She began bouncing up and down in the seat. "Rosie likes to drive," she sing-songed as she speeded up and drove straight through a stop sign.

"Rosie, stop the car! Now!"

"Why? I like to drive. I'm a good driver! I *like* this car." She bounced and wiggled from side to side, keeping her hands on the steering wheel and flapping her elbows around.

"Stop! You almost got a ticket! You could have caused an accident! I don't think Sunny would like that!"

"What did I do?" A frightened expression came over her face when she finally heard me; a tear crept out and ran down her cheek as she pulled over to the curb.

"Didn't you see that stop sign? Now give me the keys!" I was clenching my jaw to keep from screaming at her.

"Oh. I'm sorry." She quietly got out of the driver's seat, and I drove us home. That was the only time her personality change put us in danger, but it did make me realize how little control she sometimes had over which personality was going to be in charge.

Now that I understood what Sunny was all about, I wondered if Little Bear, who loved almost everyone, stayed away from her most of the time because he sensed, or was confused by, her personalities. He often just sat and watched her, making no effort to interact, quite unlike his usual commitment to be a great hostess to any guests in the house. When I thought to wonder about it one day, I realized Sunny, who adored cats, never catered to him like she did to Sami. Was Bear more sensitive to her moods than anyone else in the house, and did she instinctively know that he was on to her?

Briefly, I hoped that the worst personality trait of her "others" was just being crabby. I had admired her for her hard work, her intelligence, and her gentleness long before I understood. I wondered how scary it must be for her to wake up never knowing who she would be that day. I was amazed that she could operate as efficiently as she did. Sadly, my knowledge seemed to have created a small gulf between us, and Sunny began spending a lot of time away from the house. When she was home, Rosie came out to play less and less. I missed them.

Chapter 17
PSYCHICALLY SPEAKING

Oak Hill, Texas. Spring 1998. Besides doing psychic readings at home, another source of Sunny's income was doing readings at special events. She announced one day that there was a Natural Health and Psychic Fair coming, and she had rented a booth space. She asked Amy and me to help her.

Getting the booth ready and energized enough to suit Sunny was just my cup of decorating tea. We shopped for days for just the right shiny fabrics, glitzed the booth with anything that sparkled, arranged amethysts, rose quartz, and crystal objects to promote love, healing, and "auspicious energy" in her area. We ran out of material stores in Austin and took a trip to Mexico to raid their more showy wares. By the time we finished, it was impossible for anyone to miss the booth. I was the promoter, or circus barker, amazed at how my shy personality disappeared when I was promoting.

"Come in for the most accurate readings in Austin by a seventh generation psychic. She'll tell you your future and how to make your fortune."

Almost a year after our meeting, I finally was able to watch Sunny doing her readings. The curious came, paid their money, and got on the waiting list. Sunny's readings were very private, and I heard little of what she was saying. Within seconds of the start of a reading, though, I would see clients cry or smile, and, overcome with emotion, get up and hug her, or vice versa.

I had never asked her to do a reading for me, uncomfortable with the possibility that, if she was right, I would feel somewhat vulnerable and naked, and if she was wrong, well, I would be disappointed. After all, I was promoting what I wasn't sure I believed in, but I could do it because I did believe that Sunny believed.

As the day went on, I noticed a brown-haired woman pushing a baby stroller walking toward the booth just as Sunny took a break. When the woman saw Sunny, she rushed at her.

"Do you remember me? I've been looking all over for you!"

"Of course." Sunny smiled, and they hugged. "I read for you about a year ago."

"Yes," said the client, "and you told me I was going to have a baby boy. Since everyone from my mother-in-law to my OB-GYN had told me it was a girl, I had painted all the walls pink. And I had a boy! Just like you said! Meet James!" she said as she pulled the blue bundle from the stroller. "Will you read for me again?"

I took out the memory of that event and contemplated its truth. I had reserved judgments about psychic stories but always remembered my mother telling of watching hands-on healings in a revival tent when she was young. Did I believe? Or did I not? Maybe. Or maybe not.

The one demand I had bargained for when Sunny asked my help with her booth was time off to go to any of the advertised mini-lectures. I was astounded at all of the categories, things I had never heard of: *Heal with Reiki, Phrenology-Your Head Says It All, Essential Oils-Smelling Your Way to Health* and many more, all sounding interesting. How ever could I choose? Then I saw the heart-stopper. *"Do You Wonder What Your Pets Are Thinking?"* Oh! Yes, indeed! How many times had I studied Bear and Sami, wondering what was going on in those cat brains as they sat so quietly, focused on me, or gazing off into space for hours. I eagerly read the rest of the announcement: *Val Heart has been talking with animals since she was a small child. Hear her tell about her fascinating conversations with animals big and small. Find out how you, too, can talk with your animals.*

I headed for the room at the appointed time and, quite unlike my usual self, sat as close to the front row as I could get. Enthralled, I listened to the stories she told of her conversations with cats, dogs, horses, and even some singing baby squirrels.

Our practice exercise was short. Close my eyes, relax, clear my mind, visualize my cats, relax, breathe deep, relax... By the time Val began speaking again, I had experienced... nothing.

After the lecture, as other attendees rushed up to talk with her, I stayed put, feeling goose bumps, thinking of how amazing such an ability must be, but crushed because I had not been able to it.

Finally, Val was free, and I hurried up and booked a private session with her at my home for the following week. I felt as excited as a child on Christmas Eve each time I considered how the conversation would go. No matter what I was doing during the intervening time, I would get off course trying to think of things to ask. I went from excited to panicked and back, making the trip multiple times a day. *Will Bear tell her I didn't clean his cat box yesterday? Will Sami tell her I was yelling on the phone at that obnoxious telemarketer? And, oh dear, she said the cats sent her pictures. Would Bear tell her what I looked like in the shower or sitting on the commode?* I was having second thoughts about the appointment, but they were quickly overruled by the excitement of my first thought. Now that I knew it was possible, I *needed* to talk with my cats as much as I needed sleep.

Finally! It was time. Val, a petite lady with big blue eyes, arrived at the house on a bright Sunday morning. I introduced her to my cats; Sunny had elected to be gone from the house. After giving the communicator a sniffing welcome, Sami and Bear hopped up into their wicker chairs as though waiting for the show to begin.

My first question to her was why had Sami stopped religiously using the cat box ever since his head injury a couple of years before. Could she please ask him to go only in the cat box? I told her of the incident when he peed on Sunny's chair. I waited as she seemed to be conversing silently.

"Oh, dear. Sami says his head hurts badly and has since the accident; it never totally goes away. When I look through his eyes, it's like looking through a Kaleidoscope, the kind that just breaks a scene up into a lot of little boxes. He feels he should have died then. He feels very off-balance and is often confused," she continued. "Somehow, he thinks he *is* always going to the litter box."

I gave a small involuntary cry from the pain that sprang into my heart as I realized Sami was having such distress, and I hadn't even known it.

"What can I do to help him?"

"He is requesting that he be able to go outside more. It helps him feel more grounded to feel the earth beneath his feet. He could "use the box" outside, he says."

"I don't let him out because of the loose dogs, the stray cats, and the traffic. The yard has a privacy fence, but he can get over it easily."

"He says he must go outside more; it calms him down and makes him feel less confused and more centered."

Was he really telling her that, I wondered? Or was it just a guess because most cats want to be outside more? OK, I'll play along. I wanted so to believe, but I could feel the perspiration on my palms, I was so nervous.

"If I let him out, will he agree to stay in the fenced yard?" I asked, thinking that was pretty far fetched, but still...

"He wants to go out in front, but promises to stay under the bushes there and won't go any further than the houses on either side. He also would like to go out in back whenever he wants and agrees to not go over that fence."

"Will he agree to come in at night when I call him?"

She checked with him. "Yes, he promises."

I thought about it for a minute, then, with a great deal of doubt and trepidation, I agreed. "Please tell him I agree to try it, but if he wanders off, he will have to stay in the house from then on." *Would he really remember such a promise, if indeed that was what he was "saying?" How could I relinquish my fear and agree to this?*

We moved on to talk with Bear. I told her there wasn't anything in particular I needed to know; I just wanted to know if he had anything he wanted to ask or tell me. I was watching her as she began the conversation. Her eyes opened wide and she took an involuntary step backward as though the words had pushed her.

"Wow!" she said. "This is *amazing*! All cats know what is going on in the room around them, even if they are asleep. Some cats know what is going on anywhere in the house, and some know what's happening in their yard, but not much beyond that. But Little Bear! He is telling me about what is going on in the whole neighborhood! He says someone is moving out."

I was astounded! "Yes, that's true! I noticed a moving van parked around the corner Friday when I came home from work."

"He also wants to go outside more, he likes the walks, but he hates the harness."

"Well, too bad, if we walk, he's in the harness and leash. This is not negotiable. But, perhaps I could let him go out in the yard without a leash when I'm with him if he promises not to go over the fence."

She checked with him.

"No, he says he can't promise that. If he can go over the fence, he will. He's being very honest and says he could not resist the temptation."

I had not told her about the many times he had been outside rambling around, harness on but lead not attached to anything, just dragging it around the yard as I worked. Then, suddenly, he wouldn't be beside me, and I would see him sneakily ambling closer and closer to the fence. Then it was a race as to whether I would catch him before he jumped to the top and went over. Usually I managed, but a few times I'd had to hunt him throughout the neighborhood.

We talked about a few other things: their favorite cat food, if the litter was OK, how did they like Sunny's cats. The conversation came as easily as if she was talking to them on the phone and translating for me. She hadn't done any mysterious voodoo things like lighting candles, hadn't even done any obvious relaxation, and her eyes were open most of the time, but her head was sometimes tilted, as though she was listening intently.

Bear and Sami stayed in their chairs for the rest of the consult, although Sami appeared to be dozing. Bear was watching us, eyes big and round with excitement. She explained that they were both totally attentive to the conversation, even Sami.

Finally, the financial meter ticked out, and she left. I hadn't felt this excited about anything since the night my husband had proposed to me. I felt like my whole life was changing and something wonderful was about to happen, as indeed it was.

As promised, I started letting Sami out unattended, though I was nervous the whole time. When I went to look for him, though, he was either under the front bushes or in the back yard. He *always* came in as soon as I called, and, to the best of my knowledge, never wandered away from the yard—just as he had promised.

Bear and I continued our walkies, he with his turquoise harness and bright pink leash. When we walked out the door, he would take off, and I felt like a sled dog musher, so strongly and explosively did he pull me along. By the end of the cul-de-sac, he would slow down, and then nose-investigate every single flower. Or bush. Or tree trunk. Or rock, or bird feather, or the neighbors' tires. We usually made it all the way around the block in about an hour, a long way for a cat to walk steadily, but he wouldn't quit until he collapsed. With all that hair he wore, if it was at all warm, he'd suddenly plop down and pant; I would have to stand there and let him cool down, or pick up his eighteen hairy pounds and carry him the rest of the way home, which he seemed happy to have happen.

We never ran into any loose dogs, but barely escaped being run over when a driver tried to see what was really on the end of the leash. On one night's walk with Sunny, we were strolling down the middle of the street. We walked by a house and, suddenly, the black and white cat that had been sitting in the driveway came tearing toward us. I was in shock, remembering that first time as a child in the barnyard when I had been attacked by that calico cat. I started screaming, knowing this was not a friendly visit.

"Sunny, watch out! That cat is attacking us! Bear!"

Bear, busy making bug friends, had no idea he was in danger. I grabbed him, protesting, up into my arms. Sunny tried to divert the attacker. It was not a brief engagement. That cat would not give up, leaping up on my jeans, screaming insanely, going after Bear! It took several minutes before we could divert it by stomping our feet, yelling loudly, and Sunny swinging her jacket at it. Finally and fortunately, it decided two yelling women were too much, and the cat went back to its driveway. I could feel Bear shaking in my arms, and the adrenaline was rushing through both Sunny and me. I was so glad Sunny had been with us; I knew there would have been blood had she not diverted the cat. When I settled down, I again realized that taking a cat for a walk in a harness was unsafe—I was essentially dragging along a hunk of meat for the taking by any animal.

In keeping with Bear's promise, or failure to promise, I vowed to always keep him on a leash, even in the back yard, because he could disappear in the flash of a fly. I felt so mean, but I was now always hyper-vigilant anytime we were out. Despite that, I couldn't stop because it gave me so much pleasure to give so much pleasure to my boy. Sadly, for Bear, outside always included a harness, a lead, and me. This was the best compromise I was willing to make. Bear apparently understood. When he wanted to go for a walk, he'd meow at the door. If that didn't work, and if he could find his harness, he'd drag it through the house, accompanied by deep-throated, guttural meows seeming to come from his lower stomach, and drop it in front of me, exactly like a dog. He'd stand passively while I hooked him up and then take off for the door the second he felt the last tightening of the underbelly strap that signified we were ready.

His enjoyment and enthusiasm were so contagious I would force myself on a walk even if I felt too tired had it not been for his encouragement. I would stroll around, taking the time to actually notice little things—the green caterpillar on the sidewalk, the strange blooming plant, a luscious patch of grass. Until Bear moved on to another site.

We were in a tranquil period. Sami was happy being outside, and always stayed close to the house. Bear was happy with his walkies and being with Sami, and Sunny and I were getting along well. I was never bored with learning new things from her. Except for my job with the State of Texas, which I loathed with every capillary in my body, life was interesting, tranquil, and stable, qualities that had rarely been present in my life for any extended time period. Apparently, the Feng shui Man had done his job well—we all had good energy. But I also had a growing hunger, an insatiable thirst to talk more with my cats.

Chapter 18
PROMISES

Oak Hill, Texas. August 1997. About a month after Val's conversations with the cats, I arrived home from work and noted Sunny's van in the drive, and Sami curled up under the front bushes.

"Hey, Sami. How did you get outside? Did Sunny let you out?" He didn't answer, but unfurled himself and followed me into the house. As soon as I walked in, I knew something was wrong. The house felt empty, as though no one lived there, and Bear wasn't at the door. Sunny's lectures on "feel the energy" were finally taking hold.

"Sunny? Sunny! Where's Bear?" I yelled. She didn't answer. I peeked into her area; only her cats were there, asleep on stacks of papers on her desk. I went out back, still expecting to see a woman and a cat in the yard. Nothing. Nothing there except a bright fuchsia lead with an empty turquoise harness dangling across the top of the fence. I headed for the garage and a ladder, envisioning Bear hurt, and Sunny trying to fix him. I visualized his body laying in the road somewhere. Or in convulsions from a snake bite. Maybe he wasn't even with her.

What to do? If they came back while I was hunting them, I wouldn't know they had come home. I should stay put, in the house. But I couldn't stand just sitting and waiting. I ran back through the house and out into the cul-de-sac, yelling loudly for Sunny and Bear all the way. At the street, I saw Sunny half a block away, heading home. But there was no grey cat with her.

"Where's Bear?" I yelled when we were close enough that I estimated she could hear me. She lifted her hands in the universal "I don't know" gesture.

"He's not at the house! His lead is in the yard, where is he, what happened?" I felt a flood of fury wash over me. If Bear had been outside, then she had *left* him there when she went for a walk! How could she!

She again held her empty hands out in an I-don't-know gesture. Now close enough to be heard, she hollered as she neared, "I let him outside in the back yard. When I checked on him he was gone. I swear he was only out a few minutes. I've been all over the neighborhood for the past hour, and I can't find him anywhere."

I felt sick, even as I calculated that Sunny's "few minutes" could have been hours if one of her multiples had taken over.

"Where have you looked?"

She pointed east, west, south, and north—every way possible except up and down.

"Go that way, check under the bushes!" I ordered, and I took off in the opposite direction. I trotted into people's back yards if I could find a way in. If their garage door was cracked open, I banged on their doors. Half an hour later, we'd had no sighting of a big grey and white cat. It would be getting dark soon; my night vision wasn't very good. There were no streetlights in the subdivision. I'd never find him if we didn't do it within the next hour or so.

My brain worked frantically for an answer as to how to get help; then I remembered Val Heart. I ran back to the house and sighed with relief when she answered her phone. I explained, somewhat incoherently, that Little Bear had gone missing. "Can you help?"

"I'll try," she said. "Calm down and breathe; you need to be centered, or your energy might affect my being able to contact him," she soothed.

Oh, god, more energy lectures! I tried to slow my fish-out-of-water gulps of air to deep breathing and waited. It took a minute or two. Then she began translating.

"Yes, I have him. He's OK. In fact, he's quite enjoying himself. He's not far from home; he knows where the house is, and he can hear you calling. He is quite excited because he caught a bird."

I was both relieved and incensed. He was all right! He was enjoying himself! *Enjoying* himself? He caught a bird?

"Tell him to get his butt back home *now!* We've been worried sick."

"He says he'll come home when he's ready, and he's not ready yet." I refrained from the expletive that was on my tongue.

"He knows how to get home, he says, but he's not finished exploring. He really *is* having fun, and he's quite all right. He says he'll come home by dark. Just go in the house, sit down, and send loving thoughts on a golden cord right to his heart."

Now *that* was going to be a stretch, I thought, my heart still pounding and my hands shaking, every part of me wanting to first put a golden cord around his neck, shake *him* until his whiskers rattled, and then hug that chunky, furry body.

He was all right! That was the huge relief, but... he wasn't home. In my mind, that meant he still wasn't safe. But there was really nothing else I could do, except wait. I promised to send Val a check and hung up.

I sat down, breathed, then jumped up and went back to pacing the house. Sunny came home, looking distressed, empty-handed, shaking her head negatively as soon as she saw me. I relayed the conversation I'd just had. I told her to sit down and concentrate on calling Bear home since she was better at this psychic stuff than I was.

We waited; she sent out energy, and I tried to. Dusk came quickly. Bear did not. Darkness arrived, still no Bear. I called Val again and asked for help. She quickly connected to him.

"Oh, dear. Now he *is* disoriented. He says he's very close to home, but he doesn't know which way to go. I'd say he was within a block of the house. Go outside and start calling him again. He says he will hear you." I went outside as far as the phone cord could go, calling for him as I walked.

"Yes! He says he can hear you, and he'll be home shortly, but keep calling to him."

I thanked her again, hung up, collected Sunny, and we went out with flashlights, yelling, coaxing, going up and down the cul-de-sac. Then, out of the corner of my eye, I thought I saw a small streak of white zooming out of the blackness. Had I blinked, I would have missed it, but I was sure it was Bear, headed for home, but refusing to head toward me.

"Sunny! Come back, he's headed home!"

He was sitting at the front door when we got there, with nary a feather with him. Bear was home! I scooped him up and hugged him as I carried him into the house and then examined him for injuries—none. I examined him joint by joint for swelling, then his eyes—phew, all good. I felt myself relaxing.

In the gentlest voice I could muster, I told him, "You were a bad, bad, *bad* boy for scaring us like that. Don't. Ever. Do. That. Again. Not ever, ever, ever!"

And then I hugged him again, holding him so close he protested. Apparently the bird hadn't been filling enough, because all he was interested in was wiggling down to get to his food and water bowls. He'd been outside at least five hours which meant he had missed several meals. I gave him an extra helping of kibble.

I was so relieved that he was home safely, I even forgave Sunny for not keeping a closer eye on him. After all, she was just trying to be nice to him by letting him outside. Exhausted from the physical run around the neighborhood, emotionally wrung out from carrying around all the panic and terror I had felt for hours, I slept well that night. Bear, safe, was now in his usual place at the foot of the bed, on guard, and Sami was tucked into the back of my knees. All was right with my world.

That was the first, but far from the last time I resorted to calling a communicator when my Bear disappeared, an all-too-often happening. Sometimes he was hiding in plain sight, like the Cheshire cat. I would look at a shelf, and he wasn't there. I would blink, and he would have materialized, staring at me with what I knew was an amused look on his face, as though he had planned the joke. *How could he do that when he didn't have any moveable facial muscles?* Other times, I couldn't find a trace of fur or whisker—he would simply be gone, and I would start another neighbor-by-neighbor canvass. Like the horse in the book *The Pony That Would Not Be Broken*, Little Bear was *The Cat That Would Not Stay Home*.

In my life with cats, I became very familiar with the feeling that accompanies the expression "my heart sank." It sank another time when we were out in the yard. Bear was in his harness, on yard duty, attacking bugs and chewing off the grass. The phone rang, and I ran inside to answer. After ascertaining it was just another sales marketer, I went back outside. And I knew, just knew, that Bear had escaped again, even before I saw his lead hanging over the fence, pointing the way to his escape route.

When my cop neighbor answered my pounding summons on his front door, I pointed to the blue harness still dangling down his side of the privacy fence to prove my cat was in his yard. Or had been. They had a designer yard, with a pool, lush greenery, and a waterfall. The neighbor was more than happy to let me in so that I could get the contaminating cat out of his paradise.

Bear was still there, gently poking his nose into a big orange hibiscus blossom, like a hummingbird sipping happiness. And once again I felt like a pleasure-destroying ogre as I grabbed him up and carted him home, noting the sprinkle of yellow pollen on his little black nose. I seemed to always be spoiling his fun.

In an attempt to impress upon him the potential dangers in his explorations, I called Val, but she wasn't available. By now, I had found a backup communicator, just in case, and I called her.

"Please, tell him that I recognize he is very brave, but even brave cats can be hurt by other animals."

"All right. I've told him," she said. "But he says he won't get hurt."

"We have dogs, coyotes, snakes around, and possums and raccoons and stray cats in the yard, so yes, he *could* get hurt! Does he understand how little he is compared to other animals?" I was strident in my tone, hoping he would understand how serious this was.

He says, "I know I'm a cat, but I'm not little. Most cats are small. But I'm not small, and I'm very strong. So I'm not afraid." Her voice was flat, substituting for his. Clearly, he was not going to listen to me.

Having already gone up against his stubbornness and sense of invincibility, I conceded. I'd just have to reconcile Bear's determination to roam free with my selfish determination to do all I could to keep him home safe. And if ever a cat was bent on escaping, Bear was. I don't believe he ever had any desire to leave, or he wouldn't have let me find him; he just wanted to explore and be free to see what was going on in the rest of his domain. His innate self-confidence made him fearless.

He went over one fence so often that one neighbor took to calling me to let me know Bear was visiting before I even knew he was missing, which was never more than a few minutes. Sometimes he'd slip the harness, a few times he snuck out when I was going in and out of the house, then there were the times when he was *right next to me* in the yard, and then gone. When he disappeared on those occasions, I went from panic to terror, hoping he would at least keep his collar and tags on. I felt ridiculous for being so worried, but I couldn't help it. I carried a fear with me that, because I loved him so much, I was choking the life out of him, but I just couldn't stand the thought of losing him.

I did sometimes wonder—were my cats special? Bear had taught me so much by refusing to make a promise to stay home so he could go outside without the hated leash. Sami had shown his integrity by following our agreement to never leave the yard and to come in when called. It was obvious to me that both cats fully understood and kept the promises they had made, or, in Bear's case, held true to the promise he *hadn't* made. How many humans had I known that thought nothing of breaking their word! My respect for my animals grew by cat leaps and bounds.

I felt humbled at the ability of my cats to trust and voluntarily live in harmony with me after the centuries of abuse their species had endured from human hands and feet. Shouldn't fear of us be in their DNA by now? How could they love and trust humans more than ten times their size who could easily, and often did, hurt them many ways? The novel idea that they had a code of honor was contrary to everything implied in the sentiment "like an animal" which humans uttered with condemnation toward another human; it seemed to me that that expletive was actually a compliment.

Finally, with certainty, I understood that the world had lied to me, perhaps not with intent, but through misguided judgment, pure ignorance or stupidity, maybe an over-inflated sense of human egotism or self-importance. All those who advocated the idea that animals were soulless, unfeeling, incapable of human emotions and standoffish were very, very wrong no matter who they were or what authority they thought they had. When this realization slipped in, I vowed that I would never make a promise to an animal that I was not positive I could keep.

My world view, my life values—everything had been on a slow evolution since I had put an ad in the paper for a renter, and then went to a psychic fair and listened to the animal communicator there.

Chapter 19
THE AVOCADO TREE

Oak Hill, Texas. August 1997. That day blazed as hot as every other Tuesday in August in central Texas, the temperatures over 100°F as I lugged the cats into the vet's office. While other mothers were getting their kids ready for back-to-school with required shots, I was taking my kits in for their annuals.

In the vet's office, it was assumed I wanted to stick it to the kitties with the "essential" vaccines. I knew the cats hated it; they always showed signs of illness or pain the next day. Sami, especially, had had reactions from the shots, limping for several days afterward as if his shoulder hurt. But the law was the law and yearly rabies shots were mandatory, and I wanted to be a good caretaker.

For several days after that vet trip, I was very busy, gone most of the days and evenings, which is the only excuse I have for not noticing sooner that something was wrong. When I got home each night, Sami was usually curled up in his chair, but sometimes I would have to hunt for him—odd, but not enough so to worry. He kept turning up in unusual places: behind the couch instead of on it, on the bathroom floor instead of in the tub where he liked the coolness, on the floor beside the bed. I couldn't say he seemed sick—there was just something that felt a bit off, or, as Sunny would say, his energy wasn't quite right. But when I called him, he always came, ready for his "din-din," the small can of wet food which served multi-purposes—a before-bedtime treat, and a head count so I knew both were in safe for the night, and it seemed to make them sleepy.

On Friday, Sunny and I were fixing lunch when Sami staggered into the kitchen. He was obviously very off-balance and having difficulty staying upright, looking as he had after the motion sickness pill episode on the Christmas trip. I called the vet's office, demanding a same-day appointment.

I put him in the carrier and sped to the vet's office again. "He was fine when I brought him on Tuesday," I told the vet. "But since then, he's been quiet, sleeping a lot, and doesn't seem quite right. It wasn't until today that I realized there is something *really* wrong."

This was a female vet I hadn't met when I was in the office before. She examined him, asking unproductive questions. "Has he ever had this before? Has he thrown up? Could he have gotten into poison or anti-freeze?"

"No, no, and no! No way on the antifreeze, and we don't use poisons." *Thank you, Sunny, for your "natural" philosophy of avoidance of all killer chemicals.* "Could it have been a reaction to the vaccines? This seems like a pretty radical thing to happen out of the blue if it's not connected," I said.

"No, we've never had any problem with the vaccines. They're completely safe," insisted the vet, not stopping as she continued her exam. I was totally unprepared when, after watching Sami stagger around the office, mostly going in circles, she announced her death sentence. "I think it is possibly a brain tumor. There's also a disease we've seen before with these symptoms. Unfortunately, there's really nothing we can do for either one. Either of the tests is very costly, and even if we determine the cause, there's no cure or even any treatment."

I stood in shock, unable even to ask questions. Then the tears began, running down my cheeks and off my chin. I managed to pull out a charge card. I remember thinking, *why was I again paying to get such awful news?* I bundled up my baby and drove him home, a huge knot in my throat all the way.

The only place he wanted to go was into the back of my walk-in closet. He kept staggering toward it, and I would deter him, instinctively fearing that could be a one-way trip. He tried again, and I finally picked him up and carried him there. I fixed a soft pallet, brought in his favorite wet food, his litter box, and water. For the next several days and nights, I spent as much time with him as I could, sitting on the floor with him in my lap. Every day I brought fresh food and water, and the next I replaced full bowls with new ones. The litter box was always pristine. Little Bear would come in to visit and lay quietly with us. Sunny stayed away.

Finally, I made a desperate call to Val which she took right away. "Can you please talk to Sami? He's sick. The vet says he's going to die."

"Sami says he *is* very sick, and feels he will die soon," she said, as I clutched the receiver. "He's very, very weak, very tired, and extremely dizzy."

"Is he in a lot of pain?"

"No, he says he just feels very sick because of the dizziness."

"Is there anything I can do, anything he wants? Tell him I'll get him anything. I love him so much."

"He says he just wants to sleep, and the dark feels better than the light which makes his headache worse. And he loves you."

I hung up and went into my office, forcing myself to leave him alone, not bothering with a light. The darkness felt right to me, too. I cried for a long time.

By the following Thursday, I knew our time was short. Sami hadn't ventured from the closet at all for almost a week and now couldn't even stand up. His breathing was labored; he no longer even lifted his head when I went in to sit beside him. Less than a week after I had noticed his obvious symptoms, I held him close and whispered to him how wonderful he was, how much I loved him, how happy he had made me during our time together. He was limp in my arms but purring. I thought that might be an encouraging sign, though I had been told that purring was also the way cats comfort themselves when in pain or ill.

"Sami, if you will come out of the closet, I will take you outside tomorrow. You know how much you like to watch Bear play. Would you like that? You come out of the closet, and I'll take you outside, and we'll stay as long as you want." I didn't tell him that I was going to take him out whether he was able to get out of the closet or not, though I was worried about the daylight in his eyes. I thought if he understood, and got up, that maybe, just maybe, he would get better. The pessimist was trying so hard to be an optimist, grabbing at any possibility, asking for a miracle. And I knew if he didn't get better then, I would have to say a permanent good-by.

After lots of kisses and hugs, I put him back on the blanket, left the closet and went to bed, collapsing in tears, the knot in my throat so big I kept gasping for breath. Bear climbed on the bed, and I put my arms around him, holding him, something he usually didn't tolerate. I even prayed, something I hadn't done in a long time. Sami was only eleven, and he had been so vibrant just two weeks before—surely this was a mistake. I slept in snatches, feeling death hovering; it was the first thing I became aware of when I awoke the next morning.

I sat up, wanting to get to Sami right away. I swung my legs out of bed and put my feet—on Sami. And gasped! Sami was in the bedroom, next to the bed, and I had almost stepped on him! First came the question—how? How in the world had he crawled all that distance—from the back of the long walk-in closet, through the long double-sink master bathroom, and across the big bedroom—when he had not moved in over a week, had not eaten or even drunk water?

How much he had wanted to be with me and to go outside to do that long crawl! And instead of just grabbing him and taking him outside, I had made him come to me. I was devastated by my stupidity.

Either he *had* understood my words and wanted outside so badly, or he wanted so much to be with me that he somehow found the strength, the will, to crawl out of the safe place in the closet. He couldn't walk, he couldn't stand at all. He had to have traveled that distance inch by inch. Crying my eyes out again, I threw on my housecoat, picked him up gently in a towel, and carried the lightness of him to the little patio at the back of the house. We sat in a lawn chair in the filtered, mid-morning sunshine under the sprawling branches of the big Live Oak tree.

As I held him close, I reminded Sami all about us, retelling him the stories of how funny he was as a kitten, and what a wonderful teacher he had been for me and for Little Bear. His little round head was unsteady so I propped it up on my arm. His now small body was totally limp, dead weight, what there was of it.

"Do you know I never did find all those earrings that you made disappear? Do you remember how much you liked those ants in the bathtub? And when I brought Little Bear home for you and how much you hated me? And then you guys were best buds, always playing games with each other. You've been the best kitty anyone could ever ask for, Sami, and such a good big brother to Little Bear. I don't know what I would have done without you. I never really expected to love you, but you were so special, I didn't have a choice."

As I talked, he purred and purred, getting louder by the minute, until I could feel his chest rumble. He turned his head to the blue jays that were squawking, and the doves that were cooing to each other on the rim of the birdbath. He tried to follow the flight of a butterfly that landed nearby, and he adjusted his head slightly in order to watch Bear chasing bugs, ignoring us. After awhile, the purring lessened, and then stopped. I felt he was tired, so I carried him back into the house and put him beside the bed while I went in to take a quick shower and dress, hoping that his outside trip would be a turning point, and he would start getting better.

"Sami? Sami are you OK?" I whispered to him when I came out of the bathroom. There was no response. I checked on him, afraid I would find him dead; he was asleep. I left him there on the floor while I finished dressing. About ten minutes later, I came back into the bedroom just as Sami was having a grand mal seizure, his body convulsing off the floor, his limbs going every which way, froth coming out of his mouth.

"Sunny! Sunny! Sami's having a seizure! Call the vet. I'm taking him right in!"

I heard her on the phone as I grabbed him and bundled him in a beach towel. I knew from my work in a State Hospital that he would not be aware of the seizure and was numb to any pain. I knew that, but watching him made me frantic to get help for him to make the seizures stop—I *had* to stop them!

The vets took forever to get to us—on some other emergency. I wanted to grab Sami and take him home, to hold him so close, to do anything to keep the bad things away. I couldn't stand to see my vibrant, wonderful kitty lying there, having seizure after seizure.

The vet finally came in. They had difficulty finding a vein because he was seizing so badly. I was frantic at my inability to help him. He stiffened one last time as I stood close, and then he was gone. My first "child," my wonderful Sami, was no more.

"Do you have a place to bury him? We can cremate him, if not. You know it's illegal to bury him in town. You will need to dispose of the body right away," they told me. "The heat, you know."

"No! I'll take care of him." I didn't know, and I was amazed at how fast I thought of the lie. "I have a cousin with a farm, and I've made arrangements."

I could not have had Sami's body cremated or stuck in the earth in a distant grave far away from us. I knew it was stupid and irrational, but I wanted him to have every chance to get back home—I, who didn't even believe in funerals, now wanted to believe there was an after-life.

Once again Sami was making a hated car trip, but this would be his last. At the house, I carried him out to the backyard and into the copse of oak trees near Bear Rock. With a great deal of huffing, cussing, and sweating, I hacked out a shallow grave through two inches of what Texans called dirt, and then dug and hacked into the soft caliche rocks until I had a space deep enough and wide enough. The heat was like a cloud, my tears adding to the humidity, making it difficult to breathe.

I kept trying to coax Bear over to the grave as I dug so he could see and smell the body. I guess Bear knew his friend was gone. He stayed very busy nosing through the grass and weeds far away from the hole in the earth, like a person in denial.

Sunny helped me dig and, in her tribal tradition, we helped Sami on his journey, tossing in some blades of grass, a few pieces of kibble, his favorite kitty treats, catnip, his collar and tags so he could always be returned to me, and a shiny twist-tie. I hoped he would arrive on the other side of the Rainbow Bridge with everything he needed. There was only one other thing left to do—burying the body and making a marker for his grave.

I had been babying an avocado pit for months, curious to see if it would grow in a jar, toothpicks stuck through it so that only the bottom of the pit was in water. It was now about eighteen inches tall, spindly, but with leaves, a good root system, and a straight little trunk. I knew my Sami, whose favorite thing in the whole world next to banana ice cream was licking the guacamole bowl clean, would like it near. We planted the little tree on top of his grave as a marker, although I knew there wasn't enough sunlight for it to stay alive for very long. And my loyal little companion and Bear's best buddy slept the sleep that would not end, his cherished earth around his body, under a protective avocado tree.

During the next week, each time I let Bear out to roam a bit, he would go directly to Sami's grave at the back of the yard and sit there, facing the fence, his back to the house, rocking. Ten minutes, twenty, he would sit and rock. Perhaps they were talking, perhaps he was crying. Then he would get up and start his yard exploration.

I held out for a week, then succumbed to my longing; I called Val again, asking her to ask if Sami was OK.

"This is very odd. He hasn't arrived at his destination, even seems to be lost. I've never seen this happen. Let me see if I can help." She communicated silently for several minutes, then said that he had arrived across the Rainbow Bridge. "He's all right now," she assured me. "He is where he is supposed to be."

One week after Sami died, still hurting in my heart and having breakthrough crying spells, I awoke to the shocking news that Princess Diana had died in a car wreck. I was dismayed at my reaction. I was not a person who paid much attention to celebrities, but no one could have missed the constant reports of Diana, her trials, tribulations, and accolades, nor the reports of all the scandals. Until I began crying, I had no idea that I'd had more than a slight feeling of attachment to her, but I found myself grieving for her as deeply as I was grieving for Sami, a continuum of the deep emotion. Only for my grandmother's passing had I grieved as deeply. With some sense of curiosity at this intense reaction, I finally realized that, as far into my life as I was, I was very unfamiliar with literal death. I had seen the death of dreams, of my marriage, of other relationships, but with so few relatives, I had never been to a funeral. I was too young for Grandfather's and, living in Alaska, too expensively far away from Nebraska to get to Grandmother's. But Princess Diana had been electronically in my living room with all the details on TV almost every day for years. It had taken a cat and a Princess to show me the deep grief of losing a beloved.

Little Bear continued to grieve, too. He still played with Funnel, begged for "walkies," chowed down on his food, but he didn't seem as enthusiastic about anything as he had before. He abandoned the chair he had claimed as his so long ago and now sat in Sami's chair. The rocking at Sami's grave continued. Every day it was the same—first the trip to the grave, the sitting, the rocking, then, finally, going about his business. He was faithful to this routine for months, only gradually spending less and less time graveside. There was no doubt in my mind that this animal—supposedly something with no feelings and little memory—was grieving as much as this human was.

The house felt so empty with only Bear and Precious. Sunny's tuxedo cat, BB, had died months before from the after-effects of a rattlesnake bite when they had been on the reservation. Sunny said that she and a shaman had done healing work, and BB had finally recovered. However, according to the vet Sunny took her to, there had been damage to the heart muscle, and BB simply wasted away, reinforcing for Sunny the powerlessness of modern medicine.

Sometimes, I would forget that Sami was gone. I'd see Bear or Precious, and get that quick, heads up feeling, and realize I hadn't seen Sami in a while. I would involuntarily and immediately go into "missing kid" panic mode. Then I would remember. And get that knot in my throat again.

Against all odds, the crazy avocado tree stayed alive in this climate where it shouldn't grow, in the deep shade of the other trees, protecting and identifying Sami's grave—not thriving, but not dying. I'd visit it each week and give it some water, and assure Sami it was still protecting him.

A week after Diana's burial, I found a lump on Bear's leg. I rushed him to the vet in a complete panic. The vet's response after her exam was nonchalant.

"Oh, it's just a reaction to the vaccine. We don't inject the shot into their shoulders anymore, because we've found it can cause cancer, so now we give the injection in the leg. That way, we can just amputate if it becomes an injection-site sarcoma."

I was speechless. They were trying to tell me there was no connection between the vaccines and Sami's death, while assuring me that if the shot caused cancer, they were ready with an amputation? But what could I prove? I barely knew where to begin to research for answers other than the ones the vets were giving me. But I began anyway. I read every book in the library relating to vet medicine—all two of them, and found no answers. I had no outlet for my anger, but I knew in my heart that the vets or the pharmaceutical companies were lying, and that Sami would still be alive had I not let them give him the vaccinations. I was sure it was not just a coincidence.

Bear's lump went away after a few months, and I finally relaxed again. In the meantime, I found out through a friend that there were two different rabies vaccines—a three-year shot and a one-year. I had never been asked by any vet which kind I wanted, and I hadn't known there *was* more than one kind. In the fall, I again took Bear in for his annuals, but this time I questioned the vet. "I understand there are different rabies vaccines, one and three year. Is that correct?"

"Yes."

"And which kind have you been giving my cats?"

He leaned his tall, lanky self back against the stainless steel table, his dark arms crossed over his white-shirted chest and, after a hesitation, admitted, "The three-year."

I asked, "Why would you do that? Aren't you double dosing them?"

He shrugged. "That was what I got from the drug company, and I am doing what is recommended."

"But it's just common sense that giving a shot that will last for three years *every year* means that by the third year, the cat has three times the equivalent of a one-year shot all in his system at the same time!"

I waited for him to speak, but he was silent. I felt a surge of revulsion at the thought of what the vets had done and were continuing to do, deliberately, endangering my cat and everyone else's. It took every piece of self-control I had not to give way to the rage I felt.

"I want to know what I need to do to make sure my cats *never* have to get annual shots and boosters again."

"It's the law," he said. "Yearly vaccinations."

I just looked at him. He stared back.

"You will not vaccinate Bear *now*, and you will *never* vaccinate *any* of my cats again." I took Bear and stormed out of the office. I made it my mission to explain to everyone I knew about the dangers of, and the ways to avoid, getting needless vaccinations, especially for indoor cats. I found out that, under Texas law, cats that are ill, or very old, or had become ill after the injections—*were exempt.* Sami had not had to be vaccinated at all as he *always* showed major side effects for days. I had to try very hard not to get sick to my stomach as I drove my boy home.

Then I went to a lecture by Dr. Martin Goldberg, DVM, a holistic vet and author of the book, *The Nature of Animal Healing.* He showed before and after photos of animals brought to Cornell University's vet center, animals literally on death's door. The vets there changed diets and stopped all vaccines. The after pictures were of beautiful, sleek, and healthy animals, barely recognizable from the before picture. As I read, I had a realization that the primary reason shots were "mandatory yearly" was to force pet owners to take their animals to get an exam. Without that requirement, most owners wouldn't, and the vets, taxing authorities, and pharmaceutical companies would lose money. I had finally found a symbolic bra worth burning.

Now, I understood why Sunny so distrusted doctors and drug companies. Her life motto was, "If I'm bleeding, if I'm having a heart attack, or if I'm broken, take me to a doctor; otherwise, keep me the hell away from them." The more I heard that, and the more contact I had with the medical and veterinary profession, the more it sounded like a really good idea. Obviously, different circumstances dictated different treatments—an outside, at-risk pet needed extra protections, but inside animals were, in my newly-formed opinion, more in danger from the shots than any disease the shots could protect against.

That conclusion did not end my visits to the vet for yearly check-ups, but I never again allowed any of my kids to get stuck after their baby vaccinations. Sami had presented me with another chapter in my life lessons. Because of his unfortunate reaction to the vaccines, I now distrusted and researched anything and everything to do with vet diagnoses, with pharmaceuticals, and even with pet food manufacturers. More and more I sought out alternatives in the holistic healing community any time the cats were sick. "Distrust" became my healing motto.

Chapter 20
MAGIC FLOWERS

Oak Hill, Texas. November 1997. Another newspaper article, the same as many I had read before, told of beloved pets who left signs that they had returned after death. If that really was possible, I knew Sami would let me know he had come back. But I noticed nothing.

One day, I asked Sunny, "Have you ever felt like Sami has paid us a visit?" I was sure, with her psychic abilities that she would know if he had.

"No," she said slowly. "I don't think so. A few times I've seen something, sort of out of the corner of my eye, and then it's gone before I can actually see it. I don't know if I imagined it or not."

"It would be a comfort to know he was checking in with us. Maybe all the stories of life after death, reincarnation, and contacts from the other side are just wishful thinking or a desperate refusal by us humans to let go of a loved one."

"No. I don't believe that," she said. And hurried away from the conversation as she often did in the face of my non-magical mentality.

We had been calling him Mr. Bear since Sami's death—it just seemed right as his grief lent him a dignity that hadn't been there before. "Could he really be a senior *already*?" I kept asking myself, sometimes doubting it so much I would check on the calendar where I kept the cat adoption dates. He was, at eight years old, a senior cat according to cat food packages.

Sami's babyhood was still so clear to me that I had trouble realizing he had passed his eleventh birthday a few months before dying. I had been a cat mom for more than a decade and was beginning to recognize how rapidly my own mortality was approaching. But Mr. Bear was in his prime and could be summed up in one word—magnificent. His square, muscled body was covered in a solid grey coat with silver tips that shimmered, giving him a halo effect in the sun. His stocky legs ended in snow-white paws the size of snowshoes, and his thick, feathery, usually waving tail took care of most of the low-level dusting in the house when he passed by. His most striking feature, his mane, framed his face like a Victorian ruff before tapering into the white hair on his chest and belly. Petting him was an orgy of sensuality—his fur so fine and silky it was difficult to feel it when I rubbed it between my fingers. How had that scrawny, striped, ugly kitten turned into this stately-looking specimen?

He still begged to go for walkies, hunting down his harness and dragging it to me. He still slammed his funnel over the tile floor and was still first at the door to greet visitors. Since Bear had reached adulthood around his fourth birthday, his weight had stayed between seventeen and eighteen pounds. It was around that time that I had decided he was a full or at least part Maine Coon breed—the large ears, the long whiskers, the mane under his chin, his personality, all fit. My only disappointment in him was that, while all these other changes were taking place, his beautiful adult chartreuse-green cat eyes that I had fallen in love with after he gave up his baby blues had disappeared, replaced by a deep-golden color, a phenomenon the latest vet swore she had never heard of.

His personality was changing also; it wasn't just that he was older. I still fretted about his sense of invincibility. He had no fear of anything in his relatively small world—I envied him his utter self-confidence. Now, though, he moved with more of a sense of purpose and quieter enthusiasm than before Sami's death. And he was still almost always friendly and accepting of everything and everyone. Or so I had thought.

The forecast was calling for a massive storm arriving within an hour or two, to bring torrential downpours with flooding for up to a week. I was rushing home when I saw the yellow lab meandering along the no-shoulder street in a forty-five mile per hour speed limit that designated our subdivision from the unclaimed land around it. Brush grew close to the road, and I was concerned the dog could be hit if a driver came along in a pouring rain.

"Why me?" I groaned as I slowed the car. The dog trotted up, a collar with no tags, of course, around its neck. I was at a loss as to what to do. Where could we house a dog—and two cats—in our open-floor-plan house for days and days. The garage, where the cat boxes were located, was windowless and totally packed with yard implements, way too many boxes of storage items, spare tires, and all the things for Sunny's fair booth. We didn't have a porch, a shed, or even a roof overhang except a postage-stamp sized one above the front door; there was no place the dog could get out of the weather except inside the house where the cats were. We could easily have managed for a few hours, or overnight, but for up to a week as the forecaster predicted? Furthermore, if someone was looking for the dog, they would not be able to find it at our house. Hanging "Found" signs around with the incoming weather would be impossible. Still, I couldn't just let it wander, so I drove slowly home, calling, and it willingly followed for the long block to the house. I let it into the privacy-fenced back yard and headed for the back door.

"Hey, Sunny, keep Precious in your area and corral Bear. We've got a dog outside," I yelled as I went inside to get it water and something to use as a collar and leash.

"Where did we get a dog?"

"It's lost. Do you know where Bear is? We need to keep him out of the kitchen."

I was too late. Bear, unbeknownst to me, was rounding the corner into the kitchen as I had come into the house, closing the screen door behind me and going to the sink for a bowl of water. The dog was standing patiently on the other side of the screen door, waiting for something to happen. It did.

Bear flew by me with an incensed yowl and hit the screen door with the fury pictured in those cartoons with the outline of a cat on a screen, all four feet, head, and tail in a different direction to show where it had gone through. Until that moment, I'd never considered that this could actually happen. The only thing that saved the dog's nose was the screen which held strong and bounced Bear back onto the floor.

The poor dog just stood there looking astonished, confused, and totally non-threatening as I reacted and threw the water on Bear; then I dropped the stainless bowl with a clatter and grabbed him by the scruff of the neck as he made another flying leap at the door.

"*Bear!* You stupid cat! *What* are you doing?"

Barely able to hang on to him as he writhed every which way, I hauled him into the bathroom, his hair still standing on end, legs flailing about, yowling sounds that alone could have scared something to death. I realized then that Bear had probably never seen a dog, and certainly not up close, not in all of his life with me, which meant probably never. I was perplexed at his violent attack. Never had I seen him making even a marginally aggressive move toward *anything*. I could only explain this dog-hate as some atavistic trait that had come to the fore based on an ancient scent-of-dog memory, or his willingness to protect us against any uninvited guest.

Sunny and I tried to figure out a way to keep a dog for the any number of days the torrential rain was expected to last. The only way we might be able to find an owner would be to call in an ad to the paper and wait a couple of days for it to be published and delivered. As we were trying to decide, thunder started rumbling. I felt wretched but couldn't come up with anything other than calling animal control. At least it would be out of danger from rain-blinded drivers, and confined to a safe place where an owner should start looking for it.

The dog catcher arrived in less than an hour. By then, the wind was strengthening, the lightening almost overhead. When I went out to meet the official, the friendly dog trotted up—the one I had left *behind* our privacy fence that didn't seem to be capable of keeping *any* animal in. I was sure I didn't imagine that the dog gave me a reproachful look as it was loaded into the truck.

I was upset for days, crying as I looked out the window at the sheets of unremitting rain and flooding, cursing and yelling out with anger at stupid owners who attach collars but can't be bothered putting ID tags and contact information on them. I also wavered between being proud of Bear for protecting me and ashamed of my perfect Bear's hostile behavior.

In the meantime, there was another behavior in the house that was upsetting me. Sunny's psychiatrist was attempting to re-integrate all the personalities. The Ruth personality was coming out more and more. Ruth and I did not get along; she was rigid and bossy, a mean nun without a habit. The good thing about her was that she kept order. It was Ruth, I now knew, who paid the rent, cleaned the kitchen, and organized, doing it all with a pained and forbidding look on her face. The more I saw of Ruth, the less I saw of the delightful Rosie and her effervescent personality; the adult me was not happy with Ruth, and my inner child missed our former interactions with Rosie.

"Let's go buy a fish. You want to come?" Rosie would ask.

"Sure," I said.

"I want to go shopping—you want to come?" I'd ask, even knowing that it could lead to a shopping trip for "good energy" stuff before we got home. And so it had gone, as our "little girls" went out to have fun.

Besides Ruth in the house, a new personality was emerging—the teenager. I couldn't do or say anything to please her. If she responded at all, it would come from a face with a sneering mouth and rolled eyes.

"Sunny, can you help with the cleaning tomorrow?"

"Does it *have* to be tomorrow? I've got things I want to do," and she would stalk off toward her bedroom. Now I truly knew what mothers complained about. My teen-age cats had *never* been this exasperating.

Fortunately, we both had a number of interests that kept us busy separately. When the "nice" personalities were out, we would lapse back into being good friends, and I would forget my growing frustration.

Then Sunny disappeared for a weekend with no notice to me; Rosie returned, so excited she could barely stand still.

She talked so fast I had trouble understanding her. "Look what I learned this week-end it's about flowers, flowers are so magic, they can heal anything! Look, there are thirty-eight remedies and the doctor in England found them, and they are good for all sorts of things, they will make you happy if you are sad or make you feel safe when you are scared."

"And what *are* these flowers?" I felt my forehead wrinkling as I tried to rein her in to get a reasonable explanation for her excitement.

"Bach Flower Essences. They have been around for a century in England and you know what? They can help kitties, like when Bear was so scared of the dog?"

I thought she had that backwards, but still, if something would help the cats, I'd listen.

"You just pick some flower petals and let them sit in water, and then you bottle the water with vodka, and they heal things."

Oh. *Another of her magic things.* I sneered inwardly. Sometimes she was so naive! But I continued to act interested as she told stories of snarling cats making up, and the dead resurrected after a few drops of one essence or another.

"What kind of things?"

"Everything. Rescue Remedy helps when you are really upset, like in an accident. Or we should have given it to Little Bear when Sami died. And we can give them to the plants when we transplant them, and they will grow and not go into shock. But the other remedies help other things. Olive is for mental and emotional strength, when you are just worn out, and, and... Here." She thrust a brochure at me. "Here is a test you can take, so we can see what you need."

I obligingly took the test. She determined I needed thirty of the thirty-six remedies, from Aspen for my fear of flying, to Willow for a rebirthing of faith and optimism. With a maximum of five remedies at a time, taken for a minimum of a month, it was going to take a long time to cure what ailed me. I took the ones she prescribed, somewhat haphazardly, not believing much in magic, and I waited. In the meantime, Sunny began flowering everything, from the cats, to me, to the shrubs outside; the only thing she might have missed, I think, was Bear Rock. Needless to say, with all her personalities, she was taking something from every bottle every day.

A week later, we went for a drive in the country. She saw the blot before I did, and I slowed down when she yelled, managing to stop before I hit the big tortoise that was smack in the middle of our lane of the highway. Sunny jumped out and rushed to the non-moving bump.

"Can we take it home?"

I looked at it doubtfully. "Where is its head? Maybe it's just an empty shell."

"I have Rescue Remedy with me. They said they put it on the bird that was dead, and it woke up and flew away. Oh, no! The shell is cracked." She dug into her purse for the essence and proceeded to drip Rescue Remedy on it. We waited and watched. Nothing happened. She picked Tortoise up and carried it to the empty box that had been riding around in my back seat, apparently just for the purpose of housing a half-dead terrapin.

We got back into the car and resumed our journey. Sunny kept checking the back seat.

"Look! Its head is out! The flowers helped!"

Big tortoise sat quietly all the way home, probably stunned into silence, but it *did* keep its head out. We called Wildlife Rescue, and they came to get it. They would super-glue the shell back together, watch it for a couple of days, and then release it to the wild, they said. They thought it would survive with no problem. Maybe the Rescue Remedy helped the tortoise, maybe not, but it did make both of us feel less incompetent at nursing wildlife. Perhaps we *had* found a magic remedy after all. Maybe.

I obediently sipped away at my no-more-than-five-a-day remedies, any that Sunny had on my menu to cure me that day, and waited for change. I wasn't asking to grow taller or repair my eye, but I was hoping I would be calmer about financial issues, able to make decisions easier, and to get rid of my fear of heights. I couldn't tell that anything happened.

Sunny put remedies for removal of jealousy in the cat bowls for Precious and Bear, but I didn't see any difference. I didn't feel any more optimistic or any less achy. I finally pooh-poohed the whole thing, threw the bottles into a drawer, and moved on to other educational pursuits more in the realm of my possible realities, with no magic attached.

There were many possibilities to explore. In my entire life, I had never heard of energy healing; now, suddenly, everywhere I went, everyone I met, seemed to be talking about it in general and in specific terms. I started taking yoga classes, and I got more acupuncture done that helped with my general health. I took a class on herbs, another on color therapy, and bought gemstones.

Then I took a class using energy healing. The instructor, from New Zealand, had come to the United States to promote his system, sponsored by a church I occasionally attended. We met in a private home. He instructed the class in the use of the dowsing wand to find the stuck energy that was causing the pain or other problem. There were twelve students and each of us gave another a simple "treatment," similar to a-laying-on-of-hands process. I was one of the last to give the treatment, my usual doubt foremost but willing to try. The young man on the table was in very poor health, trying to recover from cancer and its treatment of chemo and radiation.

After I completed my energy manipulations, I stood there waiting for something to happen, or some sign that I had helped. The instructor looked at me and said, "You didn't feel anything, did you?"

I acknowledged that as truth. The patient then chimed in, saying he had felt a very powerful surge of energy, and immediately felt less pain when I had worked on him. I looked at the instructor for affirmation.

"That's the way it is sometimes, with some people. Your treatment was one of the strongest we did today, yet you felt nothing. I can't explain it, but trust that you *do* have healing abilities."

Trust was not one of my major personality traits. Maybe my spirit guides that Sunny insisted were always present around me had sent me the techniques; unfortunately, they didn't send any patients. I slowly abandoned the pursuit of mastery as I sought other methods, information, and confirmations of alternative healing. I felt I was going to college again, the classes more pertinent to my life than the ones I had attended at the University. With each thing I investigated, I learned more that made me question my life-long beliefs. And I liked these new beliefs better—they felt more spiritual, more than any church service ever had, and I didn't come away feeling like a failure—a sinner. These ministrations were gentle, and left the patient in no worse shape, and usually better, than the pharmaceuticals passed out by the doctors, and one major attraction for me, of course, was that they honored all life, not just human ones.

Then I found my true love. One of the special healers that came into my life was essential oils—the frankincense and myrrh of Bible testament. I had gone to a holistic healing fair and smelled the most wonderful aromas I'd ever encountered in my life; I described them as "heavenly." I followed the scent to a booth, stopping every few feet as I approached, waiting for the chemical reactions I had to colognes, laundry products, and air fresheners, but nothing happened. Eventually I arrived at the booth and picked up the blue bar labeled "Pain Soap." The smell was so wonderful I couldn't think of anything else as the scent invaded my brain with none of the harsh undertones of grocery store soap. After a long discussion with the seller, I bought a bar of "Pain Soap." I took it home that night and showered with it. I had the best night's sleep I'd had in a long time. The next morning, I showered again and was able to bend and reach the floor, my usual stiffness greatly reduced. I went back to the booth to find out how to order.

"Well, we don't do individual sales except at these health fairs. Do you want to become a distributor? You only need to buy a hundred bars."

What could I do with one hundred bars of soap? I was sure Bear wouldn't cooperate in a bath. I bought them anyway. And started my own little business, knowing nothing about selling and not much about essential oils. I spent hours on the phone with the soap makers who generously shared their knowledge about the oils they used, about the enhancements with gemstones and herbs they incorporated. I practically lived at the library. I was soon buying hundreds of bars of soap at a time, selling them with the enthusiasm of a circus barker. I hungered for the wonderful scents as much as for food; the scent of them lingering in my nose and mouth and filling my senses, even cancelling any desire for food.

One of my first customers bought six bars of Varicose Vein soap. A few weeks later, she came back and ordered six more, saying they were for her mother in Mexico. When I was ready to place another order, I asked her if she needed more.

"No." I felt a wave of disappointment before she continued, "My mother used the ones I gave her and is now wearing shorts for the first time in twenty years—the dark veins have almost disappeared!"

I studied essential oil precautions, then delved into the healing properties of the oils. While generally safe, there were some that needed to be handled with care, especially for babies, pregnant women, and people with seizures. I read that the oils could be lethal to cats. The dog owners, though, were awed when the fleas disappeared after they gave their dogs baths in the Flea Soap.

After many months of sitting in my office with hundreds of bars of soap, I noticed I was not so overcome when I accidentally got around manufactured perfumes, cleaning products, and colognes; much of my aching and stiffness which waxed and waned from day to day went away, and I was feeling better than I had in years. Of all the modern medicines I had tried that had failed to help, or helped but had horrible side effects, and all of the alternative healing modalities I tried, some with success, some not so much, the essential oils with their magical healing properties were the ones that became closest to my heart.

Finally, and amazingly, I found another life-changing thing. I got a home computer, one that was connected to that big library in the sky—the Internet. It was a godsend with its ability to retrieve information with great speed—all kinds of information elusive to non-computer users. I knew I'd never begin to have the amount of healing knowledge that Sunny did, and I would always be less trusting in alternative therapies than she was, at least until I had proved them for myself, but now I had a way to do research besides ransacking the local library.

I vowed I would take the time and make the effort to research everything I could—for the health and safety of my Bear. Acupuncture, the Bach Flower Remedies, homeopathy, energy healing, these were safe for every living being, and I relied more and more on them for my own health. I read websites and labels like some people read the Bible, and spent hours researching foods or checking pharmaceuticals.

When I took Bear in for his annual check-up, the labs showed his kidney's were starting to fail; he refused to eat the food the vet recommended. Based on my hours of research, I switched him from the better-than-grocery-store food I had been feeding to a new dry cat food based on my recent education of nutrition for cats. I put Bear on it. Within weeks, his coat was even silkier. When I took him to the vet for a re-check of his failing kidney functions, the vet kept rechecking the lab work—there was no evidence that his kidneys were failing. He refused to consider that it was only a change of food though he had no other explanation to offer. I had changed nothing else about Bear's care.

Chapter 21
ANIMAL TALK

Austin, Texas. Spring 1998. No matter how much I learned about alternative healing, I thirsted for more knowledge about interspecies communication. It was always on my mind, this urgency to prove conversations with my animals was a real thing.

I went to the library, but neither "Animal Communication" nor "Interspecies Communication" was a subject in the card catalog. The bookstores had no idea what I was talking about. I was at a standstill, having exhausted all my resources.

The computer was promising, but I was a novice, so intimidated by the black screen with nothing but the *: >c* blinking at me, waiting for me to do *something,* that I spent little time with it. Finally, months later, I stumbled upon a book review in the newspaper: *Communicating With Animals: The Spiritual Connection Between People and Animals* by Arthur Myers, © 1997, published six months before Sami's death. I couldn't find it in the stores, but finally a bookstore clerk took pity on me and closed her cashier's line to research it. She was diligent, and I was patient. She finally found that one book title, but no others. I ordered it immediately. I was so excited I went around telling everyone—even complete strangers—about my discovery. They smiled and nodded but didn't ask any questions or even, disappointingly, act interested.

Finally, I got the call on a Saturday—the book was here. I stopped what I was doing and hurried to the store, returned home, sat down, and read it straight through that same night, even ignoring Bear's pleas for walkies.

Mr. Myers's book was a series of interviews with Animal Communicators about the stories the animals had told them, and the changes in their belief systems that occurred after those conversations. In the back of his book, he had listed contact information for over forty Communicators and their specialties, such as dog behaviorist, lost animals, sick animals, or communicating with those that had crossed over. *How could this be such a secret!* Forty people, at least, had told Mr. Meyers they talked with animals. Why had I, who had such an inquiring mind, didn't remember ever hearing of the process until I had accidentally found Val at the Psychic Fair? I felt an insatiable need to talk more with Bear, but this kind of talk wasn't cheap. I decided to spend time doing more research, to find a way to do it myself.

I diligently went through Mr. Myer's list and highlighted every Communicator who gave workshops. The next day, I started dialing. I got lucky on only the third call. Dr. Jeri Ryan was listed as living in California and giving workshops internationally. I waited impatiently for the phone to be answered.

"Dr. Ryan's office."

"I'm calling from Austin, Texas. Is this the Jeri Ryan who is an Animal Communicator?"

"This is her office. How can I help?"

I took a deep breath and tried to calm down—I noticed my hands were trembling. "It says in this book that she does workshops to teach people to communicate with animals. How can I take a workshop?"

"Actually, she's going to be in Austin soon, but I'm afraid the workshop is full. You could sign up on a waiting list, or call the woman in Austin who's handling the arrangements there."

I immediately called Pamela, the local contact. I rushed through the introductions—who I was, why I was calling, and then I began begging.

"Jeri Ryan's assistant told me you were arranging a workshop here. Can you tell me the details?" I was sitting on the very edge of my desk chair, practically willing her to give me good news.

"Yes, it's the first weekend in June and..." She told me the cost. I know I gasped out loud and immediately saw my dream die. "But," she went on, "we're not sure where it's going to be held because the person who was to host the group just cancelled."

I was stunned. Things didn't fall into place for me like this... but that psychic had been right about the house. Maybe...

"I have a really nice big house! Could, would it be possible for me to do the hosting? And would that reduce the fee any?"

"If you were hosting, the workshop would be free to you and anyone living in your home. We have the necessary minimum enrollment of twelve people, so we will definitely be doing the class. If you want to volunteer, that would... "

"I'll do it! I'll do anything!" I interrupted.

She couldn't resist, any objections she might have had flattened by my enthusiasm. We ironed out the major details, then the small wrinkles, and it was decided.

I told Sunny about the workshop, that she could attend for free, and told her I'd need her help at times. I hated asking, but her help equaled her reduced rent. I was shocked at her reaction. "Just keep them out of my area," she said, and slammed out of the house.

"I will definitely do that," I told the closed door. I was very disappointed and puzzled at her lack of interest. Her comment was totally inappropriate—I had never been in her area since she moved in, only occasionally sticking my head in, after I was bid to enter, to tell her something, or looking for her when Bear had disappeared again. However, as her moods had been getting worse and worse, her reaction was not totally out of character, or, rather, characters.

Slowly, so slowly, the two months crawled by as I marked off as accomplished final arrangements for guests, accommodations, food, and other details of the workshop.

Finally, Thursday evening and the introductory night of the workshop arrived, as did eighteen people consisting of students, spouses, Dr. Ryan, and Pamela. There were people sitting on the floor, on the couch, on folding chairs, and dining room chairs. I was exhilarated that I could accommodate so many people wanting to learn about helping animals. Animal attendance at this first night of the workshop was discouraged because of space issues and to ensure the safety of all the animals and humans. The rest of the workshop would include humans and their animals; if any of the animals might have difficulty getting along with the other animals and/or humans, their persons were asked to bring photos instead to use in the communication exercises.

On this night, Bear didn't seem to want to attend and chose to stay in the bedroom. I kept busy being hostess, impatient to get the socializing over with, silently urging everyone to finish with their pizza so we could start.

At last, Pamela moved forward and made the announcement I was waiting for. "OK everyone, let's get started. As you all know, we're here for Dr. Jeri Ryan. Jeri is a psychotherapist, an Interspecies Communicator, an internationally renowned teacher of telepathic animal communication, and founder of the Assisi International Animal Institute in California. She was a student of Penelope Smith, one of the first communicators to introduce this work to the public in the 1970's when she worked with animals at the San Diego Zoo. Let's all welcome Dr. Jeri Ryan."

As she finished, I remembered! A long ago TV news story on *60 Minutes* or similar, back when I was still married, about a crabby tiger at the San Diego zoo with a sore foot, and the woman who helped find the problem when the vets couldn't. It had to have been Penelope Smith! I had been fascinated and tried to find out more at the time but couldn't unearth anything, and had gradually forgotten all about it. Now, the subject and answer had just appeared. In holistic healing, there is a belief that "when the student is ready the teacher will appear." Had the fates, or my spirit guides, or the animal gods decided I was finally ready? I felt goose pimples at the thought.

Dr. Ryan was dressed very casually, unlike what I had expected of my first near-celebrity. She had graying hair, shoulder length and styled casually. She wore black leggings, a tie-dye T-shirt, and Birkenstock sandals. With her calm energy, she was my idea of Mother Earth, exuding peacefulness and nurturing. I wanted to crawl into her lap and stick my thumb in my mouth.

Everything and everyone was silent as Jeri began to speak in her soothing voice. There was an electric quality of excitement in the room, and I knew Sunny would be glad to hear I had felt it. Sunny, who had not shown up.

"The workshop runs for three days. We'll discuss the why and how of interspecies communication, the history, and the ethics of working with animals. We will do a number of practice sessions, and you will be having conversations with the animals by the time you leave Sunday afternoon.

"You may bring your animals, but they must be leashed or contained. Please, no cats because the stress of keeping them in the carriers for so long isn't good for them. Cats living in the house may attend. How many of you will be bringing your animals?"

Ten hands went up; only two students weren't bringing any of their pets. "Please do not bring more than two."

Two? Two dogs times ten people was... twenty dogs! In my home! With Bear! Ohmigod, what had I done? What had I been thinking! And why had this not penetrated before? I panicked. *What would Bear do with so many dogs in his house? This workshop might not have been a good idea. Twenty dogs!*

I forced my mind to tune back to Jeri, who kept us mesmerized with her personal journeys into interspecies communication, and the changes in the lives of animals and their keepers after sessions with her.

She explained several things, but the one that resonated most in my heart was when she told us that, years before, she had been sitting outside with her dog, looked into his eyes, and realized she was looking at another soul. I was sure I had seen that in my cats' eyes, but "they"—scientists, preachers, teachers, said animals didn't have emotions, let alone souls. So what had I seen? I wasn't sure what a soul really looked like, but it just felt like I was looking far beyond reality to some secret place when I had looked into Sami's and Bear's eyes sometimes. Here, finally, was confirmation—if I was crazy, at least there were two of us.

Jeri went on to tell stories of the sometimes wise and wonderful information the animals conveyed to her. Two hours later, looking as dazed, doubtful, and excited as I felt, the attendees left, all moving quietly, as though leaving a spiritual gathering.

Jeri was spending the night at my house. I asked her to explain to Bear what was going on, something I should have done before all these people arrived. I told her of Bear's attack the first time he had seen a dog and tried to fly through the screen door.

"What can I do with him, Jeri? I can't just let him roam free with all these dogs. I don't want to lock him away, but there isn't any other choice, is there? I can't believe I didn't think of this before! Or maybe I did and just didn't want to address it."

"Let's talk with him and then figure it out," she said soothingly

I watched as Jeri stood silently, eyes closed, and began conversing with Bear who was curled up on the bed; then she interpreted the conversation for me.

"I've told him what is happening, and that there will be dogs here tomorrow, many dogs. I've assured him that he will be safe, and that he can attend or not. He says he wants to think about it. He doesn't like the idea of the dogs, but is *quite* intrigued with the idea of all the people being here."

"Tell him that this bedroom and bath are off-limits to the dogs. Only the people can come in here, and it is his safe place. Also tell him I'd *like* him to come to the workshop, but he can choose."

"He says he will see. He might come. He wants to know why he can't attack the dogs."

I stopped myself just in time, swallowing the urge to burst out laughing. I had hurt Sami's feelings once, and had vowed then that I would never laugh *at* a cat again after seeing how upset he had been. It had been such a small thing to me. Sami and Bear had been in the middle of the floor, Bear sprawled out on his back, stomach flat, looking like an upside down bear pelt with a head. Sami, in bread-loaf pose, all legs tucked under him, was right beside him and facing him. I sensed something was about to happen and watched, thinking Sami was probably getting ready to jump on Little Bear the way he kept glancing over, studying his friend, then looking away.

After a few minutes, Sami suddenly rolled over onto his back, apparently wanting to try out the Bear pose. Sami wasn't built for lying on his back. His sternum stuck up like a Thanksgiving turkey on a platter and his legs stuck up and out to the four winds, looking like they needed to be tied together. I had burst out laughing. Sami rolled back over, got up, and—tail and head down—went slinking away, his body language conveying unmistakably his hurt and embarrassment. I felt awful.

Bear's question was not something to laugh at, even though I found it funny that a cat was upset because he couldn't take on a roomful of dogs. I would not laugh, not ever again, unless the cat was playing and showing off for me. But I was having some trouble with that vow now as I tried to answer. Struggling to keep my voice serious, I said, "Tell him that the dogs are invited guests, and it is very bad manners for a cat to attack guests—humans or animals. And tell him that he will be very, very safe," I said, "and the people want their dogs to be safe, too."

"Let me tell him that the people really want to meet him, too." Apparently *those* were the magic words—that the *humans really wanted* to *meet him*. She was silent, listening to his response. Finally, she gave a nod to me, smiled that he understood, and I was able to relax.

Jeri and Bear slept in my bedroom. I went to the office and bunked out on the floor to sleep, which, of course, didn't happen. I went over all the details for the following day—food, cleaning, parking, and the communication possibilities—too excited to sleep. I was still awake when I heard Sunny's door close quietly when she finally returned home.

Chapter 22
LIVING THE DREAM

Austin, Texas. June 1998. The first full day of the workshop arrived for me before daylight. I jumped up from the floor and rushed to get things ready, including a quick house cleanup. As I worked, I again blessed the inspiration, and the psychic, that had made it possible for me to buy this house.

I made coffee, then put out a regular, a vegetarian, and, for Jeri, a vegan breakfast. Working up a menu for those who eat no animal products was stretching my cooking skills. By then, I was running behind time. *Where was Sunny? Had she bailed again on her obligation to help?* I knocked on her door. No answer. I looked outside; her van was gone. *At 7:30? How long was I going to let her get by with this passive-aggressiveness?* But I couldn't focus on that today—I had work to do.

I was still frantically chopping fruit when the doorbell signaled the first arrivals. I greeted Pamela with my hands full of sliced apples. Jeri came out of the bedroom, and I noticed Bear had followed her into the hallway, watching all that was happening.

"And who is this?" I said, indicating the brown dog attached to Pamela.

"This is Pumpkin, a racing greyhound we were able to rescue."

"Hello, Pumpkin. Thanks for coming." I thought I saw a slight acknowledgement wiggle in the tail held tightly against his rump. Pumpkin was huge; he stood studying me intently with his eyes at my waist level. Then the doorbell rang again, and suddenly there were women and dogs everywhere.

With everyone fed and awake from the coffee, all the humans settled in a circle, dogs beside them, leashes held securely. The twenty dogs didn't show up.

We did have a white poodle, two Australian sheep dogs, two Italian greyhounds, a whippet, a black dog (a lab?), one cocker spaniel, a golden retriever, and Pumpkin, who took up more space than all the rest put together. Including Bear and I, we had eleven animals and fourteen humans.

As hostess, I did a short welcome, explaining the house rules: "Humans can use the master bath, but, please, no dogs there, that is Bear's space, and we promised him. And please, *please,* be sure to keep the outside doors closed all the way, all the time, and make sure you know where Bear is always before you open the front door. He's a Houdini cat. You'll never see him escape, and he *really* wants to be wild and free." They nodded their heads in understanding and agreement, and, knowing there were a number of cat people here, I relaxed a bit.

I settled into the circle, exhilarated. It was possible that, here in this room, my long-held dream of communicating with an animal was about to come true. At the same time, doubt remained, a looming specter over my desires and my questionable abilities.

Jeri began the workshop again. As I studied her, I realized that there was something about her that reminded me of Jane Goodall, the anthropologist, a similar build, the same energy of mother-earth-ness.

"When you got home last night, what reactions did you get from your animals?"

"Oh, they were so excited!" "Yes, mine, too, much more than usual." "They were rubbing all over me." "They met me at the door, dancing around." Most chimed in relating unusual behavior from their animals, in a good way.

"They know something's going on. Part of that, they have picked up from you and your excitement, but part of it, they just know. I don't understand how they do, but it happens," said Jeri.

"How long have you been doing communication?" asked one of the group.

Jeri answered that and the many questions that followed. Then she told us stories of what the animals—both domestic and wild, covering almost every species in the biology books, from every country in the geography books—had told her.

"When I dropped my preconceived and scientific ideas of animals, I began listening. And my life was changed forever."

"How do you know when it's the animals talking and not your own thoughts or imagination?" asked one dog owner.

"After awhile, it comes from experience. You'll be able to tell if the voice is coming from your heart, and if it is, it will be a true connection to the animal. If it seems more in your head, then perhaps you are not "getting" all of it. For some of the conversations, you just have to trust yourself. What we look for are the zingers, as I call them. You will hear or see or feel something that you could not possibly know in any other way; that's the verification that tells you it's a true communication from the animal. You won't have any doubts after that.

"Now, let's start with introductions," she instructed. "Please say who you are and introduce the dogs that you have brought with you with their name, sex, breed, and age."

The dogs were lying around in various poses, remarkably quiet, as everyone complied with Jeri's request. At last the introductions were finished, and we were dismissed for a short break. When we returned, Jeri gave us our next instructions.

"From now until lunch, we'll do some guided meditations. After lunch, I'll instruct you in the techniques we will be using. For the rest of the day you will practice actual interspecies communication." As she was speaking, she looked at me and gave a meaningful nod toward the hallway, silently asking us to look in that direction.

Bear was creeping into the living room a few inches at a time, making his way on his belly toward one of the chairs closest to the front door. As we watched, he scooted under the chair, as far away as possible from the dogs but still in the same room. I felt a huge wash of relief that he didn't appear to be in attack mode, shuddering at the vision of the resulting chaos if he decided to break his promise and take out the dogs.

"Can anyone learn this?" asked another participant, voicing what we all were thinking.

"Everyone is born with a natural ability, but we stop using it after childhood and forget. Some of you will do it today, some of you tomorrow, some will take longer. It takes practice, like everything else."

When one question was answered, another took its place, but no matter who asked, the question appeared to resonate with all of us, heads nodding, body language showing intent listening. Jeri had answered all those questions many, probably even hundreds, of times before, but she patiently shared her knowledge.

"I don't know how the process works. There seems to be 'a great interpreter in the sky' that allows me to talk with all kinds of animals. I've been in countries where the humans spoke no English, and I did not speak their language. Yet animals, even those who have never been around human speech, are able to converse as easily as you and I, no human interpreter needed. I've spoken with almost every species, even insects and fish.

"You will get information in multiple ways; for each person it's different. Some hear words like a private conversation, sometimes the animal offers pictures, some people are able to feel an animal's emotions and even pain.

"Now, let's start practicing. We will begin by asking for help and protection from our guides and then go into meditation."

The dogs, all strangers to each other, were awake, silent, and attentive. There was no barking, snarling, nipping, not even any scratching. The young black dog even stopped his incessant panting. I gave a last glance and saw that Bear was still under his chair, awake and attentive.

I really wanted to do this communication thing, but Jeri's first instruction left me doubtful. "Lie down and relax. Then ask for guidance and protection," she said.

Belief in spiritual, or "higher" powers, was difficult for me. I didn't question if God was real or not, but I was pretty sure He wasn't interested in me. I had asked time after time, year after year, and received only no's or silence, so what was the point in asking? But I would try again. For the cats. After several minutes of indecision, I latched on to the AA/Al-Anon pledge. At those meetings, they asked you to call on help from your Higher Power, what or whoever that was for you personally—even if it was a rock in your pocket. I was a little more comfortable with the Higher Power idea; I figured it covered every possibility. I took a page from Sunny's book and included all of them—God, Allah, Buddha, Angels, Spirit Guides, St. Francis, White Buffalo Woman, Santa Claus, Fairies, and other Energies—that some people believed in, and some did not.

Jeri's soft voice issued further instructions that quietly seeped in through my meditative state, asking us to first visualize an animal, call to them to get their attention, then to try to engage them in a conversation with opened-ended questions such as: show me what you do with your favorite toy? what do you most like to do? who do you live with?

Establishing and staying with the connection was very mentally and emotionally exhausting for me, requiring intense concentration to shut out the brain talk—the unwanted voices that claimed space in my head. There was interference between what I knew for sure and what I felt the animal might be telling me.

I'd had no sense of elapsed time when Jeri called us back from our meditations and into the meeting. There were more questions as we tried to get assurance that we weren't making things up.

"Just tell us what you heard and saw," she encouraged.

Each of us reported and discussed what we thought we had heard, seen, or felt. All of us said we were pretty sure we had connected, at least a little bit. By the time Jeri told us to take a break, the others looked as drained as I felt.

Of course, Bear made it out the door during that first intermission. I had been in the kitchen putting out tea and coffee; I went in to the living room to announce everything was ready when I noticed the group of four standing together chatting, the screen door wide open. I panicked, just as I heard someone yell, "Bear's at the end of the driveway!"

Everyone went into action, scrambling to get to him. He obviously wasn't serious about leaving, because he let someone catch up and grab him. She carted him back inside, gently scolding him for wanting to leave us.

After that, a call would go out before anyone opened a door. "Where's Bear? I'm opening the door!" Only after someone reported that they had him in sight would the door be opened. I relaxed, convinced they now believed I wasn't just a paranoid cat-mom.

As the morning progressed, so did Bear—around half of the perimeter of the room, sliding silently from under one chair to another, only avoiding the far area of the room where several animals and the panting black dog sat. Bear never allowed himself to be out in the open, but I was so proud of his fearlessness—one little cat encircled by strange humans and so many dogs, trusting in Jeri's assurance to him that he would be safe. Could I have exhibited such trust based on a stranger's word? I didn't think so.

Then it was lunchtime, and I was in the kitchen readying food. The black dog's owner came up and asked to *please* use the master bathroom as there was a line at the guest bath, and she couldn't find anyone to hold her dog. Distracted with dishing up food for a dozen people, I responded in an automatic good hostess agreement, "Yes, it's fine."

About five seconds later, my answer filtered into the rest of my brain, and I realized what I had just done. I dropped the spoon and whirled around; she and the dog on a leash were across the living room heading for the off-limits bedroom, while Bear, head thrust forward, ears clamped to his head, tail down, *stomping,* followed them. His body language was eloquent and unmistakable. Bear was *enraged,* as angry as I had ever seen him!

I was horrified! I had broken my promise after he had trusted Jeri's word implicitly that my bedroom was *his* safe space. I rushed after them, but they were already in the bathroom by the time I could get there. Bear was on the bed, tucked into the far corner, his back turned to the room. I rushed over and apologized, making soothing sounds, using his name over and over, petting him, but his body was rigid, and he refused to look at me. I knew I had messed up really badly.

I sought out Jeri and explained what I had done, pleading for her help. "I feel horrible! I can't believe I was so unconscious. Can you please talk to him and tell him how sorry I am?"

She agreed, but said we'd wait until after the workshop; I went back to hostess duties in the kitchen, cursing myself.

The black dog and his owner returned to the living room, Bear again following in a stalking pose. He threw himself under a chair, across the room from the trespassing dog and human, his hair seeming to bristle with his anger.

I rang the dinner bell, then went over and babied Bear while everyone else was eating. "Bear, I am *so, so* sorry, I'm not fit to be your mommy. You were so good and kept your promises, and I didn't. It was an accident, I just forgot." How could a healthy heart ache so?

He finally stretched out and relaxed a bit, but still kept his face turned away. Maybe I was communicating, or the chin rubs I was giving him were good enough to make him forgive me somewhat.

The after lunch portion of the workshop began with Jeri asking that we select an interviewee from the photos the participants had brought of their at-home animals. We could ask general information or specific info that the owner wanted answered.

I decided on Pumpkin, a dog unlike any I had ever met, in size and in life experience. Before starting into the meditation prelude, I observed his rear end on the floor in the living room, but his head was in the kitchen behind the counter; I couldn't see him from where I sat. I relaxed and cleared my mind of all the important things it was busy working on, like, *did I turn the oven off?* I meditated, then tried to "call" Pumpkin with my mind, but I didn't feel a response. I tried again, sending little balls of popcorn at him to get his attention. Nothing. During the other exercises, I'd felt the nearness of the animal, even when I didn't feel like I was actually communicating. Now, I might as well have been in the room by myself. The time allotted for the exercise was progressing, but I wasn't. My frustration and anxiety grew—that day's workshop was ending in only a few hours, and I didn't feel I had accomplished *anything.*

After several more attempts that ended futilely, I got up and went to the kitchen to try sitting next to Pumpkin. There I found out it was not just my bad technique causing the communication disruption.

Sunny had very quietly returned and was now sitting on the kitchen floor, Pumpkin's head in her lap. No wonder I was not feeling any response from him as he was obviously loving the attention and petting from Sunny. Jeri had assured us that animals could carry on a conversation during early and late stages of sleep, but apparently that didn't apply when being petted by Sunny.

I felt a rush of anger at her intrusion into the workshop she had not wanted to attend and had not helped me with. I went over to her, leaned down, and whispered in her ear in the meanest voice I could muster, "Leave. Now." She got up and slammed out the door, full skirts awhirl.

I stretched out on the floor again, my stomach churning. Finally, I was able to get back into meditation mode and again tried to connect. This time, Pumpkin responded, or so I felt.

"Do you like living with Pamela?"

"Oh, yes. She's very good to me. I like the other dogs, too." I hadn't known she had other dogs.

"What's your favorite thing to do?"

"I like to lie on Pamela's couch. And I like to run in the park."

During the subsequent confessions of our conversations, Pamela confirmed that when she looked for Pumpkin, he was usually draped over her forbidden sofa, dealing with the same space problems as *Marmaduke*, the comic strip Great Dane. Further, he loved to run in the park with her and her other dogs. Maybe I had gotten it right, but still, this wasn't much to go on. I felt disappointed.

Meanwhile, Bear was always somewhere in the middle of the workshop, still sliding from his place under one chair to another, trusting enough to be there, but not trusting enough to come out into the open. As far as I knew, he hadn't even gone to the cat box or eaten the entire day. By the time we began our last exercise, he had traveled almost half way around the circle, ending up under Jeri's chair.

We all felt frustrated as we reported our last conversations, sure that we had not really connected. In many respects the exercises were so easy—just lie down, relax, and try to carry on a conversation in your head—which happened to me almost every night as I worried myself to sleep. But trying to pluck responses from out of the animal, trying to hear with the intuition I had let become very rusty, was exhausting. That seemed to be the consensus of the group. We vowed to try again the next day, after a good night's sleep.

Later, after everyone left, Jeri spoke again with Bear, repeating my apology out loud. "Your mom is *so* sorry, Bear. She made a mistake. She was very busy and distracted, but she also knew you would be completely safe."

Silence. I waited for Bear, via Jeri, to say something.

"He's listening, but not answering," she told me. "We won't let it happen again, Bear. Every one is very impressed with the way you have been attending our sessions. You are very brave to sit with all the dogs around."

She paused for a few seconds, apparently listening, then, "He's still not answering, and his feelings are still hurt," she said to me. "You know your mom would never do anything to put you in danger, Bear, she loves you very, very much."

Another short silence before she reported, "Well, he's hearing; he's still a bit huffy but accepts the apology."

I felt a huge release of the guilt I was carrying, literally, like a physical boulder rolling off my shoulders. After being confronted with Bear's integrity, I felt like an unworthy parent, even more, an unworthy person—one of my rules was to never ever break a promise, and I had broken that promise even to myself.

"He has a question," said Jeri.

"What is it?" I asked, eager to answer any request.

"He wants to know just how long he's going to have to do this good host thing. He says he's getting quite tired of it!" Once again I struggled to keep from laughing as we assured him only two days more.

He seemed mollified. I left the bedroom to Jeri and went into my makeshift bedroom in my office. Bear slept with me that night, so I felt I had been forgiven. I was so frustrated with myself for not paying more attention. Such a simple thing to do, distracted, caught up in a moment, but not the right moment, and with such severe consequences. Bear, an animal, had proven himself more trustworthy than his human.

Chapter 23
KING OF THE DOGS

Oak Hill, Texas. June 1998. Yesterday, Saturday, had been a repeat of the first day. Now, on this third and final day of the workshop, the humans were still all there, but we were down to eight dogs. All heads, animal and human, pointed toward Jeri as though they knew she was the center of attention. No bad attitudes or yappers here! The black dog sat panting again, but the owner, who had told me she hoped to train him for rescue work, kept him on a tight leash.

Mr. Bear appeared after everyone was settled. We watched him quietly crawling from under one chair to another until he arrived next to Jeri where he curled up opposite the black dog and again settled down, giving up access to any escape route except right past the dogs. We continued with the routines we had established, delving deeper into the process, trying to get the hang of going quickly into a meditative state.

Just before lunch, Jeri said it was time again to select a photo of an at-home animal. One owner introduced the photo of an all black cat. Jack was a domestic shorthair, neutered, around four years old. She said nothing else.

I went through the meditative routine, then attempted to introduce myself to him, asking politely, "Are you willing to talk with me?"

I was startled by the voice I heard—a deep, manly baritone, with a Scottish accent. *Surely not! We were in Texas.* I had no connection to anything in Scotland except through TV shows and had never been there. How would a Texas cat end up talking like what I thought a Scottish bard would sound like? But I was almost sure it *was* a communication, and that I was hearing an actual yes response.

"Could you please show me what you look like?"

The image was of an all-black cat sitting, like a human would, in a library wing chair, one hind leg crossed over the other, a book in his forepaws. He wore only a green plaid waistcoat with a gold watch fob draped across his belly, a proper member of aristocracy, as I imagined one. What *was* this? Even if I was a person with a big imagination, this didn't seem like a reasonable scenario to come up with. This made no sense. *It must be the lack of sleep or the organic tea I'd had for breakfast.*

The owner had not requested any specific information, so I asked a few generalities—about food, his places to sleep, anyone else in the house. I didn't get a zinger. The answers were generic: blue food bowl, likes to lie on the chair I was seeing him sitting in. I didn't feel any confidence in the answers. But the voice and accent were just *not* something I could imagine myself inventing. I was very puzzled.

After Jeri called us back into the meeting, I reported my findings and probable failure to the owner.

"I can see that as Jack's personality. He is a bit of a stuffy cat, and holds himself aloof, and a bit superior from the others. His food bowl *is* blue, and his favorite lying place *is* in a chair like that," she said.

Of course, she could not verify anything about his deep voice and brogue—a meow is a meow, American or Scottish. Our conversation had been very catlike, i.e., one that could come from any cat. I realized I had forgotten to ask him open-ended questions as I had searched desperately for a topic that would interest my first non-human. I had no explanation—I was sure I had been awake the whole time—but I also could not imagine myself having come up with such a conversation through my own imaginings.

Later, I asked Jeri, "Why have I been only seeing pictures before, but today I also *heard* the black cat?"

"Everyone has intuitive ability, but each person may experience it differently. When you've heard the voice whisper, 'Don't do that, you're going to drop it' and you do it anyway—and drop it, that's the same voice. Or you think, 'I need to give Mom a call' and the phone rings a second later with Mom on the line. This is the voice called the intuitive, or sometimes, the psychic, voice. This is what we use in the interspecies communication—the knowing without knowing how we know."

I glanced around the circle and noted there was unanimous agreement, all the students nodding understanding of what she was talking about.

"Some communicators hear the voices as clearly as a conversation with a friend. Some receive through vision, like looking at a movie, and some are so tuned in—they just know and experience as though they *are* that animal.

"You might feel as though someone touched you, or you might smell something that's not around you, or even have a taste that the animal lets you experience. It depends upon the person, the animal, and the situation. Some communicators who are very good at helping with health issues actually feel the animal's pain which can make it extremely uncomfortable for the communicator."

"I guess I'm glad I'm only hearing voices and seeing pictures," I said, thinking of the bird Bear supposedly ate, or even that smelly cat food he liked.

This last day went by slowly and rapidly—the exercises so mentally and emotionally exhausting that we all felt drained and sluggish, even on a physical level, yet the lectures went by so fast we were reluctant to take a break. Most of us, still not able or not willing to believe completely, were sure that any connection was just our imagination and a desperate wishing for it to be true before the workshop ended.

Then Jeri called for another break. Bear had proven himself to be a good student; each time I had glanced at him, he had been awake, lying quietly under the chair next to Jeri throughout the lectures. Now he got up and went back into his bedroom.

The sound of our chatter was like the buzzing of bees as the students shared their experiences—and anxieties—with each other. When break was over, we drifted back to our places, even Bear.

Jeri began introducing this very last session of the workshop. Suddenly, her voice trailed off as she looked down toward the floor. We followed her gaze. There was my Bear, moving out from beneath her chair and walking, tentatively but determinedly, toward the very center of our circle. His tail was at half-mast, revealing that he might not be as nonchalant as he wanted us to believe. He reached his target, his chosen spot, and settled down carefully in the exact center of the circle, sphinx style, front legs stretched straight out, head alert and chin up, that fluffy tail curved tight around his lower body, back legs tucked under him. He could have been a statue except for the movement of his head turning slowly from side to side as he surveyed the circle of humans and dogs, all watching him.

Bear sat there in the breathless silence long enough to make his statement: "See, I'm not afraid of these dogs... they bow to me."

Suspenseful seconds ticked by as everyone waited in wonder and total silence to see what this cat, totally encircled by eight loathsome dogs, would do next. Even the black dog's usual panting ceased as he sat with his eyes targeted on that audacious feline. The human participants sat unmoving. Pamela had slapped her hand over her mouth as though to silence her breath. All were watching and waiting in an air of expectancy, amazed at this display of trust and bravery.

For a moment, perhaps even two or three, the room was completely silent, nothing moving. Then, having successfully established himself as the master of all he surveyed, Bear calmly got up, turned his back directly to the black dog and walked back to the circle's perimeter. His gait was slow enough to make sure everyone knew he wasn't retreating, just giving up ownership of the group now that he had established his rule. He settled under Jeri's chair again. We humans breathed, a collective breath felt and heard around the room. The dogs shifted about a bit, and the black one went back to panting, tongue lolling.

I found it hard to concentrate on the next, and last, exercise, my mind still trying to grasp the full significance of Bear's actions.

Then the workshop ended. Everyone seemed tired, most professing disappointment in their performances, but hopeful we would achieve true communication some day. We promised we'd get together, and it did happen with the in-town people once. But as these things go, discouraged by the lack of zingers and Jeri's encouraging presence, we left the communication to the experts and went our separate ways.

There was one mystery that remained for me. I finally asked Sunny on one of her less hostile days, "Why didn't you come to the workshop? I really wanted you to be a part of it."

"Well," she huffed, "I couldn't afford it."

For a minute, I was speechless. "But, Sunny! It was free for you since you lived here. I *told* you that when I asked if you wanted to come. And asked if you would help."

"Well, I wasn't much interested anyway, and I had a lot to do that weekend."

Are psychics jealous and protective of their abilities? Was Sunny afraid she wouldn't be able to "do it?" Or did one of her alters take the message and forget to give it to her? Or maybe she felt it was beneath her abilities? I was disappointed in her reactions and explanation, as well as her failure to keep her promise about helping. I knew her tenancy could not last much longer; it was just a matter of waiting for... something. The longer she was here, the more strained things were becoming. I had no idea what was wrong, and, therefore, no idea how to fix it. I decided to sit back and wait, but even I could foresee the future—perhaps I *was* psychic.

=^.-.^=

A week after the workshop, I received a greeting card from the black dog's owner. On the cover, a fluffy Maine Coon with a typical lion-like ruff sat full face to the reader, a gold version of my grey Bear, with his adult green eyes, and the same very long white whiskers. He looked quite satisfied with himself under his ten-gallon hat as his twirling lasso snaked across the sky. In the background, a number of longhorns grazed in a brown field. The caption read, "Guess I'll go out and brand a few doggies today."

I laughed out loud and kissed Bear, who was sitting next to me, on the top of his fuzzy head as I showed him the card. "Ah, Bear, I think they thought you were amazing, and so do I."

He turned his head, reached up, and licked my chin. I was pretty sure he had finally forgiven me for my lapse in promise keeping.

Chapter 24
CRAWLIES & CREEPIES

O*ak Hill, Texas. June 1998.* A few weeks after the workshop, I was sitting on the patio enjoying the late spring evening with the earthy smells of growing things, the subtle rustling of the tree leaves, and the light from the full moon. The yard light was on, attracting moths and other insects. Bear was in his harness, and I was hanging on to it but letting him enjoy this dark-time outing. I suddenly paid attention to some translucent-winged bugs flying around—a plague of them. I tried to deny it; I had never seen any like this, but somehow I knew, deep in my insides, with an age-old instinct, that these were *termites! Termites in swarm. Nothing else swarms. Not again!* I well-remembered my other house invasion by these destructive, crawling insects.

The next day, I placed a call to an exterminator for an appointment. I waited as he crawled around the house for a while, and then said, "You know the good news, bad news trick?" He didn't wait for a yes. "Well, the good news is, you don't have termites. The bad news is you do have carpenter ants."

"What? How... ? No, these things were *swarming. Ants* don't swarm!... Do they?"

"Yes, they do. It was carpenter ants swarming, not termites, though they look a lot alike when they're flying around. They swarm for a short period in late spring, early summer. They can do almost as much damage as termites."

He gave me an estimate. *Oh, dear.* What was I going to do? I told him I would think it over and get back to him. *What to do, what to do?* I went over to the back of my house looking where the bug man had shown me the ant trail marching into the house; they were still there and seemed very busy. What *was* my karma with ants? The fire ants my first day in Texas, the leaf cutters in my first house. Now, carpenter ants in this house. *It was not fair!*

I went to bed that night, hoping my subconscious could come up with a solution. I came awake suddenly in the pre-dawn morning with a possible answer right there at the forefront of my brain, just like had happened back when I thought to buy a big house for renters. I waited impatiently for it not to be too early to call California, then grabbed the phone, made the call, and got Jeri right away.

"Do you remember when we were at the workshop, you mentioned you had an interesting conversation with some mice? And were able to persuade them to move out of a house?"

"Yes, I remember."

"Do you suppose you could negotiate with some carpenter ants that have invaded my house? Or is that a really stupid idea?"

"I can certainly try; it's an *interesting* idea."

We negotiated a fee considerably less than the five hundred the exterminator wanted. I prayed that this would work.

"Hmm. OK, if you are asking something of them, what do you want, and what are you willing to offer them in return?"

"Uh, life? If they stay, I'll have to get the exterminator back, and they will die. So I'm giving them a chance to move away. Please tell them that I can't have them eating my home. If they don't leave, I will have to have them killed which will make me sad, but I must do it."

It was a somewhat lengthy negotiation which Jeri did silently. "Oh, dear, they are quite alarmed, but they say that it is their home now too, and they don't see why they should have to move."

"I didn't invite them here. I was here first. I'm giving them fair warning to leave so I don't have to hurt them." I waited in silence as she relayed the information to them.

"They want to know how long they have. They don't know where else to go."

How did ants measure time? "I can give them two weeks." *How did that translate to half-past ant time?*

There was more silence. Jeri said they were having a conference. We waited.

"They say they don't understand, because they aren't hurting anything. They say that they have nowhere else nearly so nice to go."

"They *are* hurting something, and the something is *my* house. I was here first. I can get some wood and build a small woodpile at the end of the yard, out by the fence. They can live there and chew the wood as much as they want."

"They are talking it over." After a wait, she reported, "They said they will go, but you must be patient."

I agreed, truly doubting my sanity. *Sunny, what in the world did you to do me?* It was one thing to communicate with animals, but asking insects to cooperate by moving out of my house? Spending money to do it? *The exterminator's fee had at least included a warranty.* I told Jeri to thank them for their cooperation and hung up, not reassured.

I scrounged around the neighborhood where some new houses were being built and found several armloads of refuse wood. I hauled it home and put the stack at the back fence, filling the spaces between with branches, sticks, and limbs.

The only evidence I had ever seen of the ants was that trail into the house the exterminator had pointed out. I waited two weeks, checked, and there they were, still busy at work. *So much for this trick.* I decided to wait one more week before calling for an estimate from a different exterminator. I was very reluctant to do the extermination. Along with my concern about poisons in general because of the environment, I had the cats to think about, and my own issues—already chemically sensitive to all kinds of things that didn't bother normal people at all. How much would another poison around the house compromise my safety?

I made an appointment for the following week, and the new bug man crawled around, under, into, and through every opening in the house that he could get to, then gave his findings.

"Well, ma'am, you have some definite evidence of carpenter ant damage in that one area at the back of the house in the attic. It's not real bad, looks like they weren't there very long. You don't need my services now, though. There's no sign of any current carpenter ant activity anywhere."

The awe I felt at Jeri's abilities overwhelmed me, but, even more than that, at the cooperation of the ants. This seemed so farfetched—talking to *ants! What else could have caused them to leave without chemical inducement or an anteater, though?*

I was so grateful, I convinced myself it had happened, but I knew that I wouldn't tell my friends. If they already refused to believe that someone could converse with my cats, what would they think about insect persuasion? The ants were gone, and my bank account still had money in it, even after paying Jeri's fee. However it had happened, whatever had *made* it happen, I was grateful, and I had a new respect for the animal kingdom. But I knew I could never tell anyone that a communicator had talked a herd of ants into a promise to move out of my house and home, and they honored it.

Shortly after the removal of the ants, I took a look around the yard and decided I needed help. The weeds were turning into small trees and the plants that had grown up in the little tree islands were a gnarly mess. I hired a day laborer with a thick Mexican accent to clean up. I was in the kitchen when I heard him yelling something indecipherable as he came running toward the house, waving a hoe. His swarthy face had turned as white as an Anglo's, his speech high and with a note of hysteria.

"'*nake! Es 'nake!* Come from árbole, from tree, fall on me! I scared of 'nakes.'"

It was obvious he expected me to do something about this 'nake' problem. I didn't know how to tell poisonous from the nonpoisonous kind, but I was pretty sure the poisonous ones—rattlesnakes and copperheads—didn't attack by dropping out of trees. Did they? I cautiously headed toward the area where the man had been working. He followed behind me, pointing toward a large, upside-down clay pot about ten feet in front of the fence. The ground underneath the pot was uneven and one area of the rim was raised just enough to let a snake slither underneath.

He motioned toward that hole with the hoe. "There, 'nake go there."

When I had seen snakes in zoos, the second they started moving, I had been filled with fascinated revulsion, but unable to turn away. Today, though, I felt very calm as I stopped a few feet away from the pot and considered what to do. I didn't feel any animosity toward the snake, I didn't want to hurt it, but I needed it out of my yard, for several reasons—the scaredy-cat inside me, the scaredy-cat behind me, and the two cats in the house that probably wouldn't be scared enough.

Remembering my animal communication instructions and the assurance that "all things are connected," I decided to try to make contact, inept as I still felt about my abilities even after the workshop. I closed my eyes and waited, trying to figure out what would motivate a snake.

"Snake, this is my territory. It's not safe for you here, and I want you to leave." I waited and listened to the intense silence, then tried again.

"Snake, I want you to be safe to hunt for your food, but you must leave this place now. There are dangers here, my cats might try to fight you."

Suddenly, a shaft of pure terror snaked through me, like a streak of lightening hitting nearby. A part of me was calm, removed from the situation, emotionless. Another part of me felt pure panic and my arm hairs were sticking straight out. Strangely, this did not feel like *my* fear, and I didn't think the feeling was coming from the gardener. That left the snake. I took several deep breaths to try to calm down.

"Snake, please don't be afraid. I want you safe, but you must leave here, or you could be hurt or even killed." Okay, I was stretching it a bit, but I wasn't sure what other threat to use. I tried to exude a sense of calmness as I stood there. The terror in that one part of me was ebbing bit by bit. I was trying to breath through it while the rest of me was observing. I waited, remembering what Jeri had said about some people being able to feel and become a part of an animal. Was that what was going on here? I didn't feel snakelike—at least not as I imagined a snake would feel. *I* didn't feel particularly afraid, just calm and still, except for that encapsulated part that was still holding on to some terror.

I tried to radiate feelings of gentleness and non-aggression as I waited with an amazing amount of patience, for me. "Please come out from where you are, go away from me, go to the fence, and go under it. You'll be safe there. There are no dogs or cats in that yard. I promise we will let you go in safety."

I didn't feel like I was establishing communication, but I was amazed at how calm I felt, especially with a Mexican man who was holding a hoe standing directly behind what he probably saw as a crazy woman just standing there staring at a flower pot. Since I was using non-verbal communication, he would not "hear" me talking. I suspected he was hanging onto the hoe as much for protection against me as against the snake.

Still not receiving anything, I decided to give it one final try and then to... well, do *something* else. "Snake," I silently visualized a pointed head with slitty eyes resting above the circular mound of its wound-up body, staring at me. "I promise we won't harm you in any way if you just go."

No response was forthcoming as near as I could tell. Giving up, I began to turn away just as the yardman yelled. My eyes popped wide open, I glimpsed the snake, well—"snaking" speedily toward the fence and disappearing under it into that neighbor's yard, a neighbor who was rarely home and had no animals. I stood stunned, my mouth hanging open, the terror evaporating, but the part of me that had been calm was now amazed. Had I communicated, or was it coincidence? I wasn't sure about the snake following my instructions to leave, but I was totally convinced that the terror, and not my usual revulsion, had originated from the snake, not from within me. Seeking safety away from us would make sense, so maybe it hadn't been my warning. Or maybe it had.

Well, great! I had signed up for communication classes to talk to my cats and instead I had possibly communicated with a snake while my cats still ignored me.

Chapter 25
THE MYSTERY OF BELLA

Oak Hill, Texas. June 1998. A few weeks after the workshop, I received a call from one of the attendees. I remembered her introduction as a vet's wife who often rescued stray cats. She had seemed nice, though I hadn't had much time to visit with her, or anyone else for that matter. Now, after exchanging pleasantries, she revealed the truly sneaky nature I hadn't been aware of.

"I remembered overhearing you tell someone that you thought Bear needed some company. We've been raising a litter from a feral mother. They're eight weeks now, old enough to be adopted. Would you be interested in one?"

"You mean a wild cat?"

"Technically, it means the mother was domesticated and then went wild after getting lost or being abandoned. We found the kittens close to our clinic. The mother may have been killed, or just abandoned them. All are females—one calico and two torties."

"A tortie? You mean tortoiseshell? Oh! They're beautiful," I said, remembering India, and reluctantly interested. Bear and I were doing OK, but still—he had lost some of his spark and playfulness since Sami's death almost a year ago.

"Yes. If it also has white, then it's a calico. I know you had mentioned getting a male, but these are very sweet girls. I could bring them to the house and let Bear see what he thought of them." I opened my mouth to decline and instead heard myself saying, "When?"

With the arrangements made, I hung up, then wondered what had possessed me. Bear was the only male energy in the house. If I got another cat, it should be a brother. Why was I thinking about a female? Ironical, really—all that hunting for a female for years and not finding one, now one showed up. Bear, and Sami before him, were much more loving than Sunny's two girls, but... .

Sylvia arrived with three tiny kittens. Bear sat in the hallway and, uncharacteristically, watched from there instead of being in the middle of things in the living room.

"These are the tortoiseshells," Sylvia announced as the first two kittens, looking like twins of Bear's India, tentatively came out of the carrier and began exploring.

"Oh! They're gorgeous, but so tiny!"

"And this is Minnie. She's called a muted calico—grey and beige with white instead of the usual black and tan with white."

Minnie was a patchwork quilt cat, like that first cat that had moved onto our farm, just lighter in color, whose zillions of progeny had incurred my fear and hatred. I knew if I chose any of these for Bear, it would be one of the torties now playing quietly with each other in the corner.

Minnie headed straight for Bear. He greeted her with an unfriendly hiss. As I watched them all, I got a feeling this was not a good idea. Sylvia left to go shopping, as arranged, telling me to call her with my decision. Minnie walked around exploring, trying twice more to get close to Bear who continued to rebuff her. Finally, she gave up and went to the hassock-sized toy box filled with Sami's and Bear's favorite things. She rummaged around for a bit, her long Siamese-looking legs working hard at moving toys around, her elbow working like a piston as she rejected toy after toy. When she pulled her head out, the last toy I had gotten for Sami, a yellow plastic coiled spring, was in her mouth. She played a bit with it while Bear and I watched her, and the other two kittens went to sleep.

Exhausted from all of her activity, she gauged the distance up to the seat of Sami's chair, considerably above her little head, and made a big leap onto the pillow, laid down, wrapped her tail around her nose and fell immediately asleep. *This was very odd! She was interested only in the things that Sami had been interested in: Bear, Sami's swirly toy, and Sami's chair.*

I left them alone and went to the kitchen. When I checked back ten minutes later, the kittens were all still asleep. Bear was watchful, on guard, though all three kittens wouldn't have made even half of him.

An hour later, with things still the same, I called Sylvia and told her to come get them all. While I waited for her to answer the phone, something tickled my bare foot. I looked down to see Minnie draped across my toes, as though pleading with me to keep her.

"Hi, Sylvia, we're going to keep Minnie. Come get the other two." I slapped my stupid head—once again I was getting a cat I really didn't want. I hoped it would work out as well as the two previous adoptions.

The first night Minnie was with us, she climbed up the bedspread to get on the bed as though she had always belonged there, then curled up against me, just as Sami used to do. Bear stayed at the end of the bed where he usually slept. I got very little sleep, waking up over and over to assure myself I had not rolled over and smothered Minnie. *She was so tiny!*

I liked the name Minnie. I thought it was a cute name for a cat—like Minnie Mouse. But I wanted to be as sure of the name as I had been for Sami and Bear. I finally found five names to try: Bella, India, Daisy, Callie and, of course, Minnie. During the next several days, I took turns calling her by each of them, mixing them up, in no order, with different voice inflections, tone, and volume each time I called out to her.

"Indiaaaaaa." She played.

"Minnie?" I crooned. No response. Strange, if she responded to any, it should have been that familiar one.

Finally, I called "Bella!" I had taken Spanish and knew it meant beautiful.

Bella came. I petted her, I told her she was wonderful. I repeated the test and each time I called "Bella," she stopped what she was doing and came running. I remembered the months it had taken for Bear to answer to his name with any consistency, and months before Sami learned his name and then only by using his vitamins. Bella chose immediately.

Little Bella, dainty and sweet, followed Bear around, trying to make friends. All he did was trot away. Precious, Sunny's cat, was still trailing after Bear like he was her boyfriend though I saw no indication that Bear agreed. Precious was not happy, even appeared jealous when Bella came near. And as much as Sunny had loved Sami, she didn't like Bella right from the first day though she never gave me a reason why.

I had never felt Sami's presence after he died, but Bella was so like him! Siamese are known for their talkiness. Now, here was a calico who loved to talk to me. She sat and hollered when she was displeased, and cried for me when she lost me, just like Sami had done, using a huge Siamese voice from her little bitty body.

I had talked to Sunny about the way Bella exhibited behaviors so like Sami's, even showing the same likes and dislikes right down to his eating habits.

"He could have come back as a reincarnate," said Sunny.

I'd heard about reincarnation in those late night discussions decades ago with friends, usually after a glass of wine, when we were young and trying to define life. But reincarnation—even the idea was against what my religion had taught.

So little Bella would play and play all by herself, then stop and run to me, clamber up my chair, and throw herself across my chest right under my chin, and go instantly to sleep. There was never a "bonding" period between us; for her part, she bonded the minute I said I'd take her, or maybe even when she first came out of the carrier.

From that first day, when I came home, Bella always met me at the door, shoulder to shoulder with Bear, though he acted like she wasn't there. She used the cat box perfectly. She had adjusted easily and quickly, and there was no reason to doubt it—it was as though she had lived with us her whole life, *and maybe the one before?*

Then came the day, about a month later, when Bella *didn't* meet me at the door. Only Bear was there.

"Bella?" I called. When she didn't come to me I knew something was wrong. "Bella!" I went through the house shouting and calling. Bear followed but gave me no clues. Finally, I found her huddled up on the floor in a far corner in my bedroom behind the bed. She didn't appear sick. She did appear to be terrified, dazed, even catatonic, squeezed in on herself, and her eyes dilated. I picked her up and cuddled her, at a loss.

"What's the matter sweetie, what happened to you? Are you hurt, does this hurt?" I felt her all over, moving her limbs, pushing on her stomach, but saw no pain response.

I knew, without a doubt, that Sunny wouldn't hurt her. Sunny saved spiders, even—ugh—cockroaches. But I needed clues. I refused to even imagine that Bear had attacked her, though I wasn't sure about Sunny's Precious.

"Sunny, do you have *any* idea why Bella is hiding in the bedroom and looks so scared?"

"No, I wasn't home much today, but I didn't see her around when I was. Actually, I don't think I saw her all day."

"Was anyone else in the house, any clients?"

"No."

I looked at Bella and tried to ask her mentally, but my little bit of communication training failed me. I could not come up with any explanation other than an attack from Sunny's cat, possibly when Bella was in the litter box, because, whatever had happened had resulted in this perfectly litter-box trained kitten suddenly refusing to use the box. I dragged her to several different vets' offices, going to one three times, another twice, and still another, all during the next six months. They all continued to diagnose her with urinary tract infections but could find nothing else wrong. They gave her antibiotics, and she would get a little better for a few weeks. Then I would find pee in strange places around the house, and the cycle would start all over again.

Finally, I decided to contact a communicator. The vet visits and the medicine were expensive, and they weren't helping that much. A few months after Bella's arrival, I had been referred to a new communicator out of Houston, and I called her. She said she could do a consult right then.

First she spoke with Bear, "Hey, Bear, how do you like Bella?

"He says, 'She's all right, but she runs around a *lot*.' Hmm. Wait. There seems to be something else bothering him She's too little, he says. He doesn't seem to know what to do with her."

I felt so disappointed, for him, for me, and especially for little Bella. "She is little now, but she will grow," I coaxed.

"He says again that she's too busy."

Disappointment flooded over me. "I'm sorry, Bear. I chose her for you and thought you'd like her. She really wants to live with us, I think. Please don't ever hurt her, and try to watch out for her?" I requested the communicator translate to him.

"He says, of course, he won't hurt her! He'll watch out for her, but he'd rather she go away. He's a bit indignant that you asked about hurting her," she said.

It took me a minute to swallow the lump in my throat when I realized my good intentions for Bear had made him unhappy, and that Bella was suffering for it, an outcast in her new home. I apologized to both of them through the communicator, telling them I loved them both very much.

Then I asked her to talk with Bella. I explained about all the ways in which Bella exhibited behaviors so like Sami's, even having the same likes and dislikes. I also did ask her to try to find out what Bella's connection to Sami was, if any. I explained the series of random events that seemed to be more than just coincidence: Sami had had a very traumatic head injury resulting in litter box issues; Bella, who had used the box perfectly for weeks after coming to us, began missing the box the day I had come home and found her so traumatized. Sami adored "stringy" things, like snakes; the last toy I had gotten him was Bella's first choice out of the overstuffed toy box. Further, out of the three kittens at the house, only she had unhesitatingly gone to Bear with no fear whatsoever while the other two had huddled in the corner. Bella had never attempted, even on that first visit, to climb on any of my furniture forbidden to the cats, as though she already knew the house rules and simply claimed Sami's chair. Bella had a very loud, totally Siamese cry, impressive in its volume, especially coming from that tiny calico body. For months, I would hear her hollering and immediately think, "that's Sami" before remembering it couldn't be. And when she was upset, she had the true trumpeting of a displeased Siamese. I chuckled whenever I thought of Sylvia's description of her as a muted calico, the mute obviously having to do only with her coat color and nothing to do with her voice. Even Bella's physical form had Siamese traits, her legs and tail longer than they should have been for a domestic short-hair cat, and with that languid cross-over of her front legs, like a model's walk, just like Sami's

The communicator asked Bella my questions, and then waited. Then she asked again, and waited again.

"There's only silence," she reported. She tried several more times. Finally, she said, "I've been practicing communication since I was a child. There have only been two other times I haven't had a response when I've tried to initiate a conversation with an animal. If Sami is there, he's not willing to talk to me, and either Bella doesn't know or isn't talking."

I was very surprised. The other communicators had never talked about this, had never had any trouble carrying on a conversation with Sami or Bear and had connected immediately, just like answering the phone. This communicator had been highly recommended. What was going on?

"Why don't you try calling an associate of mine. Maybe she can get through to her, or them," she suggested. "Just tell her I referred you."

I called, and that was the beginning of my acquaintance with Carol Wright. I introduced myself, then asked her a bit about herself. She had been doing communication since she was a child, she said, before she even understood what it was. This sounded good enough, especially when I realized that she had been one of the communicators featured in Arthur Myer's book. She said she could do the communication now while we were on the phone. We agreed on a price that I could handle. She asked the cats for permission and both agreed to talk with her.

The first issue was the mystery of Bella-Sami. Carol also said she couldn't get any definitive answer, not because Bella was refusing, but because she didn't know, and Sami, if he was there, wasn't answering. We gave up on that issue and went on to the not-using-the-litter box issue, both the peeing and the recent diarrhea the vets couldn't seem to find a reason or a cure for but which did, thankfully, end up in the cat box.

"I sense a lot of confusion. It's odd; she thinks she is doing everything right, and really wants to please you, and she doesn't understand why you are upset with her." She paused for a minute, then went on. "You know, it's almost like...

I don't know... like, there is something wrong with her brain. She does tell me it burns when she goes to the box to pee, though. You need to get a urine sample and take her to the vet."

"We've already been there," I said, recounting the number of times that had happened already with no long-term resolution. "I just can't believe that she is having this many urinary tract infections and that that's the only cause of the problem. Does she know why she is getting them?" I suddenly felt foolish for asking that—how would I answer if my M.D. asked me that question?

"Umm, no, she doesn't. She says it just feels like a pressure, and then she has to go, and it burns. Sorry, you're going to have to take her to the vet on this one."

Well, none of this was revealing. More money down the drain with no answers. I felt my faith in this process wavering. I thanked her and hung up, even more frustrated than I had been before. And went to the vet and got more antibiotics.

Weeks passed, and then months. Bella grew to her giant adult weight of six pounds; Bear began tolerating her being in close proximity for a few minutes before getting up and walking away. I continued cleaning up after her, hoping for a miracle.

I eventually found a few answers and suggestions for natural remedies and tried them with her, but none worked. Bella continued to try to make friends with everyone in the household, without too much success, and continued to pee anywhere she took a mind to, or so it seemed to me.

Bella also had some odd characteristics and actions. She loved to climb though neither of the boys had exhibited that; she also seemed to "go wild" at times. She would come tearing into the living room and attack the walls. A few times I caught her sitting on the floor, staring at the wall and yelling her head off, staccato screams with real anger in her voice, like she was ready to tear something's head off... but there wasn't anything there. Unless she was seeing ghosts.

I was truly torn. Bella was my nemesis, but she also had curled up in my heart with her sweetness, and the high spots in many of my days came from Bella's antics. She had replaced my alarm clock. Now, instead of awakening to a cacophony of loud music and dire traffic predictions on the clock radio, I awoke to Bella playing with the wind chimes hanging inside my bedroom window. The thought of the gentle notes chasing the evil spirits away made me smile even before my eyes opened, and I always had time to spare to turn off the alarm before it began its jarring morning clatter.

Unable to connect with the other two cats, Bella unexpectedly found a friend. She was assisting me as usual, never far from what I was involved in. I opened my jewelry box to try to find any earrings that Sami might have left me two of. Bella was on the bathroom counter, anxious to see what was inside. As soon as the lid went up, she dived into the box and, with her paw, hooked out a one-inch square of red felt that had no purpose for being in a jewelry box. She lifted it up to her mouth in her cupped paw, like water, then she clamped down on it, and it was hers.

Red Thang became her blankie, her constant companion, her baby, just as Bear's Funnel had been, and still was, for him. I rarely saw her without it. She slept with it, ate with it next to the food bowl, ran around the house with the end sticking out of her mouth giving her the appearance of having red lipstick on.

One morning I woke up and immediately panicked. There were red spots on the white sheets. As I scrambled out of bed to investigate more fully, I realized the spots were too bright red to be blood. In fact, the spots were the same red color as, as... *Red Thang!* I deduced that she had given her baby a bath in her water bowl, then brought it to bed with her where it had bled onto the sheets.

"You would have been a wonderful mama, Miss Bella." She leaned against me, lips closed around Red Thang, and preened and purred, apparently discerning that the words were a compliment.

There was so much heart in that little girl and so much determination. After watching her sometimes, phrases from *Maria*, the Rodgers and Hammerstein song in *The Sound of Music* would pop into my head, and I would feel empathy for the nuns as they wondered what to do with their will-o-the-wisp girl, Maria. Indeed that *was* Bella.

I couldn't make a judgment about the possible reincarnation of Sami, or even if Sami somehow had been involved in sending her to me as a gift. I did come to believe that Bella, the gift I got for Bear, was a gift to me—a catharsis for my lonely childhood. I identified with her too much. I, too, had been a gentle child who didn't fit in. I'd watch other kids kill bugs, or hit dogs, or even hit each other, and I could never understand it. Without any playmates, no girls in school my age, only boys, I had played by myself for hours.

Now, here was little Bella, playing always by herself, trying so hard to make friends, being ignored by the other cats. I would watch and dissolve into tears, unable to explain the devastation I felt, the intense need to comfort her—or more correctly perhaps, to comfort my own childhood hurts. With Sami and Bear I had not had this sensitivity of actually feeling their hurts as I did with her. I could have convinced myself I was just anthropomorphizing, but the feelings were too personal for that to be the case.

Despite her sweetness, she was not beautiful in the way that some cats are. Over and over, visitors would come into the house. They would meet Bear and exclaim over how gorgeous he was. I would introduce Bella, and they would give an obligatory greeting, then go back to interacting with Bear while Bella sat and watched. I ached for her.

I was coming to believe that my cats had come to heal parts of me that I didn't know were damaged. Sami helped me go from that cat-hater to cat-lover, taught me confidence as I learned how to be a cat-mom, and how to put someone else's needs before mine. He reminded me how to play again and allowed me to protect and feel protected.

Bear brought me a connection to another soul in a way I had never experienced before, not even with my husband whom I had loved passionately and dearly. Bear made life interesting and kept me busy trying to keep ahead of his next bit of mayhem. I loved both of them, and they both helped me learn to nurture and care for another being, and vice versa.

And then Bella came, my first girl cat. She had a streak of sheer joy and a streak of wildness. She loved to run and climb and tried so hard to please me and everyone else. She made my heart ache for the things I had missed out on; watching her was like watching a video of my childhood. The other cats ostracized her. Even Sunny, who loved cats and kittens, continued to ignore her despite how hard Bella tried to be liked. If tears can wash away pain from the past, then Bella did a good job of helping me purge many of the hurts, even as I cried for the unfairness that surrounded her. And she helped me find many recipes for eradicating cat pee.

Chapter 26
THE CROSS MY HEART PROMISE

Oak Hill, Texas. July 1998. I got a small bonus at work and knew immediately what I would spend it on—my new addiction. Carol answered on the third ring.

"Hi, can you talk to my cats again?" I asked. She agreed.

"I need to start with Bear. He's very lethargic, not eating, and sleeping a lot."

"Bear, are you feeling sick? Do you need to go to the vet?" she asked. "He says he is sick, but he doesn't need to go to the vet, he'll take care of it."

"He'll take care of it? Is he saying that just because he doesn't want to go to the vet?"

"He says he can take care of it, and he's quite firm about it."

I decided, shakily, to trust.

"I also want to talk with Bella, about her being able to go outside in the yard with Bear. Bear's always on a lead, but Bella is too little for one. She goes to the door or jumps on the windowsill and watches Bear and Precious outside having fun, and she seems so lonely. Is there any way you think she might promise to stay in the yard? Does that sound too far-fetched? It doesn't feel right to keep her inside."

I was desperately hoping to hear Carol say yes. I felt like a flower in my brain and heart and soul was opening to possibilities, and now I had to step out of my many preconceived notions; it felt right to do so on behalf of my cats.

"I'll ask her," said Carol. "Hmmm... she says she wants to do what you want, but she doesn't understand what a yard is. Can you show her?"

Somewhat taken aback, I wondered, how does one "explain" a yard? To a cat? In cat language? Then I had an inspiration.

"Okay. I know! Tell her I'll carry her around to all the places she can go. She can go anywhere from the back door of the house to the fence, anywhere in between. She must never, ever go over the fence, though. Except she doesn't like to be held much any more like she used to; she'll sometimes panic if I hold her more than a few seconds. Tell her I'll have to carry her, and she needs to let me do this so she will understand and be safe."

It wasn't until later that I realized if she didn't know what a yard was, it was unlikely she could understand the much more difficult concepts of between and over.

"She says she'll try to let you, but some of it she has no control over."

I bit my lip in indecision and looked at her little form sitting on the floor, looking way up at me with such trust. Her personality was so big that I often was taken aback when I realized how tiny she was physically. I decided I had to try.

"Can you hold on while I try to take her out?"

"Sure."

I grabbed Bella so quickly she didn't have time to object and hurried out the back door. Holding her in my arms, we circled the entire yard, walking along the side of the house to the fence, then following the fence around the big yard, along the back of the house, and then back inside. Bella's little round head bounced around like one of those bobble-head toys, but she stayed quietly in my arms, apparently fascinated by this big wide world she'd never experienced before. She must have been so interested that she lost her usual fear of being held.

"Okay, Carol, we're back." I said breathlessly. "Tell her that she can go anywhere between the back door and where we went, but mustn't go over the fence."

"She promises," said Carol after a moment of silence. It was that easy. "I'm sure she will do her best. She really, really wants to please you, you know."

Well, actually, I didn't. If that was true, why the litter box issue?

I decided to try again to extract the same promise from Bear—maybe he hated the harness enough by now that he would agree. Oh, I *so* wanted to be able to trust so that he could roam free in the yard. Carol asked him, and I waited anxiously for the answer.

"No. He won't promise. He's quite firm about it. He says the fence is just irresistible, and he *has* to see what's on the other side."

Disappointed about Bear, but glad to hear Bella's promise, I hung up. *Okay, we'll see how well this stuff works. But I'm not ready today. If Bella didn't comply, she was so tiny I couldn't imagine how I could ever find her again. Surely, I was crazy to try this.*

A few hours later, I heard a terrible retching from the other room. I rushed in, alarmed, just as Bear finished presenting me with an almost four-inch long hairball. Yuck! But he was right, he totally took care of the problem himself, and then trotted off to his food bowl.

Finally, a few days later, I got brave. I let Bear outside, tying his lead to the clothesline so I wouldn't have to keep track of him, too. I escorted Bella out, staying right beside her. She wandered around sniffing, went to Bear to nuzzle him which he was finally allowing these days, then walked along the fence. She walked around investigating, smelling, rubbing everything. Finally, I couldn't take the suspense any more and grabbed her and brought her back inside, praising her, holding her close. Enough for one day!

Soon it became a routine—Bear out with his lead tied to something, Sunny's cat out if she wanted to roam, with Bella bringing up the rear. I was now relaxing somewhat when I opened the door for her. She religiously came when I called her, popping up from wherever she was, then barreling toward me, prancing as she pulled up in front of me like a horse refusing to take a jump. I was ecstatic—the best of all worlds was watching them on yard duty, playing, enjoying the outdoors as cats should, without having to curtail their freedom. At least, not too much.

Then it rained, another Texas gully washer. All the cats stayed in for several days, sitting on the windowsills and trying to catch the raindrops scuttling down the glass. Finally, the clouds left. I let the cats out and went back inside for a few minutes, just a few minutes. When I came out—Bella was gone! I called, and she didn't come. I panicked. Her neck was so tiny, I hadn't been able to find a collar for her; she had no ID. She was totally defenseless! *Stupid, stupid me.*

Quickly running around the yard, then along the fence, I made a plan. I would follow the fence, checking behind and up the trees in the tree island, and under the bushes. If no results, I'd get the ladder and try to see over the fence. She was such a good jumper. I turned the corner of the house and passed the Lady Banks Rose bush, now covered with small yellow flowers on its long streamers that flowed gracefully to the ground. I stopped abruptly. Something felt odd, though all looked normal. I ducked down under the bush. There—behind the bush! One of the fence boards had turned up at the bottom, probably from the rain, leaving a hole much bigger than little Bella would need to get out of the yard.

I started running, along and around the end of the fence, through the gate, thank god it was unlocked, and into the neighbor's yard. And there was little Bella, her head bobbing along between her narrow shoulders, practically touching the fence, like a blind person following a wall. She had kept her promise! She had not gone over the fence, only *through* an opening—and that was not a warning we had given her. I quietly walked up behind her, realizing that she was trying to figure out how to get back to me with a fence that she wasn't supposed to go over blocking her path.

"Bella." I said it softly, so as not to scare her. I noticed my knees felt weak as I reached for her. "You are such a good girl." I couldn't resist a hug and a kiss when she let me pick her up.

I replaced the board before I let her out the next day. Bella faithfully kept her promise and stayed within the confines of the yard with no other safety measures on my part. At times, she would be at the far distant corner of the one-third of an acre lot, and I would see her start running, pell-mell. Straight across the yard. Aiming right toward the opposite fence. Then, at the very last second, she would pull up instead of making the jump, and turn and calmly prance back to me, tail all fluffy and with an "I'm sooo pleased with myself" look, while I settled my heart back into place.

And all was calm. For a month. Then Bella started peeing outside the box again, and was also having diarrhea which she did manage to keep in the box. I made a vet appointment, but decided to call Carol in case she could come up with any new insight on the peeing.

"She says it is burning again. And she has a question. She wants to know if she can pee outside?"

"Oh, indeed, Bella, anytime you are outside you can go there to pee or poop anywhere you want."

I was overjoyed. Then Carol continued, "You know, I just feel confusion from her. She is very frustrated too, because she can't understand *why* you are so upset with her."

This made me so sad to hear. I had tried multiple foods, multiple remedies, conventional medicine, alternative, and every type of litter box, the box placement, and litter I could find. I truly felt I could pass an exam for a doctorate in Litter Box. Though I now felt I was an expert on cat bathroom habits, nothing changed. I assured Carol we already had a vet appointment.

At the vet's, they put us in a treatment room, and we waited. After a while, I went outside and asked for a cat box. I, Bella, and the box waited. *Finally*, half an hour later, the vet walked in. Little Bella looked at him, *instantly* jumped off the table, ran over to the box, climbed in, and let go. It was quite a loud and smelly demonstration, but very explicit. There's no doubt in my mind that she was tired of going to vets and wanted to make darned sure this one saw what was going on; there hadn't been a millisecond of hesitation between his entry and her demonstration.

The vet, a strapping Jamaican man, studied her for a moment, then gave her a dose of the pink stuff often used for children with upset stomachs, cautioning me, "I give her this, not you."

I nodded my understanding; I knew by now that most human medicine couldn't be given to cats, and, if it is used at all, the dose is critical—literally a matter of life and death. We went home, Bella cooperating, as always, with taking the medication he prescribed.

Within a week the diarrhea was gone, finally. That was the good news. The bad news was that she continued peeing outside the box and began spreading her wealth around once again. I found it hard to not be angry at what I could only assume was her obstinacy, despite Carol's assurance that she didn't understand.

Bella was a smart cat—what was there not to understand? I was a walking ball of frustration. I simultaneously loved her, loved her personality, her gentleness, while almost hating her for causing all this work and upset, and for not being more like Bear. I was tired of doing laundry, cleaning carpets, floors, and litter boxes, spending any spare money on recommended resolutions. And very angry at myself when I blamed her.

My optimism and feeling of success at nurturing was severely dented. It was a good thing I hadn't had real kids, and a good thing that Bella was not my first cat. Here was proof in six pounds of cat fur that I would have been awful at being a mother I realized as I looked at her sitting there so innocently. I cried out of frustration and weariness as I went to get the rags and the carpet cleaner. Again.

Chapter 27

COMMUNION

Oak Hill, Texas. November 1998. I continued to attempt animal communication many times, but there simply were no zingers, no sense of absolutely knowing that I was engaging in communication with an actual animal and not my own imagination. I still felt there was a possibility that I could succeed, but always it came back to the doubt, the uncertainty. *When was I going to get it? How could I want something so badly and not be able to do it?*

"Please," I pleaded to the animal spirits, my guides or Whoever might be listening, "please confirm to me some way that I can do this, that I really heard the cat's voice and wasn't just dreaming things up. I so want to believe in the reality of this process." But I heard no answer.

Sunny and I were in an amnesty period, tiptoeing around each other when she was home, which wasn't often. The atmosphere had been tense and tentative for the months since Jeri's workshop in June. Now, Sunny had invited me to go with her to a wedding celebration on Thanksgiving Day. She mentioned something about Hindu or Buddhist, but even as I climbed into her van with her big bowl of a vegetarian meal contribution for this untraditional Thanksgiving celebration, I wasn't sure what we would be doing.

We drove through the Texas Hill Country outside of Austin, the fields autumn-sparse, little sign of green life along the rural road, no cattle, the only green from small, struggling cedar trees and some cacti in beautiful bloom in the fields. We passed the main ranch house, a sprawling, weathered building, and parked down by the hay barn where the women were preparing the meal.

On the way onto the property, Sunny had pointed out a circular building sitting on a platform.

"That's where the marriage ceremony will take place, in the yurt."

"Yurt? What is this yurt? I've never heard of that before."

"Yurts were the round tent homes of Turkey and Mongolia, similar to the teepees of the Plains Indians. This one is manufactured, though, with a canvas-type covering over the frame instead of hides as originally used. They're amazingly light inside and have great energy, very calming. Some people live in them year round here in the States.

"This one is bigger than the traditional yurts, even bigger than some apartments I've lived in. I think there will be over twenty people here. Do you want to go in before the ceremony?" she invited.

Fascinated with the idea of my first yurt, I quickly agreed.

"Leave your shoes out here," she instructed, as she lifted the door flap.

I felt as if I had just entered a church, except the hardness and formality of the churches I was familiar with was missing. Instead, a wide table across the room from the entrance acted as a setting for incense burners and vases of flowers. In place of pews or hard chairs, beautifully-patterned rugs covered the floor, topped by pillows of all sizes and loftiness, all wrapped in exotic Middle Eastern fabrics that looked like art-in-cloth. The materials incorporated intense pinks, golds, greens, reds, turquoises, and purples in cheerful profusion, accented by gold, silver, and shiny copper threads running through the designs, nothing "matching" but everything blending in a rich profusion of joyous color. The feeling was casual, celebratory, yet reverent, with none of the stiffness of a traditional Christian church.

The noon sun was illuminating the room with a bright but softened sunlight. I could feel the air—no—the *energy*, flowing softly like the clean scent after a thunderstorm. It was easy to breathe. A faint trail of incense smoke wafted upward from a holder on the altar, but, incredibly, I was not having any reaction to the smoke as I usually did. I was amazed that I understood the significance of most of the things there—the bowl for a water blessing, photos to honor the ancestors, the incense for clearing, the candles, a figurine of Buddha—even the shape of the structure itself—things I would have either not noticed or just accepted as eccentricities a few short years before.

"It feels much bigger inside than it looks outside, bigger than our living room," I said. I realized my voice was hushed, though I hadn't planned it that way.

We left the yurt and walked to the old barn. The greetings between Sunny and her friends were quiet, unlike the more boisterous reunions that were undoubtedly taking place between friends and relatives in traditional American homes on this Thanksgiving Day. The women continued working on the food as Sunny introduced me; I hadn't met any of them before.

"Can I help?" I offered, observing the piles of raw foods that looked like the beginning of an Indian meal, my least favorite food, but the smells of the exotic spices were making my mouth water.

No one took me up on my offer, not even those pulling the rose petals that would decorate the couple's path into the yurt off thorny stems. Unable to enter into the conversation of people I didn't know about other people I didn't know, including the bride and groom, I finally wandered away as it didn't look like dinner would happen any time soon. I decided to go walk in the fields and enjoy being out in the wide-open spaces on this beautiful day.

As I trod on them, the beige and brown grasses crunched and loosened puffs of dust into the air, tickling my nose. Prickly pear cacti looked like table tennis paddles with needles. Attached at the top, fat buds and deep yellow, hand-sized blooms gave some color to the landscape. Several gnarled live oak trees offered shade under thick sprawling limbs with the small, deep-green leathery leaves that would stay on the tree through winter.

I stopped when I got to the apple trees that were grouped together, still holding on to small apples ripe for eating. The past-its-prime fallen fruit huddled on the ground amid brown stalks of weeds and layers of rust and copper leaves, an autumn painting waiting to be framed. I picked up an apple and inhaled the almost sickeningly sweet ripeness. Some insect had already had a meal, probably the one that was buzzing around my head.

Wandering cautiously on a barely discernible path through the grasses, I looked more down than up, watching where I was putting my feet, concerned that rattlesnakes and copperheads might also be out giving thanks for this warm day. Hoping the ranch owners weren't raising any angry bulls, I continued to amble around. The six horses grouped ahead of me seemed to be quite occupied with grazing and paid me no mind as I pulled the cedar-pole-and-barbed-wire-gate open enough to squeeze through.

It was not lack of desire that had kept me from being familiar with horses. The Saturday night movies of my childhood had more horses than cowboys. The sturdy frontier women were my role models—women who did things other than take care of a house. The strong, silent cowboy was my hero, sweeping the rancher's daughter off her feet and onto his horse before riding away on the faithful steed into the sunset—or into some hovel where there was no point in housekeeping.

I stood now watching these horses. I was familiar with the words, but unable to tell a mare from a gelding, or a bay from a sorrel. I only knew they were brown or browner, except the white one. I looked them over to see if they looked friendly. They continued to ignore me. Impatient, I decided to try a communication with the lone white horse since it appeared to be grazing toward me, still about two living rooms' distance away.

Not feeling at all confident, I closed my eyes and tried to center myself, to get the distractions out of my head, and to concentrate on feeling peaceful and receptive. I tried several times but didn't feel a connection. When I opened my eyes, though, I had no doubt that the horse had heard me. It had quietly grazed closer and then turned around. I was staring at its white rump now aimed directly at me. *Okay, I guess I was communicating—it's pretty clear what this horse was saying.*

Giving up, I turned to leave the field and go back to the ceremony. Then I realized that one of the less-brown horses of another small group was heading straight toward me, as though it was a magnet, I the North Pole. Its eyes focused intently on mine. I felt a bit of panic—was it going to just walk over me? Then I realized I still had an apple in my hand. I threw it, thinking he, or she, would slow down to eat the apple, and I could take off to safety. The fruit landed short but in the horse's direct path. Without hesitation, it walked right over the apple and moved even faster toward me, like it was late for supper, and I was it.

Just as I was about to turn, aiming for safety on the other side of the fence, the horse slowed and stopped at a nice conversational distance between a horse and a human. It stood for a minute, studying me. I didn't sense any dangerous intent, so I stood my ground. Then the horse, slowly and deliberately, walked toward me. It stopped only when it was so close I could reach out and touch its velvety nose. *I didn't know horses had whiskers.* The horse stood there looking at me with soft brown eyes, black pupils staring intently into my own.

Okay, I'll try this again. I closed my eyes to center myself, then sent up a request for assistance to my spirit guides, asking that I not unknowingly insult this very large creature which could stomp me to death in seconds. I heard Jeri's voice again from the workshop, telling us that we should always be respectful as we addressed other species.

"Brown Horse, I think you have come to talk with me. I've read about what wonderful beings horses are. I'm trying to learn how to talk with animals. Are you willing to help me?"

Silence. I waited a minute or so. Nothing. Finally, I peeked.

Brown Horse was still standing there staring at me, not seeming to have moved at all. I closed my eyes again.

"Brown Horse," I said, trying very hard to visualize him—or her—mentally. "I've never ridden a horse before. I would love to know what it feels like to ride on your back. Would you show me that?" I kept my eyes closed, trying to stay centered, and waited. And waited.

Suddenly, I felt as if I was being transported, flying smoothly onto the back of the horse that felt as real and solid and grounded as the earth and rocks beneath my feet. I, my ordinary self, was still standing on the ground, watching and feeling another me on the horse, a split between my ordinary self and an inside self I didn't know I had. Before I had time to understand how I could have split in two, everything speeded up.

I felt myself bending forward over the horse's neck, clutching its mane; there was no saddle or bridle, but I had no fear. I knew I was safely stuck to that horse's back. Brown Horse picked up speed until it was racing over the field. Then she— I'd decided it must be a she—began running faster. Hooves hit hard on the earth, pounding upon the ground with incredible force that reverberated up into her shoulders, then through and up my legs, up my back, and into my shoulders. It felt like I was one with the horse.

Brown Horse hit her stride, running so smoothly, so powerfully—I had never felt anything like it, not ever! I was filled with some kind of emotion that resonated deep in my core being. Her mane flew into my face and entwined with my hair as I instinctively leaned further forward over her neck. My vocal cords felt like I was shouting for no reason except that I could. I urged the horse faster. I was not a thinking being, only one full of sensations—the body heat of the horse, the sun on my face, the deep, heavy breathing in synch with the rhythm of the hooves deafening my ears to anything but the heavy pounding on the earth, the intoxicating smells of dust, and nature, and horse sweat. I was balanced so securely I felt no sense of danger even though we were racing so fast. How could we be on the ground at all? I leaned back and spread my arms, then stuck my legs wide out to the sides, my face raised to the sky, only my butt still making contact with the horse's back, but so perfectly balanced I knew I was secure.

And I laughed, a great deep laugh that came up from my heart and even deeper. I instinctively knew that I was laughing with joy, a feeling that spread from my chest outward, going straight up to the heavens.

My other self, the part that did not get on the horse, still stood on the ground, watching and feeling everything through some kind of osmosis with my horse-rider self, experiencing an intensely emotional, mental, spiritual, and physical attunement, totally in the moment. Long ago I had seen a picture of a child riding down a long country hill on a bicycle, arms and legs akimbo, head thrown back, a look of such ecstasy on his face I knew I would remember it forever. He had looked just like my now horseback-riding self must look, reveling in the sense of freedom, going faster and faster, barely attached to the ground through the horse, and then the stride so smooth, I knew we *were* flying.

The part of me that was acting out this scene was so focused, I could have stayed in that place forever, riding, feeling freedom, feeling invincible. But eventually—too soon—Brown Horse slowed, then stopped, sides heaving, and the quiet thunder of her breathing echoed into the very essence of my being before it slowed and quieted. And Horse lowered her head and began grazing, as though this ride was all in a day's work.

Somehow, without my active participation, I had merged again with my real self, like that feeling of awakening after an intense dream and realizing I had been dreaming about myself, and the dream and I were one. I was still standing in the same spot where Brown Horse had found me. I felt tears, my cheeks wet, my eyelashes spiking together, not from sadness, but from joy. I finally found the words over the huge knot in my throat.

"Thank you, Brown Horse, thank you," I whispered. "You have given me such a wondrous gift."

Brown Horse lifted her head and looked at me; I reached out and scratched the velvet nose, under the chin, behind her ears. She gazed at me a moment longer, gave a snuffle, then turned and ambled away, and she looked like an ordinary brown horse again.

I slowly reintegrated the rest of myself from that ether, or other world, I had disappeared into. I was still where the ride had started, an ordinary person in a dusty field. But I no longer felt ordinary. I had been on that horse ride without ever moving from my original spot. I had communicated in the most visceral way with an animal of another species. I bowed my head in silent obeisance to Jeri, to Brown Horse, to the animal spirits and guides who had made that ride, that merge, possible.

There was no doubt in my mind that I had just experienced the definition of true joy for the first time in my life. I knew now that it wasn't just happiness, as I had always equated it; joy was far beyond that. The full-throated hymns finally made sense, "Joyful, joyful, we adore Thee. Hallelujah!"

I recognized that something miraculous had happened. I stood quietly, recreating the feelings, replaying the ride and the sense of freedom, the incredible power, the joyousness, over and over.

"It" was real—the act of intensely communicating with an animal, allowing an animal to communicate with me. There was no more doubt, not about the process nor about my ability to touch the soul of an animal. Jeri was right. When it happened we would know—I *knew*. I *had* communicated in a way without boundaries, with an ordinary brown horse in an ordinary field on a day of thanksgiving. And I would never ever forget it, or question whether two souls, even of different species, could wordlessly communicate.

Was this sense of freedom, this melding with another world, what Bear felt when he was flying over his fence? I felt it was. I had seen the excitement and happiness in his eyes whenever I retrieved him from the other side. Now I understood why he would refuse to make a promise to never go over the fence even if it meant being outside only when entrapped in his harness. Like Bear, I would break every promise I had ever made to take that ride again if Brown Horse offered. How could I ask Bear to promise to voluntarily stay in his mundane yard? But how could I risk letting him go free? What if he never came back because he wouldn't, or worse, couldn't? The angst I felt at letting my fear hold him to me even more closely was so much worse now.

I felt that Brown Horse was watching me as I walked quietly back to the celebration. In the yurt, I sat and watched the beautifully simple ceremony as two became one. Afterward, I ate, but held myself apart from the others there, not ready to talk, knowing I couldn't share this experience with anyone, not yet. Nothing bad could touch me. I was changed. For this while, I knew perfect peace.

Chapter 28
THANKSGIVING

Oak Hill, Texas. Thanksgiving Day, 1998. After the wedding, Sunny drove me home and then left for another event. I'd been having such a lovely day I wanted to share it with Bear, so I put him in his harness, and we strolled away from the house, leaving Bella looking wistfully after us. He was more than ready, galloping down the cul-de-sac with me in tow. We strolled steadily for over half an hour before he was willing to quit and head for home. As we started into our cul-de-sac, I noticed that the corner neighbor's *For Sale* sign had tilted over. To straighten it, I dropped Bear's lead, put the sign upright again, a time consuming endeavor of approximately fifteen seconds start to finish, and turned around.

Bear was gone. The last foot or so of his neon pink lead was slithering down into the storm gutter even as I watched it go.

I ran over and knelt down, peering into the five-foot wide horizontal slit in the concrete of the curb, with an opening just high enough for my fat cat to be able to slide through. I dropped to the concrete. Even with my face against the opening, there was barely enough light to see Bear's white bib in all the darkness. He appeared to be sitting on a ledge only slightly below street level, at the back of a gaping hole. Between us was a pipe opening, probably thirty-six inches or so wide, farther than I was going to be able to reach across.

I didn't know a lot about drainage systems, but a couple I had seen before as a kid had some kind of floor which stopped all the leaves and small trash; there was no such floor here, just that opening into a pipe imbedded in concrete which must be what Bear was balancing on. I was pretty sure the next cut in the curb would be way down the street, and equally sure that the pipe eventually would empty into another pipe or culvert taking the rainwater, and Bear, into a lake or river. I had no idea how he managed to dive through the slit and not end up being swallowed by the pipe already; he must have just managed to get a grip on that ledge and pull himself up on to it.

The end result was that Bear was truly caught. He still had his harness on, the lead now dangling down into the void. If I could get hold of anything, his harness or the lead, I would still have to try to lift him *across* the pipe opening and *up* toward me, all the while making sure he didn't slip backwards out of the harness. If he slipped out, he would fall into oblivion—there was nothing blocking the yawning opening. Besides pulling him across and upward at about a thirty degree angle, I would need to bend his head at another forty-five degree angle to pull him through the slit and back up to the road. After really looking at the situation, I couldn't imagine doing what I would have to do to rescue my baby. My fear came out as anger.

"You stupid cat! What where you thinking! You are so big, I don't know if I can even lift you from this angle, one-handed, far enough to get you out. What am I going to do? That stupid vet, he said you didn't need to lose weight. Who has a damn eighteen-pound cat? I'm too old to be doing this. Thirty percent chance of rain tonight they said—if the streets flood, you'd better know how to swim in the Colorado River!" I was raging, letting the anger flow to keep away the fear.

There was no response, no meow, no whine, no sound, no movement. *Think, think!* If I didn't figure this out correctly, and soon... I was having trouble focusing, my mind skittering around rat-like, looking for any out. I sat up and took another look around the neighborhood. There were no cars in any of the neighbors' driveways. I was on my own. My brain raced from escape plan to escape plan, to what could happen, and to the realization that I truly might lose him because of my ineptness—that fifteen seconds of non-attention—as a guardian.

"God Bear, what *have* you done? What's down there? *How* am I going to get you out?"

I flipped myself with my head changing places with my heels, squeezing as close to the curb as I could, then shoving my left arm into the horizontal slit. *Wasn't one arm or leg supposed to be longer than the other?* Nope, that arm wasn't any longer. I almost had my entire left shoulder jammed into the opening, my fingers waving, trying to find something to connect with. As I started to pull out, I felt skin come off. I had pushed so forcefully I had almost gotten my arm trapped.

Trying again, I flipped back around and stuck my right arm back into the hole. Who knew what was in that pipe—a black widow or brown recluse spider, scorpions, roaches, snakes—all kinds of leering heads popped into my imagination, ready to eat my Bear. And me. The shorts and sleeveless tee I wore were too hot. I sat up, wiped the sweat and gravel off my cheeks, then stretched out against the curb again. I wiggled around on the concrete, stuffing myself as close to the curb as I could get, squinting into the semi-blackness for another glimpse of him. His eyes glowed dimly in the dark

The image of a horse being hauled up by a rescue helicopter came to mind. The horse's chances of rescue—a straight-up pull—had been better than my cat's, but maybe it would work. All I needed to do was grab the lead, work my fingers down to the halter, hang on to it while also grabbing the skin behind his neck with my only available hand, and pulling a fat cat through a small hole, both toward me and up at the same time. And somehow, I had to do it all with the only arm I could get into the gutter. And do it without knocking his head off. There was no way I could get both arms out in front of me and through the narrow opening and still see what I was doing.

I resumed my pushing of my arm, trying to get my muscles to stretch just a... little... bit... more... more... *yes*! I felt a few hairs but ran out of fingers before I could get to his skin. I relaxed, then tried again. I was pushing so hard my breath was coming out in puffs. *It was futile*. No! No, it couldn't be! I *had* to find a way.

"Stay there, Bear, just stay put. Please, please, please don't decide to jump until I can get hold of you."

I again thrust my arm as hard as I could into the rectangular slot. I felt him! *Ohmigod, I had him, I had him!* I latched onto some hair, then walked my fingers down to the roots, just a bit more—ah! Skin! The back of his neck! Grabbing what I could, I worked my fingers down his back under his harness to get a better grip. Now what could I do? *Think, think, think! Make the harness as tight on him as possible to keep him from sliding out. Keep it pulled tight... upwards.*

"Oh, animal spirits, please help me. If his body slides backward out of this harness, he will be gone. I love him so much, that just can't happen."

Lying there, praying for courage and strength, I mentally tried to will this to work. I couldn't go on much longer. This was the last chance for a miracle. I took a deep breath, held it, braced myself and pulled sharply, jerking him off the ledge with the skin on his neck and a portion of his harness. I had him! Angling his head and shoulders toward the slit. Now! He was almost at the street opening, but his hind legs were still in the hole with nothing to get a purchase on. *Almost, almost. Come oonnn Bear. Yes. Almost.* He had sense enough to duck his head toward the opening for that last forty-five degree exit. I pulled harder, everything straining to get him up and out. His head came through, scraping against the top and bottom of the slit, it was that narrow. *That's a good boy.* Almost... damn! Stuck! His shoulders were too thick for me to pull him through.

I realized I was crying when I had trouble breathing through the snot in my nose, but I refused to let go. I was not a contortionist—I couldn't figure out how to get my other arm into a useful position to help. I kept tugging, tugging. Finally! He pushed his front legs out of the opening far enough to grab onto my shirt with his claws. As he tried to haul himself out, I got the fingers of my other hand around his bottom and pulled, falling backward, drawing him across my chest. His hind end came out, and he popped out of the hole!

"You're out! You're safe. Oh, sweetie, you had me sooo scared. Don't ever, ever do that ever again!"

I sat up and wrapped him in my arms, rocking back and forth, trembling with relief as he wilted quietly into my body. Unlike other times, he did not resist my embrace. Bear was back where he belonged.

Finally, I calmed down enough to realize we ought to get out of the street before some turkey came zooming around the corner and ran as down. This whole fiasco probably hadn't lasted longer than ten minutes, but it felt like I had been squirming there for hours—no, for eons.

Hoisting both of us up, I walked back to the house, refusing to relinquish him to the ground despite the adrenaline coursing, my hands shaking, and my legs wobbly. When we got inside, I unclasped his harness, expecting him to rush over to the food bowl as he always did after a walk. Instead, he headed directly to his chair, climbed up, curled up, and went instantly to sleep, confirming my suspicion that he was as undone by the ordeal as I had been. My tough guy had been truly afraid for only the second time I could remember, the first the night of the cat attack. One good thing—I was sure I wouldn't have to look for him in any gutters ever again.

I sat down and contemplated the day I had been through—from the totally sublime to the totally terrible, from the heights to the depths—and I gave a prayer of thanksgiving to every entity or God or angel that might be listening.

Chapter 29
DEPARTURE

Oak Hill, Texas. December 1998. Sunny and I made it through the Christmas season, though there was always tension in our relationship now. Christmas itself was smack in the middle of another mysterious—to me, anyway, "Mercury Retrograde," a period of significance to astrologers and psychics that occurs four times a year. According to Sunny, when Mercury is in its weeks of being retrograde, anything to do with communication, finances, or transportation can get way off track. Perhaps it was just one of those theories like more accidents, more divorces on full moons, or Friday the 13th. Perhaps it wasn't. It seemed to me that every time I was cursing about my computer messing up, the car not working right, and the check book not balancing, Sunny would take out her ephemeris calendar and invariably report that, yes, we were in another Mercury Retrograde period.

As she had warned me that another Retrograde was coming up that would include Christmas, I put the cause of our communication and transportation issues down to the stars.

I was at work, but dealing with a major cold and finally had to pick up some antibiotics my M.D. had phoned in when the few alternative methods I knew about at that time didn't seem to be working fast enough. Thus began the train of events that became ludicrous.

I got a call from Sunny, saying her van was stuck in the drive-in at the bank. Could I come pick her up on my way home and then take her to work later that night? I said I would.

Then, just as I was leaving work, I got the call from the pharmacy where my doctor had called in the prescription for the cold-that-wouldn't-quit, saying it was ready, but they were closing early. Further, the pharmacy had moved into a trailer in the HEB parking lot because the store was under reconstruction. If I wasn't there by 6:00, they would leave the key to the pharmacy with the store manager.

When Sunny and I got there at 6:30, the trailer was closed, the store manager knew nothing about the keys, and the store was closing at 7:00 for Christmas Eve. There was nothing they could do except let me go to suffer through my misery until the following afternoon when they would be open again. They did give me some cough drops.

Sunny had to go to work at 11 p.m., a recent job in a nursing home. Amy, who lived elsewhere with a roommate, was on the same shift. Sunny and I decided to go to a Christmas Eve supper, then I'd deliver her to the nursing home, and Amy could bring her home in the morning.

As we walked out of the house, we noticed that the cop neighbor's garage door was open—and we knew they had gone away for the holidays. We went back into the house and called the in-town cops, who came quickly and decided there was nothing wrong except a malfunctioning door opener. They closed the garage and left.

Sunny and I got into my car, now one hour hungrier than we had been when we started the journey. I turned the ignition and... dead battery. We called the tow truck people for a jump and were soon on our way up the highway to the restaurant ten miles away. By the time we got there, they were out of most everything except for one very half-drunk, obnoxious customer who was harassing the waitress. After the dinner of Christmas meal substitutes, we went out the door to view the beautiful holiday night sky. And got into my car. And turned the ignition, and heard nothing.

The parking lot had few cars in it. We called for another jump start. "Fifteen minutes," they said. Thirty minutes later, after singing off-key carols into the cold night, we called again. "He's on his way."

Our knight arrived an hour after the initial call. I'm not sure why. Why he arrived, not why it was an hour later, though that was curious also. It turned out his truck had been broken into that afternoon, probably by someone else needing a jump start, as they took his ignition cables. At that moment, one of the employees exited the restaurant and rescued us with his jumper cables.

I took Sunny to work, and went home, leaving the car running for over half an hour before finally going to bed before Santa could get there. The next morning, the phone rang at 8:30. Amy was supposed to give Sunny a ride home, but Amy's roommate had taken her new car in for a tune-up the day before, they had done something to the oil and had killed the motor on her new car. Like Sunny's car, the roommate's was parked for the duration of the holiday. So Amy had to go take her roommate to her job. Could I come and pick up Sunny?

No, it seemed I couldn't. Once again, the battery was dead. It was Christmas day. Amy finally brought Sunny home, and we had a little gift exchange and ate lunch and Sunny went to bed. Merry Christmas.

Early the next day, after Christmas, I again had to call for a jump. Obviously this was not a simple dead battery; probably an expensive alternator instead. After getting the car started, I dropped Sunny off at her car to meet with another towing company, and I got a new alternator put in, picked up my pills, and went home and to bed. Out of four cars belonging to four people, in this Mercury Retrograde, only one car, Amy's little "Toy-ota" had made it through the holidays intact and useable.

The Retrograde communication part might have been responsible for Sunny moving out at the end of February. For weeks even before Christmas she had looked stressed, ready to cry one minute, almost manic the next. I knew she was seeing a psychiatrist frequently, and that they were trying to reintegrate her; I had the feeling it was not a successful endeavor.

Her rent had been late twice, in November and December, for the first time in her three years with me. Then, in early January, we went to a health fair. While there, she bought three *very* expensive dresses. When I saw the price tags that added up to more than her rent, the last straw settled on my back. Had we been getting along OK, I could have forgiven it, but by now I wanted her to move. I was afraid of what might happen to her without the safety of a confirmed living space, but I was no longer comfortable in my own home, never knowing what kind of mood she would be in. Further, she had opted out of helping with household tasks completely. I asked her for a meeting and told her it was time she moved.

She took it well. "I know. I've already talked to Amy about moving in with her. She has room, it will be cheaper, and Precious knows her." She offered no other explanation.

I was distressed that she never shared with me what was wrong. She began moving, assisted by Amy, with both of them dragging out armfuls of her belongings several days a week throughout January and February. Finally, three years after Sunny and Amy had moved in for "three to six months," Sunny's van rolled out of the driveway for the last time, bulging at the seams and leaving little puffs of smoke behind, appropriate for a medicine woman, I thought.

Sunny had carried Precious out under her arm on her last trip out the door. She never said good-bye to Bear or Bella. Or me. As the last puff of smoke disappeared into thin air, I felt a loss that we had not shared a peace pipe to resolve our differences, whatever she thought they were.

Watching the van disappear, I simultaneously felt an acute sense of loss and a big sense of relief, somewhat like my feelings when my husband and I walked away from each other for the last time. It was the closing of another era in my life.

The house felt resoundingly empty without Sunny's swirling energy running through it. Above all, I knew I would miss the wondrous things Sunny had shown me about the energy that surrounds and is within all things, about alternative and holistic healing, about believing in limitless possibilities and little pieces of magic, about respect and honoring of all things, even rocks. She had led me into worlds I never dreamed existed, changing my beliefs about everything spiritual and the natural world. I would be forever grateful for all the doors she had led me to, the ones she had opened, and the things she had taught me.

Sunny, and even her alters, were interesting and fun, especially the fearless, charming, enthusiastic little Rosie, who had taught me how to play, perhaps for the first time ever. Rosie, who would call out, and my little girl would answer "yes," always ready to go have fun. Not only was I losing a teacher and mentor, it felt as if I was losing my very first childhood friend or that sister I had wished for—the one I had never had until Rosie, and who would never be replaced.

"Are you sad, Bear? Do you think she will ever come back for Bear Rock? I guess she left him to stand guard for us, do you think?"

He looked up at me, seemed to consider, then turned and trotted back into the living room.

So now we were back to just the three of us, two females and one male in an interspecies family. I was the caretaker, the food provider, the leader of the pack. Bella was my wild and crazy girl, climbing walls, trees, the chimney on the roof, and the highest place in the room with exuberance, with only two speeds, busy, busy, busy, and sleep. Bear sometimes extended his role as Bella's big brother out to me. He almost always knew where I was, and if he didn't see me for awhile, he'd come looking for me. He was the male energy and guardian, always first at the door when I came home, or when visitors came.

As Bear, Bella, and I settled down, calmness pervaded the house. I began interacting with the cats more, telling them about my day, a great way to vent in the absence of another human.

"Do you know what my stupid boss did to me today! He gave me this new workload—it's awful! I so want to quit that job, but I don't have enough energy to get a new one."

They acted fascinated, their eyes on me as I flung myself around the living room in frustration. Since they stayed in the room, I took it to mean they were interested in the one-sided conversation, and I vented to them often.

And Bear *was* my guardian. One day, as I was getting ready to take a shower, he charged into the bathroom to see what was going on. He slid to an abrupt stop as soon as he saw me, then stared fixedly at my head, obviously distressed, rocking from side to side. This normally not-very-vocal cat then began expressing urgent little syllables. *"Uh, Uh, Uh."*

"What's the matter, Bear?"

He continued rocking, his eyes fixated on my head, unmistakably upset. I reached up toward the area where his eyes seemed to be focused.

"The shower cap? Is this what has you upset?"

I pulled it off slowly, watching him watch my movements. Yes, the cap was definitely the problem, but—*why?* I bent down and let him smell the inside and outside of the white plastic headgear. He sniffed and sniffed, touched it with his paw, licked it. Then I slowly put it back on, stuffing my long hair inside, watching him watch me intently. When all my hair was tucked up, he took one last look, turned around and trotted away, tail up. I realized that he'd never seen me with anything on my head before. I'd had short hair for years but had been letting it grow, only starting to wear the shower cap a few days before. What a shock for Bear to see my head being attacked by a big white bubble.

To me, this was confirmation that Bear would have been a hero cat if there had been need for him to be. There was no doubt in my mind that the shower cap had narrowly escaped a horrible death, and the only thing preventing it was Bear's uncertainty of how to attack without hurting me.

Chapter 30
KITTY GAMES

Oak Hill, Texas. June 1998. I noticed that Bear and Bella seemed to react well to this calmer way of being with just the three of us. One day, I did a sort of life-review with the cats. First there had been Princess who opened the door to cats. Then Sami came and essentially turned me into a cat-mom, teaching me how to be a nurturing cat lover, showing me how to play, how it felt to come home and be welcomed.

Then Bear arrived, Bear, who connected with me on an even deeper level than Sami and who had a personality as big as his world, which, for a cat, was very big. He was not a cat who tucked his tail but rather raised it like a flag. If I wanted to know what his mood was, I just watched the tail; if he was happy, which was most of the time, that tail could have been a stairway to heaven, it stood so straight, flowing and glistening with every breeze. When he was angry, he swished it from side to side or slapped it on the floor in staccato movements. If he wasn't feeling well or hadn't gotten his way about something, the tail dragged behind him like a child's blankie.

Then came little Bella, who I often thought of as a fairy child who loved Bear, and sounds, and life, and asked Bear and I to care for her.

But even with all that, I felt that, for Bear, some spark had disappeared with Sami's death. With Bella, Bear always maintained his position as a protective older brother, periodically getting irritated with her and never engaging in the roughhousing, and never sleeping attached to her the way he had with Sami. But he always knew where she was when I couldn't find her. "Where's Bella?" I would ask.

He would look at me, think about it, and then turn his head. If I followed his eyes, I would usually find myself looking into hers, at the highest possible climbing area of the room.

Bear continued to maintain his friendship with Funnel II, and Bella continued to carry around Red Thang most of the day, almost every day, letting a little hang out of her mouth so she looked ready to entice a boyfriend. Her favorite interactive toy was a bright red boa on a stick. Scientists say that cats can't distinguish colors, except possibly blue and yellow. I don't know what kind of cats they tested, but I had no doubt that Bella loved and could identify every shade of red. When she wasn't carrying around Red Thang, she would be carrying around and playing with fuzzy red pom-pom balls, sold in multi-color packs. When I dumped them all on the floor at once, Bella would unhesitatingly grab the red ones; if there weren't any red, she latched onto the pink, ignoring the rest, including the blue and yellow. I'm not sure, though, that Bear could distinguish *any* colors, or maybe, being a guy, he simply didn't care about brightly-colored fuzzy balls and boas.

Bella had an endless array of games she played with Red Thang. I would see her drop it, and then claw at a blanket or a piece of paper to cover it up. Then she would sit there and stare at where it had been. Finally, she would claw the covering away, perhaps afraid Thang had disappeared while she watched.

In the meantime, Bear watched her. I'm sure he would have been glad to recommend her for a Las Vegas act; she was one of the most inventively entertaining cats I've ever known. She was always busy, busy, busy, while the energetic Bear just sat and watched, seemingly overcome with fascination. She supervised my every task, sitting and staring at a project to make sure I was doing it right, until it was done.

Since the scientific articles I'd read said that cats can't think, can't plan, can't reason, and can't remember, I had believed them. After all, they had done the research. But I came to know that my cats *could* think and plan, and definitely did remember, and could, as well, *execute* a plan. Over and over they proved this to me. I remember well my amazement the first time Bear and Bella ganged up on me in very deliberate fashion.

I had let both of them out into the yard to enjoy the late spring day. Since I was with them, I had left Bear in his harness but hadn't attached his lead as I planned to sit and watch them play for awhile. Bella was pacing along beside him when the phone rang. I ran in to answer it, returning within two minutes at the most. I couldn't find hide nor hair of either one.

"Bear? Bella?" I called. No response. No movement of leaf, grass, or limb. I walked around to the other side of the yard. Bella *always* came when I called her. My heart started thumping.

"Bella? Bear!" Again, no response, no movement anywhere. It was as though they had taken wings and flown over the fence in those couple of minutes. By now, though, I was fairly certain that Bella would still be in our yard, so I should at least have been able to find her, even if Bear *had* jumped the fence again.

I wandered around, looking for any sign of either one. At various times over the years, he had disappeared briefly, accidentally or, perhaps, deliberately hiding. I could just look for the pink lead that pointed directly to where he was or from where he had left, but not on this day. I saw no sign of the shaggy gray body, no sweet Bella.

I looked under the Lady Banks Rose where Bella had once disappeared. No opening, no sign of a cat. I checked through the underbrush in the tree island where Sami was buried, his little avocado tree still there. No live cats. I peered through the bushes lining the back of the house. Nothing. *Where* had they gone? I had no sense of panic, just confusion. Never once had Bella gone out of the yard, but I had worried that someday she might just follow Bear. And usually, when I called, Bella would meow back at me. Now, though, there was not a sound except the birdcalls, the chatter of a squirrel, the distant sound of traffic—nothing cat-like.

There was only one place left to look, under a big bushy spirea taller than I was, with tiny white flowers growing in profusion on each cascading limb. I'd never seen the cats over on that side of the yard, but it was the only place left. I turned and began walking toward it, knowing if I didn't find them soon I was going into panics-ville again.

Then I spied four feet in a precise line just inside the bush's shielding streamers. Two of the feet were white, big, and furry, and two were white, small, and dainty. As I peeked down, I could see the cats sitting shoulder to shoulder, both with their heads dipped down, peering through the bottom of the branches to watch my big feet, not realizing I was peering down at their fuzzy heads and hunched up shoulders. Feeling relief, I realized they were engaged in a game of hide-n-seek as surely as any small child. I decided to refrain from letting them know I had found them. I continued to walk slowly back and forth, several yards one way, turn, several steps the other way. I called, over and over, "Bear? Where's Bear? Where's Bella?" I kept watch on those white paws out of the corner of my eye; they didn't move a whisker's width. Several trips later, I went directly to the bushes, parted them, and two sets of innocent eyes looked up at me.

"Oh, look, it's Bear and Bella!" I exclaimed.

I squatted down, patted my knees, and they came rushing toward me, preening around my legs and looking very proud of themselves at having outsmarted Mommy again. I obligingly told them they were very smart and very funny.

One winter day, wiped out from a bad day at work, I came home and flipped on the lights in the living room. No cats met me. I wandered through the house calling, "Hey Bear, hey Bella! You guys ready for some din-din? Mama's cooking," I sing-songed as encouragement.

No cats. Very odd. I wandered all through the house, calling again and again. No response, not even Bella's usual answering meow. I sensed somehow that they were in the living room. I went back and looked behind the couch, under the chairs, behind the TV. Not a peep. *Where the heck were they?*

I always felt panic whenever I thought of my cats being outside, wandering around lost, being run over or catnapped, or carried off by animals with big teeth, but I was pretty sure they *had* to be inside. I was too tired and exasperated for this. I stood in the middle of the floor and had a temper tantrum, stomping my foot and yelling, "Bear! Get in here!"

And then I felt it. Eyes were watching me. I closed my eyes and concentrated. When I opened them, I looked up. And there they were, both Bella and Bear, on the very top of a six-foot tall bookshelf, peering down at my head, watching me run around and make a fool of myself. I had always heard that cats can't smile because of the muscular structure of their face. But I knew Bear was laughing at me. His ears were forward, his whiskers forward, and his eyes were sparkling. I couldn't explain it any more than that, but on a very few occasions, like this one, I knew that he was very amused at watching me act the fool. *I* was Bear's very favorite game.

I tried to make sure we played some games every day, especially when they couldn't go out because of the weather. I'd spend at least fifteen minutes getting them to chase things. I dangled or dragged around interactive toys or tossed soft toys around and let them fetch. Bear tried to swat everything down, capture, and then sit on it. Bella would leap high into the air, twist and turn, bring it down, and try to carry it off in her mouth like a hard-won bird kill.

If I was too physically tired to work very hard at playing, the game for the night was "Bug Hunt." Instead of leaving their always-present, highest-quality kibble out for them to free feed, I would take their bowls up as soon as I got home. Later, when I judged them to be as hungry as spoiled inside kitties could get, I would toss the pieces of their dinner around the living room, interspersed with their hairball-specific treats, one nugget at a time, then watch them scurry around the living room, getting some exercise, as they slurped up "bugs" from the floor.

The cats had a toy box about the size of a pirate's treasure chest, covered with embossed metal, filled with toys: wooly mice, jingly balls, Bear's spare funnels, and Bella's red fuzzy pom-poms. During the years, they had gotten to try out almost every toy in the pet store.

When Sami was alive, and Bear still young, Mother had sent them two catnip-stuffed terry cloth socks for Christmas. I recognized the outer covering as a washcloth I had used in high school, decades before. Sami and Bear had carried the socks around, licked them over and over and over, almost to disintegration. Bear especially liked to use one as a pillow after he had exhausted himself licking it, and the sock was wet with slobber. The two socks had lasted for over ten years, threads dangling, flattened after being a pillow, and incredibly filthy looking. I tried washing one once and re-treating with catnip, but the cats hadn't liked it. I finally had asked Santa-Grandma for a new one, but it didn't cut the mustard either, until she searched and found some really high-quality catnip to stuff another set with. Bear still carried them around, but catnip held no interest for Bella.

She doted on a toy that was a circle with a track around the outside perimeter, a ball in the track, and a round scratching post in the middle, known as Turbo Track to most cat lovers. She would slam the ball around the channel for seemingly hours. I would sometimes awaken in the middle of the night to the sound of the ball careening around its round plastic path. It should have been annoying, but it wasn't—it was simply my lonely little kid having fun in the middle of the night all by herself. I'd turn over and go back to sleep, lulled by the gravelly sound of plastic on plastic.

Every grocery day brought big toys into the house. I would unload a paper bag, throw it on the floor, and one cat would scoot inside of it. The other one would jump on the sack, making a frightful racket, at which point the inside cat would come barreling out, and it was time for a chase around the house until the other cat would jump inside the bag and the game would start all over.

Bella's best toy was a laser light. She'd chase it until she laid down panting. I finally realized it must be very frustrating as she chased but was never really able to "catch" the light. Thereafter, I made sure I always had one last place to shine the light where she could find a treat. We moved on to Da Bird that probably got the purple ribbon for Best Toy, or perhaps, second best after the piano-wire-and-cardboard Cat Dancer. These interactive toys let them work off some energy without my having to work very hard. I could put both my cats up as proof that spayed and neutered inside cats did not have to be fat cats, even though they got ample food and too many treats.

Another Cat Dancer, a length of very fuzzy striped material attached to a wand, was Bear's baby. For reasons known only to him, he would pick it up in his mouth, the wand and the fabric trailing between his legs, and wander around the house emitting agonizing-sounding, guttural, mournful cries, like a lost child. The cries were so deep I could see his ribs move in and out as he cried with the exertion. Then, he would abruptly stop, drop Dancer, and walk away. I tried to go into a shamanic journey once to see or feel what was happening for him. The only thing in the vision was a small island with bright green grass in the middle of a completely desolate and burned-out field, only black skeletons of trees, no sound of birds, nothing, except Bear standing there with his cat dancer in his mouth, crying. I could never figure out why that "toy" would cause such a reaction. Again, I wondered—was this really a communication or only something conjured up by my mind at hearing his mournful cries? I finally took it away from him, dismayed at the sound of the agony in his cries.

Whatever the toy of the evening was, though, both cats were very good about sharing them, with each other and with me. But one night, Bear shared something that I knew I would always remember.

Bella was sleeping in her chair, but, oddly, Bear was insisting he wanted to go out through the side garage door. There was one small area where a regular door opened out of the garage into a small fenced-off area that had been a pen for the previous owners' dogs. The house formed one side of the pen, the other three sides of the four by ten foot area were six-foot-high chain link fencing instead of the privacy fence that was around the rest of the yard. I sometimes let Bear out there, even without a harness, because he couldn't climb or jump that fence. Tonight I let him out and went to finish doing dishes.

Bear had been out only a few minutes when I heard him thundering through the house and into the kitchen, making the same sounds he had made when he found the alien shower cap on my head, except these sounds were more urgent and demanding, "Uh, Uh. Meow! Meow!"

He slid to a stop and looked up at me, and I looked down at him. His eyes were round and almost filled with his black pupils, his tail straight up—an indication that whatever was going on, in his mind, it was good. His whiskers pointed forward, practically quivering with excitement. Seeing that he had my attention, he turned and took off at a run toward the garage.

I stood there a moment, puzzled. He came racing back and again made the urgent sounds.

"Mew! Mew!" he barked.

He looked at me, both pleading and excited, rocking from side to side. I remembered the Lassie films where the great dog would ask her people to follow her. So I followed, through the house and garage.

At the doorway, I stood on the stoop and looked down into the pen, then flicked on the outside light above the door to see more clearly. In just a bit more than the blink of an eye, I watched Bear take a step closer to the part of the fence that had his attention. As he did so, the little, silent animal on the other side of the woven wire also stepped forward into visibility. They looked at each other, moved to the fence, then reached out toward each other and touched noses, tentatively, slowly, very gently, as I held my breath. The ferret took a step backward and melted into the darkness, and, like a ghost, disappeared. Bear stood watching for a minute, then turned to me and rocked from side to side again, looking at me in an excited way, seeming to say, "Did you see it? Did you see it? Wasn't it great?"

It was one of those mental snapshots that will always stay in my mind—a wonderful innocence in that moment when a big-hearted cat met another species. Instead of doing the natural cat thing of defending his territory with screams and growls, or running away, he reached out in friendship and acceptance—one small cat so entranced with meeting a new friend that he welcomed it with a gentle touch through a small opening in a wire fence on an almost moonless summer night… and called me to share this wondrous event with him. I felt very honored at being the cat-mom to such an amazing animal.

Chapter 31
THE BLUE BLANKIE

Oak Hill, Texas. June 1999. I discovered that Dr. Ryan was returning to Austin to give an Advanced Communication Workshop. I offered to have her stay with me, though the lecture was to be elsewhere.

I was struggling to clean up the house before she arrived, but even the task of plugging in the vacuum cleaner defeated me. After repeatedly missing the holes in the electrical outlet, I sat down on the carpet and cried from the frustration of being so weak. I didn't know what was the matter, but my always low level of energy had deteriorated to next to none. When Jeri arrived, I showed her where she would be staying and very inhospitably went to bed, frustrated at the missed opportunity to talk with her more.

The next morning I dragged out of bed, and we drove south out of Austin to the back of a large house tucked up on the side of a hill. We entered the home and walked through the big country kitchen and into the living room. There, a wall of floor-to-ceiling windows gave a 180° unobstructed view—side-to-side, up and down—overlooking a forest of trees surrounding the small clearing directly in front of the house. Even as we watched, ground fog rolled out of the trees, crawled across the clearing, and seeped under the deck, covering everything with a dream-like quality of stillness. I stepped outside onto the cantilevered boards, and I could have been standing on a cloud, separated from all reality except for the fresh clean scent of the moisture-laden air. Regretfully, I went back in after the hostess called, wishing I could have made time stand still in that sublimely peaceful moment.

We brought our coffee and tea into the living room and sat quietly, all of us in a semi-circle facing that window, enjoying the view. Jeri came in and sat toward the side of the circle so we could all see her but not have our view of the forest and fog behind her obstructed.

"Good morning, ladies. Are you all ready to begin?"

As she finished the sentence, instead of answering, we all let out a unified gasp. A small herd of deer was materializing out of the shrouded trees. With their feet and legs partially obscured by the fog bank, they seemed to swim directly toward us through a magical sea-cloud. They showed no hesitation, moving as a unit with a definite destination, then stopped just short of the edge of the deck, gazing slightly upward, seeming to seek eye contact with the workshop participants. The sound of my heart beating against the intense silence was all I could hear. In the space of mere seconds, there was a metaphorical touching of spirits between the welcoming delegation outside and the eager, wanna-be communicators inside. The graceful creatures contemplated us for a timeless space, then turned and morphed into the fog that closed over their ghost-like absence.

Everyone I looked at had the same expression of wonder on their faces as I felt on mine, as though the deer had been spokespersons for the animal kingdom sent to bring blessings through the trees, through the fog, and into our group. Sunny had explained the qualities that different animals are known for. I knew the deer brings gentleness, magic, innocence, intuition, and sensitivity. How fitting that it was the deer that came to us that morning bringing those so-appropriate gifts.

Shaking off the mystical moment, we twelve attendees introduced ourselves by telling of our experiences with past communications. I tried to focus on the meeting, but I felt deathly tired, barely able to keep my eyes open as Jeri gave her introduction. I heard, but most of my attention was on trying to stay awake during the morning exercises and lectures, although that magical moment with the deer kept coming back into my consciousness again and again.

Lunch came; the hostess offered us coffee, tea, and soft drinks. For over a week, I had been trying to quit my addiction to Diet Coke. I was definitely white-knuckling it through the ordeal still. And there was my nemesis, lying on top of a big tub of ice. I succumbed and chug-a-lugged it in seconds, then went directly out to the car and fell asleep. I woke up almost an hour later with barely time to make it back into class, but I felt somewhat more alive for the first time in days—about the same number of days I had been off Diet Coke, I realized.

As class resumed, Jeri gave us the usual instructions on choosing an animal's picture for a conversation. For some puzzling reason, I chose the picture of Daisy, a very plump sixteen-year-old version of that calico from the farm. Daisy was sitting bread-loaf fashion, front and back paws tucked under her, on a kitchen shelf, wedged between a box of Corn Flakes and two other plump cats. I did the required centering exercise and then began. "Daisy, I'm with your mommy. She wants me to talk with you. Are you willing to do that?"

I imagined that I heard her agree.

"Do you like where you live?"

"Yes."

"Do you get along with the other cats?"

"Yes."

"What does your food bowl look like?"

"It's red and round."

If this wasn't Daisy, it was pretty boring; if it was Daisy, then it was quite exciting, I thought tiredly, still trying to stay awake. Then I remembered the proper way to investigate anything—with open-ended questions. "Where do you like to drink?"

I saw Daisy crouching down in a low area in a patch of cement but with cement behind her, too, like a drainage ditch or a dip in a driveway. The picture didn't make much sense, but I mentally recorded it and moved on.

"What is your favorite thing in the whole world?"

She showed me a fuzzy, baby-blue blanket, the kind that started out cheap and smooth, and then got little fuzz balls with each wash. She even showed me the strip of blue satin material on the edge of the blanket. I remembered having inherited one just like it at some short point in my life, short because I gave it away. I love all colors—except baby blue. No one would be able to find any trace of anything baby blue in my home, so it was unlikely I was imagining that color because of any liking for it. I took this to be a possible answer, though, and changed the subject.

"Do you like your tail rubbed?" I asked, thinking of that spot on Bear's back at the base of his tail that sent him into ecstasy, but again forgetting to ask open-ended questions.

I "saw" her turning around to put her face toward me, tucking her tail under. I took this as a "no." Then she sat down and managed to put her left rear paw in her mouth and began chewing on it, spreading her toes and digging with her teeth into the webbing.

"Is something wrong with your foot? Does it hurt?" I asked. She gave me this incredibly offended look, got up, and walked off.

Since Daisy had ended our chat, I struggled back to reality and waited for the revelations from the group. A woman sitting across the circle identified herself as

Daisy's mom. She had come in to Austin from Dallas, two hundred miles away, which is where the cat was. I had never met her and had not exchanged any words with her before or during the workshop, nor had I overheard her talking with anyone.

I was very nervous as I started telling Daisy's mom what I had received. I felt certain that there was nothing reliable here, but, with butterflies in my stomach as though I was about to read my writing to a critique group, I reported what I perceived as my communication. The owner remained silent and immobile, giving no clues from her expression.

After I finished, she gave her feedback. She and her husband had dug out a shallow hole with sloping sides in their yard, and lined it all around with concrete to collect rainwater. It formed a pool that the cats loved to drink out of. The picture, then, of the sunken cement, was correct!

Daisy hated to have her tail touched. When she walked around the house she hugged the perimeter of the room, keeping close to the wall so the other cats couldn't run up behind her and grab her tail. Two things right!

The owner admitted that she'd had all four of Daisy's feet declawed as suggested by the vet when she first got her—before she knew any better. I felt my stomach churn at this revelation.

Declawing is outlawed in many countries, but not in the *civilized* U.S. Instead of using patience and training, the naive owner accepts the word of the vet that the "little operation" will keep their furniture and carpets safe. The declaw procedure involves removing the ends of the "fingers and toes" up to the equivalent of our first knuckle, not just the removal of the nail and nail bed. I had a thankfully short but very intense flash at the thought of waking up as an innocent cat with all of my fingers and toes amputated at the same time with no idea why this betrayal had been done to me. Human amputees report that their phantom pain remains for years, so I would suppose this is true for cats. Then the cat doesn't use the litter box because the litter hurts its feet, and it begins peeing outside the box. Then the poor cat is turned in for euthanasia as a cat with a behavior problem.

Once, I had talked to a vet tech who told me that cats would come through the spaying and neutering process with a quick recovery, but the declawed cats often suffered and bled for days. She told me about the morning she went into the recovery room and found blood everywhere, the bandages torn off by the animal crying in agony from the pain. I wanted to cry for Daisy. At least, now, the owner understood what she had done. A quote crossed my mind, "Father forgive them, for they know not what they do." They, the owners, may not have known, but the vets knew and knew how to make a little more income—to hell with the poor cat that they were sworn to protect. Instead of taking a few minutes to give the client alternatives and training, they amputated. Another reason in my bag for not trusting the veterinary profession.

Now, I didn't respond to the owner, and I tried very hard to keep my face expressionless so as not to reveal my revulsion for her decision.

She told us that, before leaving the house that morning, she had noticed Daisy licking her left rear paw. She was unable to find anything wrong. Because she was late for the seminar, and this didn't seem to be an emergency, she didn't take Daisy to the vet but was planning on doing so after the weekend. I wondered if Daisy's look of contempt at me when I asked if her paw hurt was a reflection of a recent problem or her disgust for a human left over from that long-ago declawing.

Finally, the woman revealed that this old cat's very favorite place to be was curled up in front of the fireplace. In her basket. A basket lined with an old, fuzzy blue blanket. With a blue satin stripe.

I had done it! I had my zinger! No more doubts. The blue blankie cinched it. I could not imagine my imagining a baby blue blanket—a red one, a plaid one, a green one, but *not* a baby blue one. Now, at last! I was totally, know-it-in-my-bones aware that I had carried on a communication that made sense, that answered specific questions, that was *real*—with a cat. I felt my doubts dissolving and something in my chest unfolding. Any skepticism I'd had was erased forever. Even with my communications with my cats through a cat communicator there had been some doubt, especially doubt as to how it was possible, and whether just anyone could do it. And now, I knew in my heart and soul this incredibly unconventional, impossible, wondrous exchange I still didn't understand—worked. I couldn't fathom how thoughts between species could be translated into understandable language for each, and I didn't care. The Blue Blankie communication was my epiphany.

I spoke with Jeri about my success and asked if she could explain why I was able to connect today even though I was so tired. She confirmed that for some people total relaxation put down the defenses and opened the unconscious mind to receive the messages. Since I was detoxing from the Coke chemicals, I considered that my exhaustion might have opened my receptivity. After that single can at lunch, I was definitely more alert, but still very, very tired—almost unable to think or to focus to move my arms and legs at will.

This struggle for my epiphany, or my zingers, had been a long one for me, but the results had been worth it. First, I had received the adventure of a lifetime as a gift from Brown Horse, and now had had an honest-to-goodness *verifiable* exchange of information and conversation with a cat. *I had participated in an interspecies communication—and gotten it right!*

Perhaps I would never be able to do it again, but I had my proof. However, I had found the process exhausting each time I had tried it—I hated getting into a meditative state. But now I knew that true communion between an animal and a human was not only *possible*, but real, and that I could do it with some little degree of success. I was excited, humbled, and amazed at this most magical and mysterious of all connections. As I looked around, nothing was the same as I had always seen it. Imagine— animals could express themselves in a "language" understandable by humans and vice versa. Indeed, my world view had changed, though I suspected it would take a long time to digest and recognize just how much could, would, be changed by this knowledge.

Chapter 32
THE HUMAN ZOO

Oak Hill, Texas. July 1999 - July 2001. I looked at the checkbook, then made out my list of wants for a new renter, put an ad in the paper, and soon got a phone call. I told him to come over.

=^,-,^=

HUNKY: The six foot tall, great-looking Hispanic guy who could have been a male model with his hunky build, curly black hair, and a smile with dimples, almost had me falling in love. He wore a starched white shirt, tie, suspenders, and dress pants. Trying to maintain a landlady exterior, I led him to the rooms, telling him the rules: no drugs, no excess drinking, no smoking, and let me know about extended absences. "Two bedrooms and the small bath are yours."

"This is perfect. I share custody of my thirteen-year-old daughter. Is it okay if she stays with me every other weekend? I'll always be with her, and we'll be gone a lot."

I understood without him explaining his situation and agreed. I was too old for his ex to look on me as a threat, and they'd have a built-in chaperone.

"Can I move in tomorrow? It's Saturday, so I don't have to work. Uh, I realized when I got out of the car that I forgot my checkbook. I can come back after work with the rent and deposit."

"Well, I do need to check references first."

"Here. This is my boss." He presented me with a business card bearing his name, the title of Paralegal, and the name of an old and prestigious criminal law firm. He left, and I immediately called his boss, the senior partner in the law firm as it turned out.

"He's been working for me for two years now, a fine young man, very dependable," said the attorney. *Wow, great looks and a great recommendation. This was almost too good to be true.*

As promised, Hunky stopped by, gave me a check a few hours later, and moved in the following morning in an hour, as single men are able to do. Then he left; I didn't see him again all weekend.

On Monday morning, I gave in to some sixth sense. Great references! Did as he promised with the check. How could anything be wrong? Still, I decided to call the California bank Hunky's check was drawn on; no suspicion there for me—I still had a Nebraska bank account.

"Hi, I just want to verify funds for a check."

"What's the account number?"

I told her and waited. She asked again. I told her again.

"What is the name on the account?"

I gave it to her. The woman was very helpful, trying different name variations, but she finally conceded defeat. "We don't have an account with that number, or a client with that name on file—we've never had one according to my records."

That's why my neck hairs had been rising all weekend—why everything felt just a bit off-kilter. I'd been around habitual liars before, I should have caught it, but he was slick. He had stolen or forged the check. I called him at work and mentioned his check was going to bounce.

"Wow, really? I don't know what's wrong. I'll call right away and straighten it out. I promise to bring the rent by tonight after work, in cash."

My suspicions were barking at me all day, but he showed up and handed me the cash, as promised, looking properly apologetic. Besides, he was already moved in, had signed the month-to-month contract, and, in Texas, the Landlord Tenant Act tilts like the Leaning Tower of Pisa toward all the deadbeats. I knew I couldn't evict for a three-day late payment, but I told him very emphatically that I needed money in hand before the first of each month, or I would begin eviction proceedings immediately. I knew it was an idle threat; he surely did too from working at a criminal law firm, but I wanted to at least sound like someone to be reckoned with instead of an ineffectual and wimpy woman.

For the cats and I, nothing much changed. Hunky was rarely there, gone in the morning before we were up, and home after we were in bed, if he came home. I assumed he was living somewhere else and just showing up enough to claim residency at my house. As far as I could tell, he was in compliance with all the rules. When he did come home and rushed through the house, the cats would watch him from afar, neither of them, not even Bear, making any attempt to follow or interact with him.

When the next rent was due, he didn't come home, despite having promised to bring the money that night. On Sunday, two days later, I finally heard from him.

"Hi. I'm sorry about being late with the rent. I'm in jail because I'm behind in child support. My boss has put up bail money, and I'll be there on Monday with a rent check from my boss."

He kept his promise. For the next three months everything was fine. Then the first of the month passed without a payment. He was home the following night. I went to his room as soon as I heard him and knocked. He came out of the bedroom with a very pleasant smile, but my heart was thumping. I hated confrontations. I reminded him of the rent, then said, "This just isn't working. I need a reliable income."

"I'm sorry, but I've had some money issues. I just can't afford to be here, though it's a great place. I'll move at the end of the month."

At the end of the month, he didn't move. A week later, when he was still there, I called and spoke with his boss. Again.

"He's a really good guy, he's just had some unfortunate things happen."

"I'm a single woman. His tenancy is an unfortunate thing for me because I need the money."

"Yes, certainly. I understand that. I'll talk to him and tell him to move out right away."

Hunky arrived, still looking as spiffy in his laundry-starched white shirt as the first time I saw him. He asked if he could store a dozen boxes in the garage because he was moving into his office at work and didn't have room for them. Stupidly, I agreed, with the stipulation that everything be out in two weeks; he signed an agreement.

Two weeks came and went, and I was still a storage depot; he no longer answered his phone. I left a few messages, then called and spoke with his boss's secretary, who, I discovered, was not fond of Hunky.

"I need him to get his stuff off my property—I can't sell it, can't put it on the curb, and the law says I can't even change the house locks as long as he has stuff here."

"I can certainly understand. I'll have the boss call you."

I had a sudden thought. I wasn't convinced he wasn't on drugs. What if he had packed them into his boxes? I could have all kinds of illegal stuff in there. I rushed out and opened the first box I came to, knowing I was guilty of some crime but begging leniency because of self-preservation. Right on top, I found court papers—filed by his attorney boss, asking the Court to vacate Hunky's criminal conviction for spousal abuse. I panicked. This mild-mannered man wasn't so mild-mannered. I had asked him to leave. Was he waiting for revenge? Did his violence extend beyond his ex-wife?

I called the law office, again, and asked to speak to Hunky's boss, to tell him that I needed Hunky's stuff out now! The secretary said he was busy, but she'd make sure he called me back.

A few hours later Hunky arrived with the trailer his boss had rented for him—he was definitely a charming guy. He packed, and I watched his trailer pull out of the drive with considerably different feelings than those I'd had when Sunny left, relief being the primary.

=^,-,^=

PEEPERS. My spiritual friends were always telling me I should ask for what I wanted. I now knew what I didn't want for a renter—no Multiple Personalities or a broke guy with a felony conviction. So what *did* I want? Someone who would love my house, would help me take care of it, would pay the rent on time, and, most of all, who would love my cats, at least a little bit. I wanted someone like... Sunny. Or even my ex. Without the drama. I plastered ads on all the bulletin boards I could find, put an ad in the paper, and waited. Weeks later, I finally got a call. I almost swooned upon hearing the voice inquiring about rooms, a voice even sexier than Clint Eastwood's character in *Play Misty* for me. "Tell me about yourself."

"I'm 35, divorced, have a Bachelor's degree, and work as a Security Guard at the IRS. I've been in my last apartment for several years."

Sounded good! Especially good in that voice! Oh my! Too bad he was only 35.

I explained my rules, adding, "The most important thing is to never, ever, let the cats get out. I'll knock some off the rent if you'll spend a couple of hours a week helping around the house."

"I was a janitor for six months, I can help. I don't do drugs or drink, and I love cats."

He arrived the next day. He was at least two inches shorter than I was and so skinny he didn't have a shadow when he turned sideways. A piece of white adhesive tape held his glasses together above a beautiful, lush mustache which he petted as we talked. I could hardly tear my eyes away—I wanted to touch it. Not him—it. I could see a resemblance to Wally Cox's TV character, Mr. Peepers, without the mustache, from 1950's television.

I showed him the rooms, and he gave me the rent. He was... odd, but I couldn't sense any threat in him. That weekend, he brought armfuls of clothes and loose belongings in, no boxes or suitcases. He put down his sleeping bag, set his TV on the floor, borrowed a TV tray to eat from, and asked me to help him hang his pictures—two 27 X 40 inch framed football posters—and he was moved in. He had no furniture, not even a chair. His diet was fast food and TV dinners, and he only ate from paper plates with plastic silverware. I never had to ask him to clean up a mess in the kitchen because he never used it except to microwave.

He didn't have a lick of common sense, asking simple questions that I thought any fifth grader would know about the practicalities of day-to-day living: how much did a stamp cost, how to do laundry?

I sometimes caught Bella and Bear sitting, shoulder to shoulder, staring at him as he walked through the house. Bear rebuffed any of his efforts to pet or pick him up, Bear—who welcomed guests and repair people like he had been waiting to meet them his entire life—remained emotionally uninvolved, as he and Bella had done with Hunky tenant. There were no changes in the household with Mr. Peepers there. He came home, microwaved a dinner, and stayed in his room watching sports on TV, apparently his only hobby. I emptied the wastebaskets in the house once a week. Every week, without fail, I found five or more empty containers of roll-on stick deodorant in the trash.

One day I asked him to weed a little flower patch in back of the house. I showed him the weeds and left him to finish this half hour job. I returned an hour later, and he was squatted down, picking at green stuff.

"How's it going?" I asked.

"Well, I don't feel too good."

He looked up at me; I looked at his very white face and flushed cheeks and tried to figure out a way to word my suggestion.

"Well, it *is* 90°, and you *are* in full sun. Why don't you take off your jacket and cap—they're fur-lined, aren't they?—roll up the sleeves on your uniform, put some cold water on your face, and get some water?" I was reminded of my patients at the State Hospital who couldn't follow cause-and-effect reasoning. He took his cap off, went into the house and, a few minutes later, left for work.

Then there was the mopping incident. I asked him to mop the kitchen floor and wax it. He looked at me, appearing puzzled.

"I don't know how to mop."

"I thought you said you worked as a janitor and had been married."

"Well, I only threw out the trash. And when I was married, we lived with my parents, and the maids and butler took care of the cleaning."

When I recovered, I held out the tools. "Bucket. Mop. Cleaner. One capful in the bucket. Add water to the line. Wring out the mop. Use it on the floor."

I shouldn't have left him alone for those next ten minutes. When I came back, the floor was covered, sole deep, in pretty bubbles. The next day, I waxed the floor when it finally dried. He did a few other things for me—moved some furniture—but only under my direct supervision. I was not getting a good bargain here.

Two months later, around 2 a.m., I was submerged in a computer project in the office which was in the tenant's end of the house. I had been vaguely aware of Peepers coming home hours earlier, fixing a meal, and passing by my office door as he went to his rooms. Suddenly, I felt a cold draft around my ankles. I emerged from my work into reality, looked up and around, and realized I was missing a Bear. He and Bella were always in my office when I was working. Now, Bella was on the floor, asleep. But where was Bear? And *why* was there a draft?

I went looking for the cold air and found the front door standing wide open, the screen door inches ajar. I didn't find Bear. After grabbing a coat and flashlight, I pounded on Peeper's door.

"Bear's gone," I yelled. "You left the front door and the screen door open. It's supposed to be below freezing tonight. Come help me look."

My heart was thudding as I ran out the door and down the cul-de-sac, shining the light into every dark shadow; we still didn't have streetlights in the subdivision. I was afraid to yell too loudly because all the houses were dark, but I whispered at the top of my lungs as I shook a package of treats, "Bear! Bear, come get some treats!"

Something sparkled, bright eyes reflecting the illumination from the flashlight. I ran toward them—a cat, but not Bear. I searched on foot, Peepers in his truck. Finally, my flashlight caught more bright eyes. It was Bear! I shook the treat bag, and he ambled out to get his reward.

I wasn't sure if I was madder at him or at the tenant. The security guard won. What kind of person, let alone a guard at IRS and a college graduate, can't keep doors closed? Maybe he had had butlers do that for him, too?

A few weeks later, I was working on the flowerbed, with Bear, I thought, safely in the house. When I went inside to get some breakfast, I noticed the front door wide open and the screen door ajar, again, and did not find a tenant or Bear.

"Calm down," cautioned myself. I knew I needed to send out a guiding light to Bear to lead him home. I knew those things, but I was anything but calm, and I didn't think I was going to get that way. Instead of staying put, I drove around the neighborhood again.

At the house directly behind me, inaccessible without going around the whole block or over the fence, I spied him. He stood in the middle of the driveway watching the neighbor work on his motorcycle. Bear's tail waved slowly, his ears forward, obviously very interested in this metal beast. I apologized to the neighbor and then threw my wandering boy into the car and took him home.

When Peepers came home that night, I suggested he move immediately, possibly into a tent. I'd never felt as insecure as when a Security Guard was living in my house. So much for asking for what you want.

=^,-,^=

Bear continued to jump over the fence, and Bella continued to go on her peeing rampages. I was impressed with my cleaning jobs as none of the tenants or visitors ever complained of cat smell, even when I asked them. For both of the cats, they seemed to know what was the tenant's area and what was not, and they never trespassed. Bear, other than watching Peeper's entrance and exit to the house, had acted as though the guy was invisible. Bella anointed only our area.

I continued on my job, exhausting my limited energy supply trying to satisfy the diametrically opposed instructions from the bosses: "Research everything, but do it fast, or we'll fire you," hating the work, but knowing it was necessary to keep the things I loved—my pampered cats and our house. Trying to keep up with all the work of daily living—a job, an hour's one-way commute, house cleaning, yard work, shopping, paper work—I felt like I was suffocating, and was very anxious to get some help. When had daily life become so burdensome?

By now there were many items on my repair list—honey-do things I had thought Hunky and Peepers could do as part of their rent reduction. Hunky had never been home, and after the failure-to-mop-the-floor incident, I'd been afraid to let Peepers around a rake, let alone a screwdriver or hammer, so none of the chores he was getting rent reduction for had been done.

=^,-,^=

LURCH. Someone suggested I contact a friend of hers, an intuitive nutritionist who had a large client base. I went to see her. She said an old friend from her high school was staying with her while looking for another place. I asked her to tell the woman to call me. Several days passed before I got the call.

She wanted to see the house, she said, but her car was in the repair shop. I offered to pick her up. She hesitated, which I thought odd, but then agreed.

She had a sweet face, a beautiful peaches-and-cream complexion topped by short, wavy, honest-to-goodness Titian hair so often seen in European masterpieces. The woman was taller than I by several inches and large boned. Her form was pear-shaped, probably a size twelve on top and an eighteen, at least, on the bottom. She walked with a lurching gait, as though one leg was shorter than the other, or her knee didn't work, though there was no obvious physical defect.

She got into the car and explained about her prospective tenancy. "I only want to rent for a few months, until I've saved up enough to go back to Scotland. I met this wonderful man while I was there on vacation, and we're getting married as soon as he gets his divorce."

I quickly recovered and steered the car out of the adjacent lane, not saying another word all the way to my driveway. As we came into the house, I explained the usual no-drugs/drinking/loud music or parties; make sure to keep the doors shut so the cats can't get out, most important, and clean up the kitchen after cooking. After looking at the space that would be hers, she wrote out a check and then held it, looking at it for many seconds, fondling it, before finally handing it to me. My intuition was chattering like a squirrel with a nut, but I couldn't hear any words, just the same feeling I'd had when Hunky moved in. Why did this not feel right? I totally trusted the woman who had referred her, so what could be wrong?

Lurch moved her stuff in the next day, then left the house, returning the following day with several sacks of groceries. I heard her banging pans around in the kitchen. Half an hour later, I was still in the living room, reading, when she joined me, plunking herself on my second-in-a-lifetime-new Shabby Chic facsimile couch. She began stabbing at the overly-endowed plate of slick, puffy Asian potstickers.

Alarmed, but trying to be cordial even in the face of this potential disaster of slimy food on my beloved sofa, I rose and said, "There's a tray in the kitchen you can use when you eat in here. I'll get it for you."

"Oh, I'm fine," she said.

I sat back down and watched in agitated suspense as she tried to stab one of the little pillows of Asian food. It was crafty and avoided the attack; the rest slid around to make room, teetering on the edge of the plate.

I continued to watch while trying to find a polite way to say it. Finally, I couldn't stand it. "Well, I *will* expect you to pay for repairs to the couch if you get food on it."

Without a word, she got up and lurched away, looking mad enough to dump the puffy pillows on my head.

Things deteriorated from there. When she cooked, which was rare, she made a big production of sitting and pouting at the kitchen table, hunched over her food like a prison inmate. After a week of occupancy, she disappeared for five days. I didn't know if she had vacated or gone on vacation. She reappeared intact, rolling a suitcase behind her. I met her in the kitchen.

"If you're going to be gone for more than a day, I'd appreciate if you would let me know, for your safety and mine."

"What do you mean?" She looked like a belligerent teen-ager.

"If I hear things in the house in the middle of the night, I'd like to know if it's you or a burglar. Further, I didn't know if you'd moved out, or if I should call the police and report you missing."

She stared at me with a lethal look in her eyes, then, without responding, turned and stomped off to her bedroom. The shorter this relationship was, the better I was going to like it. She gave me the heebie-jeebies. After the lesson learned with Hunky on the difficulties involved in an eviction, I decided to raise the rent drastically with the hope that she would be mad enough to leave quickly and peacefully.

When she came home and found the letter on her door advising of the rent increase, she got on the phone and began screaming about how awful I was, that I was a crazy person, that she was afraid of what I would do to her. My intuition told me she was talking to our mutual friend, and what she wanted was an invitation to move back in with her, rent-free. I couldn't imagine what the nutritionist thought of me at this point.

Within the week Lurch had moved. She left a message on my voice mail as to the exact day she was coming by to get her bed. On that day, I took off work and stayed home, keeping the cats with me in my bedroom, fearing she would try to do something to them. I heard her arrive and then the sounds of the bed being loaded into a pick-up.

When all noise ceased, I walked out into the main part of the house. Both the front door and the screen door were propped wide open, an obvious invitation for the cats to escape. I closed and locked the doors, then went into her area, fearing what I would find.

What *had* she been doing? Never had I seen such a filthy tub, multiple bathtub rings, actual mud on the bottom, wads of hair and soap rings everywhere. It was a pigpen, and she'd only been there three weeks.

Bear was standing there watching me, an anxious aura about him. "This was not a nice lady, BearBear. But you can relax, she won't ever be back."

Then, fearing the worst, I opened her bedroom door, then let out my breath—the walls, windows, fixtures, and carpet didn't appear to have been trashed. I decided to play Scarlett O'Hara and deal more closely with the cleaning and the rest of it "tomorrow."

The snake in the grass had been easier to deal with than the ones *in* my house. But what else could I do? I needed the money from the tenants to keep the house for my kitties and me. Now that it was obvious I was jeopardizing the cats' safety by having these strange renters here, I would have to start reconsidering what I could do to have more income. I went back to bed hoping I would receive a dream solution.

Chapter 33
HOUSE OF STRAW

Oak Hill, Texas. August 2001. During the years since Sunny left, interspersed with blessed vacancies, there had been Hunky, Peepers, Lurch, and a renter who moved in one week and out the next to go to acupuncturist school out of state. I decided my lovely home would have to go; I couldn't keep it without the rental income. The constant anxiety—wondering if the next tenant would be even worse than the last, could cause harm to the cats or myself, or could burn the house down—was too much. I was a mess.

Despite my attempts to meditate and do more animal communication, I couldn't relax enough to be successful at either. I loved this house more than anywhere I had ever lived but getting help and good renters was just too difficult. The cats were wonderful at helping with the weed eating, but they couldn't mop worth a darn even though Bella would probably be able to furnish the water.

I scheduled a meeting with a real estate agent for the Friday before Labor Day. To prepare for the appointment, I finally forced myself to finish cleaning Lurch's area. I'd already dredged out the filthiest bathroom I'd ever seen. Now it was time for the bedrooms. I took a step into the first bedroom and heard squishy noises underfoot. *What in the world?* I reached down to feel the carpet; it was sopping wet. *Oh, no! What had she done? She hadn't had a waterbed—had she deliberately sabotaged the room?*

When I slopped across the carpet and opened the closet, the damage was revealed. The week before, a windstorm had dumped torrential rains, pretty much the only kind Austin has, rain that had found a construction-caused leak in my roof. Lurch could not have failed to notice, but she hadn't bothered to tell me.

Instead of meeting with the real estate agent on that Friday, I met with the insurance adjuster. As he pointed out the structural problem, he told me that the leak was the original builder's fault, too long ago to hold them responsible. He poked around the house and referred to "Stachybotrys" mold in the tenant's area, and, upon further inspection, he also found it in my bedroom closet on the opposite side of the house.

"Do you want to file a mold claim?" he asked.

I had no idea. "Should I? How much is the repair?"

His answer of $50,000 shocked me so much I couldn't think, but I heard him explaining about having to replace everything on the front of the house including the framework, the bricks, insulation, and rebuilding the bedroom and closets.

How was I going to pay for this? I visualized myself at my hated job, cutting my 90th birthday cake. But that wasn't the end of the bad news. He explained that the hysteria in the insurance world was a result of a family in Dripping Springs winning a $32 million lawsuit against Farmers Insurance for failure to remedy a mold claim on their new house. The husband ended up in a wheelchair, and rich. All the insurance companies had immediately changed their policies and were now not covering more than one repair per house, or per person--forever and ever.

"You can't sell the house with mold in it. If you don't file a claim, the insurance can't cover repairs. If you do file a claim—well, insurance will pay this one. But you probably won't be able to get any insurance on any home ever again and any buyers of this house won't be able to insure it."

If I stayed, I'd need another tenant or an additional job. But who knows how long it will take to sell a house with a mold history? What should I do?

"How soon do I need to decide?"

He shrugged. "If it is Stachy, it gives off a potent neuro-toxin, and it's really not safe to be in here. And the inspectors are way backed up because everyone who sees a speck of any mold is filing a claim, even about mold that's been in a house for decades. To anyone buying or selling a house, the words mold or water are the death of a sale nowadays."

"OK. I guess I'll file and hope something changes. What should I do now?"

"You need to immediately move out of the house while we wait for official confirmation of the mold type—take about three weeks to get an inspector out here. If it isn't Stachybotrys, we'll have to repair the water damages. If it *is* Stachy, it will take a few months to repair everything."

Because of my health issues with the fibromyalgia and the chemical sensitivity, the insurance company insisted I move to a hotel. The agent said he'd been assured the cats would be fine as long as they were kept out of the areas of the house where there was active mold. The contractors replaced the outside of my house with heavy sheets of plastic, overlapping, hanging from floor to ceiling to keep the mold from the main part of the house.

I fixed up the garage for the cats: food and water bowls, snug beds, and a load of their toys, including Funnel and Red Thang. Then I packed a bag and checked into a hotel, planning to go back twice a day, wearing a painter's mask, to check on them.

On Labor Day weekend I was restless, unable to settle or concentrate, and very bored. The cats were doing fine when I checked on them, although they seemed confused when we went into the yard, heading somewhere, stopping, then turning in another direction. I totally related. I reluctantly put them back in storage and returned to the hotel.

Tuesday morning, I crawled out of bed, switched on the TV, and went into the bathroom to get ready for work, coping with my things in places they didn't belong. The loud, excited voice of a reporter interrupted the water flow. I turned off the shower and poked my head out of the bathroom to hear better.

"We have confirmed! A second plane has just crashed into the Twin Towers! The United States is under attack!"

I rushed into the bedroom, standing there dripping as I listened to the newscast of this sacrilege. I kept switching channels to make sure I wasn't just watching a movie. I was numb—too much happening too fast, too many life changes to process. Who had done this? Why? With no warning. What was happening? What was *going* to happen? Could the powers-that-be defend us? With the rest of America, I waited for the next shoe to drop.

Through all the tumults of my life, I'd been able to cope—as long as I had a safe nest, my retreat. Now, I did not feel safe. I had no secure nest—no physical home, no emotional home without the cats. The mold, the uprooting, living in a hotel, now the violent attack—I felt punch drunk and kept finding myself simply standing and staring at nothing, not thinking, and incapable of planning three minutes ahead.

The other shoe did drop the next day when the insurance agent called and confirmed Stachybotrys. The repair people came in and took down the plastic, then removed any piece of plaster or board that had telltale black muck on it. This included taking down a twenty-foot section of the front of the house from inside to outside, totally exposing us to all weather and any passers-by. The contractors wiped everything down with some kind of anti-mold cleaner, probably causing more chemical danger than there was in the mold itself, reinstalled heavy plastic by tacking it to the ceiling and roof, turned on industrial fans, and said I could move back in. Even with all that, I was grateful to be back home with the cats.

Halloween, then Thanksgiving came and went, then Christmas. Bear managed to behave himself—not a single gutter dive or fence escape. The temperatures kept lowering. Right after New Year's, a winter storm came through. I had to call the construction crew in the middle of the night to come put the plastic back up to keep the wild wind and rain out. The temperature nose-dived into the single digits. Would this chaos never end?

Six weeks later, I celebrated Valentine's by wadding up the last of the plastic and filling the garbage cans with it. At last, five months after 9/11, I had my nest back and was home where I belonged, cats in my lap. Things would get better. I knew they would. They had to.

Several months later, I realized I had been exposed to Stachybotrys, not only at home, but at my office. Even though I was better since using the essential oils, I had requested disability accommodation for my chemical sensitivity by asking that I not be seated near the other employees unwilling to stop wearing colognes and perfume. A single inhale could set off an asthma attack, often turning into bronchitis that would go on for months. The agency decided I should move to a storage room. They cleaned the boxes out and moved my desk in. The room reeked with a moldy smell. I complained. They cleaned out the vents. It didn't help. I complained again, but this agency dealing with disabilities ignored the complaints for months. Then one of the ceiling tiles fell down. The cleaning people came, then the mechanical engineers, then the Air Quality people. When they pulled the rest of the tiles down, the Stachybotrys mold poured slowly off the tiles, like very dirty, thick, sludgy black oil from a car.

I had been working forty hours a week at a disability agency in a building with, as Air Quality finally diagnosed, Sick Building Syndrome from the black mold that causes neurological damage, respiratory illness, eye problems, headaches, and fatigue. It wasn't just the mayhem of 9/11 and my mold at the house then that were responsible for my increasing fatigue and aches.

Finally, things were getting better, though—my house was intact again, and the agency eventually fixed the ceiling and moved me into another part of the building. But the country was now at war in the Middle East, and everyone in America seemed to be as uneasy, anxious, and unsettled as I felt. The stock market nose-dived and my retirement savings were in trouble, and real estate sales were at a standstill. Even installed behind the walls of my house, the only time I felt any sense of security was with the cats on my lap. At night, I dreamed of being inside a snow globe which had been turned upside down, with bits of airplane metal, dollar bills, black mold, and people and cats falling out of the sky.

Chapter 34
CHAOS & CONFUSION

Oak Hill, Texas. May 2002. I had my house back, but I just could not force myself to put it on the market again with all the chaos going on. I needed my home. No one was buying or selling anyway.

Further, in the middle of the mold chaos, I took Bear in for a tooth cleaning. During the pre-surgery exam, I asked the vet to look at the lump on Bear's back on a spot underneath his harness. The vet felt it should be biopsied, so, panicked, I agreed.

After Bear came out of the anesthesia, he was wild, licking at the open wound that was about the size of a fifty-cent piece surrounding the area where the pea-sized lump had been. The vet said he didn't want to take any chances and had excised it beyond the boundaries, just in case it was cancer. He also told me that it wasn't. I had an uneasy feeling that this had been a money operation, not a health one, but I couldn't prove it in spite of the niggling at my gut.

It was pointless to put any antibiotic on Bear's wound because he licked it right off. I finally called Carol to explain to him why he needed to stop licking it.

"Bear, you need to leave the sore alone, or it could make you very sick."

Carol waited for a response, then, "He's very upset. He thought he was going to have his teeth done. He wants to know why does his back hurt? He says that's not where his teeth are. And he says his licking will make it better so he's going to lick it. And he's probably right."

I tried to explain that the decision was an emergency one, that I hadn't known we would have to do it when I took him in. Carol said he didn't seem mollified.

It took a long time for the physical wound to heal, a scab covering it one day, and licked away to raw skin the next. When I tried to take him to the vet, though, I found he had been psychically wounded. Always before, a vet trip had gone smoothly. Now, in the carrier, Bear would yowl and cry, stand in the carrier and rock back and forth, bite the metal carrier bars, blow his coat, and froth at the mouth, all the way there and home. Every trip was now a nightmare.

In the process of cleaning out a kitchen cabinet one day, I found a bottle of Bach Flower Rescue Remedy. I had totally dismissed the remedies when Sunny had talked me into trying them several years before. I hadn't noticed any change after taking a few, so I had shoved them in the cupboard and forgotten about them. Now, it popped into my head that I should try the drops on Bear at the next vet trip. The instructions were to rub four to five drops in his ears or on his paws. I decided to follow directions. Not a good idea. He became very upset as soon as the alcohol-preserved flower water touched his ears or his feet.

I had recently been studying more about energy fields and auras that surround all living things, and, some believe, even inanimate objects. As I again got Bear into his carrier with considerable difficulty, I suddenly felt compelled to put Rescue Remedy drops in my hands and run them through Bear's aura. It was, after all, energy medicine. I dumped a few drops of water into my cupped palm, added five drops of the essence, swiped my hands together, then quickly wiped him down, from nose to the tip of his tail, on both sides, then again down his back, never actually touching him.

I waited a few seconds and nothing happened. *Of course not... how silly, putting the "essence" of a flower on him. I really needed to throw this stuff out.* At the end of thirty seconds, Bear was reclining calmly in the carrier, fully alert, but acting like it was any other day. He stayed like that all the way to the vet and back, exhibiting none of the symptoms of the last few trips. *Maybe this wasn't just another of Sunny's crazy ideas!*

A few weeks later, I pulled a box containing a fifty-pound manager's chair from the back of my hatchback. I wrestled it part way out before it slammed downward, the point of the box hitting into the dent on the side of my right hand where the thumb meets the wrist. I watched all the blood leave the area and the initial numbness return as severe pain. I danced around screaming. Then I remembered the Rescue Remedy, ran into the house and grabbed that yellow-labeled, brown bottle and wiped a few drops over the swelling area. It wasn't quite instantaneous, but almost, about twenty seconds—and the excruciating pain ceased by about seventy percent, then slowly dissipated entirely. The area never did bruise. The bottle moved to the top of my first aid kit.

My medicine cabinet now contained two magical and effective healing remedies. I still used the essential oils and now I also had the amazing physical, mental, and emotional healing powers of the Bach Flower Essences. I began more in-depth study on both, and even found a few classes. The more I learned, the more fascinated I was. Part of that study was simply using the essences on the cats and seeing almost immediate results during thunder storms and vet trips.

When I got a mailer about another animal communication workshop that would include making flower essences, I signed up. Leta Worthington, an Animal Communicator who had helped me select some healing herbs back when Sami had been my only cat, had relocated to a ranch a two-hour drive away. I and about eight others would spend the week-end there, practicing interspecies communication and learning to make flower essences.

The flower essence instructions were easy: select the right plants with the right energy, add spring water, soak in sunshine, have patience, then add preservative and pour into bottles—a simplistic shorthand explanation for the making of effective healing remedies safe for all humans and *all* animals. The hard part was figuring out what healing properties each flower could contribute. Even after the class, I didn't understand how the process of selecting the right flower's essence worked, the same as I didn't understand the animal communication process—the how's and why's that made everything happen used to be important to me, but no longer. What I looked for now was the end result: did something work for me, or didn't it? Faith had overcome my suspicion, and I had felt first-hand the amazing way the essences had curtailed pain and anxiety. Had Sunny been there telling me it would work, then the placebo effect might be in force, but Sunny wasn't there. So far, I had never heard anyone say that the placebo effect worked with animals, but the essences definitely had worked on me, and on Bear

Back at home, I found the computer a source of ongoing amazement and help, an unimaginable learning opportunity. It became a substitute for watching television, for reading, and saved me hours and hours of tedious research in libraries as I always had questions about something. The rabbit trails were there when I took the time to follow them, one website with invaluable information linking to another clue, and then to another. I began educating myself daily about alternative therapies for animals, about naturopaths, and acupuncturists, and any health information, including vaccines and food, pertaining to cats. I found vets who were actually advocating no vaccines and no dry kibble. I finally started looking deeper into everything that Sunny had told me about, no matter how crazy it may have seemed initially. I took classes in energy healing, I researched everything I could find on cat health and well being. The more I read, the more upset I became.

It took hours and hours, but finally I found an answer to my long-ago question about Sami's death—an on-line veterinary article that confirmed rabies vaccinations could definitely cause severe neurological complications. I also found that the FDA had withdrawn the type of vaccine given to Sami shortly after his death. In trying to keep my cat well, I had allowed him to be killed. The circle of anger, guilt, and grief was a terrible conclusion to a traumatic and possibly needless death.

My faith in vets, those individuals I had entrusted the health of my animals to, was completely shattered, as it had been for me for doctors by that eye surgeon so long ago. I would trust them when I had no choice, I vowed, but now I would research everything in the health field before I sought medical advice, I would ask questions, and if I didn't, in my gut, feel the advice or treatment was good, I would seek another. Further, whenever possible, I would do everything I could through alternative medicine before trusting my safety and that of my cats to the modern medical and veterinary professions, as amazing as they sometimes were, as much researched, and investigated, and approved by the FDA. I'd adapt and adopt Sunny's motto as my own, going to a hospital only for major emergencies. Otherwise, I would first seek out appropriate alternative health practitioners.

There was one thing I never found the answer to on the computer and that was the curiosity of the cats' eyes. Bear and Bella had switched eye color. I liked Bear's blue eyes when he first came as a kitten, but in short order, as he became an adult, they had turned to a beautiful chartreuse. When he was about eight, those green eyes began having brown specks in them. Slowly, they turned the deep, golden-brown of a piece of amber, the brown specks obliterating the green. But wherever he had left his green eyes, Bella had slowly found them. Most kittens have blue eyes until around three months of age, but not Bella. She had come to me at eight weeks old with gorgeous golden brown eyes, and they stayed that way until Bear's began to turn brown years later. Now her baby brown eyes were almost the same chartreuse that Bear's had been. Had I not been able to look at some of their photos, I would have thought my memory was faulty. The vet said she had never heard of such a thing happening except in the kitten-blue to permanent-adult color.

The worrisome part for me was that Bear's eyes now had many dark brown spots and specks. Although his eyes glowed with health and zeal for life, I had seen these same specks in human eyes... old friends becoming older. I was jarred when I realized Bear's specks were a sign of his aging.

I was aging, too, and the tenant situation, or lack thereof, was making it imperative I make some major decisions. I decided I would put the house on the market in November, though the price of houses was still way down... but the mortgage payments weren't. I would just have to rent an apartment unless I could find a house with a yard to rent for the cats. The realtor warned me that it would be difficult.

Then my new toy, the computer, went crazy. Its death seemed imminent; I was no nerd so I scouted for a computer nerd and finally found an ad in the paper and called.

=^,-,^=

SWEETIE. "Hi, you said you repair computers. I've got a problem that the electronics shop couldn't fix. What is your experience?"

"I have an electronics degree, and I've been doing repair work for over ten years. I just finished a repair for a well-known country-and-western singing group."

I was surprised—the voice was female; in my experience, anyone could use a computer, but I had only heard of guys who could *fix* them. I had no idea whether her description of herself made her a good candidate or not, but I had to take a chance with someone. "Can I bring one to you?"

The address she gave was a small, old-time Austin home near the University. I handed Sweetie, a petite, blonde Southern Belle in her mid-30's, my computer, listed its symptoms, and left. She told me to come back in two days.

When I went back to pick up the computer, she told me it wasn't ready. Since I had seen her last, Sweetie had added a black eye to her sweet face, not exactly a typical computer nerd enhancement. She said she had fallen into a statue at her friend's house after a big argument with her boyfriend who had told her to get out. I noticed she was a bit wobbly and had a half-filled glass in her hand. She was desperately looking for a place to move to—no job, no car, no money, but she did have computer skills. I was a sucker.

"My house is on the market, but you can stay rent-free for a month to figure out what you're going to do. You'll have to keep your area tidy in case buyers show up, and help me with any computer issues. A month—then you need to move or start paying rent. Also, I'm a mile from public transportation."

A friend dropped off her belongings, and she moved in. When I left for work the morning after her arrival, she made breakfast for me. When I got home that night, the house was straightened up. I felt very pampered and was grateful for her contributions to the housework. Finally, someone was helping! She did look for work, but everything, including the economy and job-hunting post 9-11 was in such chaos that employers weren't hiring, and I could understand how difficult it was for her with no car.

Having Sweetie in the house to help was a definite mixed blessing, but the back-of-my-neck hair was there talking to me again. Finally, one slurred word too many, one misstep too many—like the one into the middle of my just completed stained-glass project—and I understood. I had lived with male alcoholics but never a female. I remembered mother gossiping, saying that "they say a woman alcoholic is always much worse than a man." I was learning that "they" were right.

First I found the empty wine bottles in the garbage, then found the adulterated bottles of booze under the sink. They had been there, unopened, for three years, since the New Year's Eve party that was iced out. The safety collars had now been opened and the vodka smelled like water. The vodka's absence, added to the occasional stumbling walk, mumbling speech, and mercurial mood changes added up to a headline: "The Lady Boozes."

I finally confronted her when, as far as I could tell, she was in a sober state. She denied everything, saying she had to take medicine sometimes that made people think she was drunk. I suggested she not take her medicine with a quart of wine or other booze.

Sweetie was one of the nicest, kindest people I had ever met. Until she drank. Then she turned into a mean bully, demanding, almost shoving food into my mouth when I refused to eat something she had cooked. She was, though, always gentle and concerned about Bear, when she could catch him. At times he would let her pick him up, but he would brace an arm against her chest, holding himself away; at other times, he would slide under a chair so she couldn't reach him.

As others had done, Sweetie acted as though little Bella was invisible. I wasn't surprised, though I just didn't understand it. Bella was so dainty, so cute, so sweet and kittenish even after she had matured. She lapped up attention like other cats lapped up cream, loving it when someone just talked to her. Few did, just that "Hello, Bella" when I introduced her, and then they would turn their attention back to Bear. I would see her watching with hungry eyes for attention as Bear held court, then she would slowly back away and disappear. Even though she was not comfortable with me picking her up anymore, I always wanted to cuddle and hug the hurt I imagined she felt, to tuck her into my heart and keep her safe from the neglect of visitors. Of course, my brain replayed the scientific lectures about how silly people were to reflect their own feelings onto an animal, the lectures I had believed for so long, but I now knew the truth—animals did have many human emotions.

Several weeks later, I came home from work intending to discuss with Sweetie what she was going to do about moving. Bear didn't meet me at the door, and a full-house search didn't produce him. I found Sweetie passed out in her bedroom, not even answering my knock.

"Sweetie! Sweetie! Where is Bear?"

"Whaaat?" she finally answered in a confused voice.

"Did you let Bear out?"

"Nooo. 'was cleanin' the house this morning, but never shaw him."

Knowing how irresistible any open door was to my cat, I projected the scene. She went out for a cigarette break. Open door, cat slides out, Sweetie doesn't notice, comes in, passes out, and Bear is over the fence.

After two hours of scouring the neighborhood, in a panic about him and furious at her as she stumbled down the street insisting she hadn't let him out, I was frantic when I called my communicator, who answered right away.

"Carol, Bear's gone and…"

"He's close. He can hear you calling."

"… I've been calling and calling. I've introduced myself to everyone in the neighborhood—we started looking at the end of the day. Now it's completely dark and…"

She interrupted firmly. "*He can hear you!* He's *inside* the house."

"… I don't know where else to look," I said, not totally registering what she was saying.

"He's *in* the house! Just keep calling and look through the house again."

As I hung up, I heard Sweetie calling from far away, "He's here! He's in the garage."

I took off through the house and jerked the inside garage door open. As usual, there were boxes stacked everywhere, now including Sweetie's belongings that took up over half the garage, floor to ceiling, and all the things I had boxed up when I listed the house. There were a few empty boxes, too, and a few of those without lids, like the one that a rigid Bear was now sitting in the middle of, his pupils wide and round and black, ears down, obviously terrified as he looked at me.

When I saw him, I read the posture and had a flash of insight into what had happened. He had taken to sleeping in boxes lately; he must have been curled up in one when he heard me frantically calling for him. Instead of coming to me, he stayed hidden, afraid to come out, thinking he was in trouble. I had never done more to him in his life physically after I discontinued the water bottle than take a wild swat at his rear when he ran off from doing something he wasn't supposed to, never connecting with that hairy pillow of a posterior. I was sure the only thing he felt was the indignity. But, if I scolded him in a really angry voice, he was devastated, and just seemed to melt into the floor. I now had the awful realization of how terribly upsetting *my* upset was to him. How had I not recognized it before?

I finally had the realization that my hanging on to Bear this way was *not right*. I had hated cats for decades, but now, I loved one *too* much. Bear, Bella, and Sami were deeply lodged in and loved from my heart—but Bear, Bear was my soul child, too, though I didn't understand why. How could I deal with it if, or when, I lost him permanently? I had heard a conversation on a talk show with mothers all swearing they loved all their children equally. Then they all confessed that there was always *one* that was a little more loved. That's the way it was for me with my kits.

Except for her drinking, I'd have let Sweetie continue to stay, but if she could buy booze and cigarettes, I figured she should be able to pay rent. She had a yard sale and sold almost all of her possessions, then went home to her preacher father and mother on the other side of the country, still in denial that she had any kind of drinking problem.

Now I recognized that the cats had to be affected by all this craziness with people moving in and out, with the mold chaos, with one crisis after another. It had been clearly shown to me by my little teacher, my valiant and self-confident Bear, so paralyzed with fear that he sat in a box for close to two hours while I called for him.

I also had to consider that one of my sources of support for much of my life, my ex-husband, had recently died... Even divorced, we had remained friends. I had always known that, if I called him in desperation about something, he would have come through for me. I was concerned about what would happen to my cats if I could no longer care for them—would someone else accept them, understand them, and love them as I did? I re-made my Will with provisions for the cats, anything to keep some sanity and security in my life.

Then there was the rumor of a reorganization at work, no one knowing what that would mean for our jobs. The house had been on the market for almost three months without a single offer, in fact, only one viewing. The real estate market was still falling, prices plunging. The job market was disastrous, jobs disappearing like popcorn at a movie theatre. Everyone was uneasy. I felt helpless, out of control, anxious, and unable to make a coherent decision, like being inside a washing machine, with very small respites, before I started spinning again. But I knew one thing. The renter situation had to stop. Our beloved house had to go. Somehow.

Chapter 35
LIFE CHANGES

Austin, Texas. May 2003. The house had been on the market for six months with no activity. I complained that the agent wasn't doing enough (or anything, actually.) She agreed to cancel our contract. I went to work the next day very frustrated; it looked like I *would* need another renter.

Then the dominos began to fall. First, there was a note on my desk to see my supervisor. My boss had a smile on her face when I walked in. "I'm sure you've heard the rumors of the necessity for a staff reduction?"

"Yes." *Oh dear, this was not going to be good news—why was she smiling?*

"In the supervisors' meeting today, we found out that, instead of laying people off, anyone close to retirement is being urged to retire early. And they will get a bonus if they leave before September 1. Are you interested?"

I shook my head. "I'm not eligible for another five years."

"According to the paperwork I got from payroll, you *are* qualified."

I walked out of her office in shock, just like on 9/11. I had longed for the day I could say "I'm outta here," but now I felt unbalanced and unprepared. I went home to wrestle with the financial possibilities.

That very evening, the next domino in line fell. Synchronicity at work. I had a call from a sales agent.

"Hi, my niece is looking for a house, and I saw yours on our office tour awhile back, but I can't find a listing for it. Has it sold?"

"No, I cancelled the listing, but I'm intending to put it back on the market." I explained what had happened.

"Oh. Well, then, can I bring my niece to see it?"

We set an appointment, and I called the old listing agent, saying I might be getting an offer from an agent that had viewed it while the house was under her contract. She graciously said she would not hold me to any agreement.

The next day, my house was sold! The buyers secured an inspector to be sure everything was all right. I held my breath.

The inspectors came and reported no evidence of any problems, only a very small area in the attic at the back of the house where there had been carpenter ants at one time. There was no evidence of mold. Even if there had been, the insurance companies had settled down to reality again, and her insurance company would insure the house. Our home was sold! Alternately excited, sad, and scared, I grabbed up Bear and danced with him around the living room while Bella peeked at us, big eyed, from around the corner.

I applied for retirement the very next day. I had been working since I was fourteen—what would retirement look like for me? Jobs provided grounding, a connection to people and a place. That connection would be lost. I felt a bit of panic as I tried to imagine what this change would truly mean. Thereafter, my regular workday was often interrupted by overwhelming excitement and major fear at the huge change to come.

Less than three weeks later, two years after I had found the mold, I retired. The following week, we moved to an apartment. My head was swimming from all the changes, and alternately rejoicing and panicking at not having the routine of a job, even one I hated, to provide stability.

I was also having difficulty comprehending that this new life was real—jumping, or more like stumbling, out of bed, and then remembering there was nowhere I had to be. With some of the bonus money, I bought my first-ever new car. The car helped to alleviate the feeling of personal oldness that was creeping into my spirit. Retired people were old—what did that make me? Always, retirement had been an unachievable dream, signifying a change of attitude, a slowing down, as well as total freedom. I didn't want to slow down. I hadn't leapt my tall buildings yet, I hadn't left a gift to humanity. When was that going to happen? I had to hurry.

The first step was a move to an apartment. The two big single guys above me worked the swing shift. Exercise time for their very large pit bull was 1 a.m., and the exercise was chase-the-dog-that-is-chasing-the-ball-all-around-the-apartment. Bella was terrified when the ceiling started shaking, and she cowered under the bed. Bear stayed on the bed unmoving, staring up at the ceiling until there was silence again, usually half an hour later.

Bear could only go outside on a leash now. The grass patches in all the concrete were few and probably loaded with poisons. I'd clip some grass blades and take them home, and wash and feed them to the cats, which Bella loved. That was her compensation for having to stay inside now. There was no way I could let her out in the apartment complex safely. I manufactured reasons to shop just to be out of the apartment as much as possible. I really hated that apartment though I recognized that, for many people in the world, it would have been a palace, but, after my last house, there was no elbow room, no wide windows, not enough sunshine, and always, I felt a restlessness, a needing to get away. *No, Sunny, I didn't like the energy.*

I was now doing *a lot* of house hunting. I had been too overwhelmed to coordinate buying a new house, selling my old one and moving somewhere all at the same time, so an apartment had seemed a good half step. I still hadn't found a house when the six-month lease was up. I reluctantly renewed for another six months, the shortest time possible. Then I hurt my back, twisting as I reached for something the wrong way. Two months later, I was still in excruciating pain, chug-a-lugging Ibuprofen for some relief.

Both cats were there for me, in bed, one on each side of me. I would feel one get up, then hear the scratches in the cat box, the rattle of food in the bowl as they tried to capture the best morsel, then the lapping of water, and he, or she, would cuddle up to my vacant side, and the other cat would leave to attend to her or his needs. They never both left at the same time; one was *always* with me. I was in bed, knocked out by meds, except to go to my litter box or fix a TV dinner. Caring for them, the bending to put down food and water, was excruciating.

Finally, I recovered. Bear and I went back to slow walks around the complex. One day we were at the back of the apartments in a natural tree and grass space the size of a small house lot. Bear was at the end of his lead, mimicking a basset hound, nose to the ground. I stared up, almost hypnotized at the peaceful, lazy drifting of a hawk way up in the cloudless, intensely blue Texas sky. The big bird was coming slowly down in a circular pattern, the circle getting smaller and smaller as it glided on the air currents.

I went back to watching Bear nuzzling a leaf. The hawk shadow passed over us, and I was surprised at how large it was. Then the thought hit me like a physical force. The hawk was hunting! Hunting my leaf-sniffing Bear who was only five feet away! I began yelling and grabbed him, yanking him up into my arms.

"Go away!" I shouted up at the hawk as I headed for the apartment as fast as I could while carrying almost twenty pounds of hawk meat. The shadow passed over us again. I looked up; the raptor gave one final graceful circle, now down below the level of a second-story roof, then flapped those big wings and rose straight into the sky.

"Oh, Bear, you were hawk bait! Didn't you see him? You weren't even paying any attention, were you?" My voice was scolding, hoping he understood me. *Another reason not to walk a cat outside. Why ever had I thought it would be fun to do so?*

Then came the night I arrived home late and was met by silence. Bella was sitting in front of the door, waiting, but not Bear. I walked all the way to the back before I found him, stretched out on the floor. When I called to him, he didn't get up, instead looking at me, a pleading look in his eyes. I rushed him to the emergency vet's. After an endless wait, it was our turn, around 1 a.m.

The vet couldn't find anything definitive; the hip muscles appeared very weak, but his joints all seemed to be working fine. She decided it was probably a pulled muscle, gave him a shot for pain, and we went home. The next day he was back to normal.

Finally, after what felt like a decade of apartment life instead of one retirement year, I bought a house, half the size of our last much-loved home but without the need for a tenant. Life was going to be good, I thought, as the movers brought in the last box and squeezed it into the living room. "That's everything, ma'am."

"How much do I owe you?" I went over to sit in the recliner, the only place not covered with boxes, checkbook in hand. As I sat down, my foot slipped on the new flooring, and I felt something rip in my knee. "Aooowwwww! Ohmigod." I began screaming.

"Ma'am?"

"My knee!" I was crying, the pain was so intense. My check was dotted with tears when I finally was able to finish writing it, my hand shaking. Apparently embarrassed at seeing me cry, they quickly left me surrounded by two truckloads of mostly unlabeled boxes that contained my life.

I went to see the only Orthopedist at my usual Medical Association, a new, fresh-faced version of the star of the old TV series, Dr. Doogie Howser, boy genius.

"You have a torn medial meniscus. I've got some pill samples that should help the pain. Come back in six weeks, and we'll take another look at it."

"What will happen then?"

"Well, there's not much we can do."

I was perplexed. "Don't they operate all the time on people with torn menisci?"

"Almost everyone has tears by the time they get to your age, so surgery doesn't really help old people."

"So, you're not going to do *anything*? Then why am I coming back?"

"Well, for follow-up."

Six weeks later, I had used up all the pain pill samples and was still unable to tolerate the pain of walking. The pills weren't helping the pain, but they were making me sleep. I never could get the hang of crutches so I was basically an invalid. Any movement, even an inch, in any direction, was followed by such intense pain I would almost pass out, and I kept getting worse, not better.

By now, I had become severely depressed, so depressed I began making calls to arrange to give my beloveds away. I couldn't take care of them any more. I was in despair knowing I couldn't really take care of myself. What was I going to do? I had no family to assist, friends had their own families, work, and private lives. I was hiring help to pick up groceries and cat needs, and to do some cleaning and laundry, but that couldn't last for long. Then I ran out of the pain pills. I called for a refill.

Unlike the sample packets, the contra-indications were attached to the sack containing the prescription. I read them, getting angrier and angrier. *"May cause depression if taken for more than two weeks."* After six weeks, I was definitely depressed and had been for weeks. Because moving at all was so painful, I had betrayed my own rule and not looked up the pill information after the doctor's failure to warn me.

Finally, an acquaintance called. "I'm sorry to hear you aren't feeling well. There is a guy I want to refer you to. He brought this technique back from England and is the only one in the U.S. who can do it. I went to him for a headache I'd had for weeks. He just put some slight pressure on my neck and head, and I walked out pain-free. Tell him I sent you, or, I understand you are having trouble driving—I can come and get you if you want."

The person who recommended him drove me to his office and pushed me into his little treatment room on my desk chair from home. Thirty minutes, and the normal charge for a co-pay later, I hobbled out, walking more than I had in two months. After four more visits over the course of two weeks, I was experiencing only minor pain with sustained walking. He called himself a "manual therapist" and the technique was quick, gentle, and easy. Even after treatment, I had no idea what he did, though he muttered something about body fluids when I asked.

My weakening faith in the medical profession reached a new low, with a special contempt for that "doctor" who had demolished my self esteem, did nothing to help my pain, and, without any warnings, prescribed pills that could have been the source of my demise at the rate I was descending into depression.

Since I could stand again, the first thing I did was unpack, finally, enough to find a fry pan and the saucepan. I reminded myself I was retired and that it was OK to work slowly, going through one box every few days. Life was getting better again—I could walk a little bit, I could drive, I could take care of the cat mom duties, and I could stand long enough to take a shower. Things were definitely looking up.

Chapter 36
MAYHEM & A MIRACLE

Round Rock, Texas. September 2004. The house I had moved to was half the size of our Oak Hill house in what appeared to be a quiet neighborhood in Round Rock, an Austin suburb. I bought it because it was affordable, needed decorating help, and the backyard could be easily made safe for the cats. After some redecorating, including painting the walls and replacing the treacherous flooring, it was looking much better. But when the movers dumped everything into it, and I had then incapacitated myself on the treacherous new floor, I was not appreciating anything about the place, even after the seller stopped by, came in, and her mouth dropped open. "I can't believe I lived in such a pretty house," she said. Ah, Feng shui.

Unfortunately, the redecorating didn't make it grow, and once I started unpacking I belatedly realized it wasn't much bigger than the dollhouse I had bought when first arriving in Texas. Since moving in, I was hearing sirens going off day and night, helicopters flying overhead, their searchlights bouncing around the yards in the dark. The house was two blocks from a high school—I wished I had known there was so much noisy security.

After settling in, I decided to take a walk and scout out the neighborhood without Bear. As I turned onto the street behind our house, I began feeling really relaxed. The breeze blew by again, caressing my cheeks, bringing a smell I remembered from the 1970s. Ah, Mary Jane! I finally put it all together—the sirens, the helicopters, the cop cars. How could I have been so oblivious? There had been no warning from the Realtor. The duplexes lining the street just over the fence behind me must be home to marijuana users, maybe with gardens of delight in their back yards, and most probably drug dealers.

One of the reasons I had chosen this house was the wonderful backyard, with plants, a producing grape vine, flowers, bushes, all in delightful disarray—so like my grandparents' house when I was a child. There was a small vegetable garden, a little garden shed, and a nostalgia-producing white picket fence dividing a vegetable garden from flowers and trees.

I put up chicken wire on top of the privacy fence to keep the cats from climbing over or other cats from climbing in. There was only one small place that worried me, up by the house, but I was sure Bear couldn't get up there. He couldn't even climb a tree with his short legs and heavy body; he'd take a flying run, jump, grab the trunk and hang before sliding all of four feet back to the ground. And seven years before, Bella had promised to never to leave the yard. She never had, so no worries there. I felt safe in letting the kits outside as long as I was nearby, Bear finally unfettered by harness and lead.

One night, I was reading when I felt the bed dip. I looked up, expecting that Bear had jumped up on it. Instead, two big white paws were hooked over the edge of the bed, slowly sliding away. He couldn't make it onto the bed that he had been jumping up on to his whole life. I got up, picked him up and put him on the bed. He seemed embarrassed and walked over to the far corner and settled down, turning his back to me.

The next day, I got a footstool and put it by the bed to make it a two-level climb.

"Look, Bear, here's a way to get up on the bed."

He looked, turned away, and walked away into the kitchen, refusing to put a foot on that stool. It became a nightly ritual; he was unable to get enough spring from his hips to get onto the bed. He would walk around the bed and try to jump up, then go to another corner and try. Always, he could get his front paws up there, but then slid off.

Finally, I started carrying him to bed with me. I would swoop him up, give him a smooch on the head, and say, "Hey, Bear-Bear, let's go to bed. You are such a big boy, I can hardly carry you. But I can't go to bed without you, now can I?"

I praised him and petted him, hoping to make him think I was carrying him because I wanted to, not because I thought he needed my help. I was sure that he was embarrassed and felt diminished by his inability to follow Bella as lithely up onto the bed as he had his whole life.

A late night TV commercial advertised a set of plastic steps for pets. I ordered one, sure I was wasting money, but I had to try. If he wouldn't get on the stool, why would he use stairs? I assembled them, lined them up against the bed, called him, and stood back to watch.

He didn't *like* the stairs, he *loved* them. Perhaps they reminded him of the time when he and Sami chased each other up and down the long staircase in the condo, perhaps it was his idea of feeling young and empowered again. Whatever took his fancy, he would run up them and stand on the bed, head held high as though he was surveying his kingdom, then he would scurry down, turn and run right back up, over and over, at all times of the day and night. I felt glad that they made him happy, but both secure and sad, in knowing that he would not be jumping fences anymore.

The neighbor on one side of our fence was a single, employed woman with a terrier and a smaller mixed breed. I was working in the kitchen the day I heard her dogs barking and barking. And barking. I went outside, saw Bear chasing a bug, but didn't notice anything out of the ordinary. I didn't see Bella but figured she was in a favorite place of hers, behind the shed.

With the dogs still frantically barking, I decided to investigate; I brought out my ladder so I could peer over the privacy fence toward the barking to see what was wrong. The terrier was in a crate on the neighbor's patio.

But, *ohmigod*, I was horrified to see Bella on the far side of their yard. Her other, smaller dog, still twice the size of Bella was barking and threatening and lunging toward her, stopping just a few feet in front of her at some invisible line that apparently only he could see. He had Bella trapped, backed up to the fence. Her head was lowered and swinging from side to side like a maddened bull, her stance defensive, her tail a bottle brush. There was no way out! She couldn't go forward away from the fence because the dog was there. If she made a 180° turn, the dog could grab her at the moment she crouched to spring over the fence. And turning 90° would still have her trapped against the fence unless she could outrun the dog and crouch to spring over the gate before he could grab her, probably an impossibility.

Heart racing, I ran back through the house, grabbing a hammer from the garage with some vague notion of tearing down the neighbor's fence, or knocking off the gate lock, or—something. *"Come on, come on, hurry faster, she won't stay there long!"* I was in one of those movies of the person running full tilt but barely moving forward. I knew I'd never be able to get there in time. *But I had to try.*

My legs felt like pudding from adrenaline, my mind racing, looking for a solution. Even if I could get to her, I wouldn't be able to hang on to her. As terrified as she was, she could tear up the rescuer—me—as animals did in defense. And Bella *was* terrified. When I got to the neighbor's gate and peeked through the gaps, she was as I had last seen her, still backed against the fence, still swinging her head, with the dog in front of her, still yapping.

The fence itself looked like the best possibility of getting in as the gate had a big lock on it. Maybe if I banged on the boards—they were old—to loosen the nails... I jerked and pried, trying to wiggle the nails loose enough to yank them out with the hammer. It was working! First board down. Now the second. Coming down faster than the first. The nails were rusted. Dog was still yapping. *That was good, wasn't it?* I now had a narrow opening, two boards wide.

I squeezed as much of myself sideways through the twelve inches as I could. My arm went through, but then I met resistance, unable to force my head and boobs through. Bella was a perfect facsimile of a Halloween cat, hair standing up, low growls coming from her throat, bushy tail whipping back and forth. There was no recognition in her eyes that were black with panic when she turned her head toward me, looking for a way out.

The dog continued to yap and lunge and threaten. The two boards I had pulled down were old and rotted, or I wouldn't have been able to get them loose from the cross railing. The ones next to those two were newer, with screws instead of nails. I couldn't bang them loose quickly, and I couldn't squeeze through. It was up to Bella.

I called to her, doubting that she would respond. If she didn't, I had no ideas left. I could only hope that she would run through the hole in the boards, and that I could stop the dog that would surely follow before it leapt on her. I knew this was probably a futile hope. If she made it through, she would run heedlessly. I might never find her again. I kept meaning to get the new micro-chipping done but kept forgetting. But lost was better than dead. At least she would have a chance.

"Bella, Bella, honey, come to Mama. Come through the fence." I crooned and sent her mental pictures of her running to me, through the hole, jumping into my arms. I knew, though, that we were both so rattled it was unlikely she would "hear" me, especially with only my novice skills at telepathy which were now probably so panicked any message I was sending would probably be too garbled. She had gone too far into cat. I coaxed again, totally focused on that little scared baby.

"Come on, Bella, run to me as fast as you can!" I pleaded, mentally sending pictures of her turning and running, and also calling her. "Come Bella. Bella come to Mama."

Then, in disbelief, I saw her make a 90° left hand turn. She raced straight toward me along the fence! She bolted through the narrow opening. She started up my legs like the farm cats used to. Climbed all the way to my left shoulder, wrapped her front legs around me. She buried her head in my neck, front claws hanging on to the back of my shirt. The dog stood with his shoulders stopped by the boards, still yapping.

I was shocked. This was the cat who, from a month after I had gotten her seven years before, would fling herself about, scream, holler, and moan as though she knew I was going to kill her *every* time I picked her up. Except for that explaining of the yard so many years before, ten seconds was her adult limit at being held before she would go into histrionics.

Now, here she was, quiet in my arms, clinging to me, shivering, trembling, but refusing to let go. I had expected this cat, in her panic, to just blindly run and run and run toward any tiny space she could tuck herself into.

Had she not totally trusted me, this entire episode could have ended in disaster. All the house lots touching the neighbors were surrounded by privacy fences, one after another. I wouldn't be able to get into their yards to find her. If she got out, she had no street smarts—she would be totally vulnerable to any passing car or animal. A few months before, the vet had affirmed that Bella had a hearing loss. She had just done the *only* thing that day that she could have done to keep herself safe. *She trusted me!*

I blessed my habit of teaching my cats to come when I called them—always their first lesson, starting with Sami's vitamins all those years ago. When they heard their name, a reward would follow—din-din, play time, treats, and now, life. Bella, whether thru her own instinct, or hearing me call her, or receiving my mental pictures, had run to me in complete trust, relying on me for her safety rather than trusting her own wild instincts. Which meant my wild child trusted me! *Or I was a really great communicator.* It didn't really matter which was correct.

Somehow, while still holding her, I put the boards back up with one hand, enough to fake the dog out for a few minutes. I had already taken my neighbor's fence half down; I didn't want to explain to her that I had also let her dog get lost. I hobbled back to the house, only then recognizing the leftover pain from the knee injury. Bella clung to me, quiet, all the way home.

I dumped her into the living room and hurried to the kitchen to get Bear into the house from the back yard, then rushed out to the garage for more nails. Belatedly, I realized Bella could have misplaced her terror right onto Bear's nose and eyes; I berated myself for not thinking clearly, again. By the time I got back in the house, I realized once more what incredible cats I had. He was nuzzling and licking her, comforting her, and she was lying quietly, letting him.

The dogs had finally stopped barking. I re-nailed the boards. When the neighbor got home that evening, I explained what had happened, offering to pay a professional to replace the boards. She was forgiving and refused. However, I later repaid her several times over. Unlike Bear who went over fences, the terrier dug his way under the fence, and I rescued him as he ran down the street—twice.

She told me that was the reason he was in the crate that day, because he kept getting out. I always shuddered at the realization that, had he been loose, Bella could not have saved herself from two dogs.

For days, I kept coming back to this incident, marveling over and over at the way things had happened. For seven years, Bella had wandered the yard of the other house, never breaking her promise to Carol and I that she would always stay inside the fence. I realized, too late, that I had never asked Carol to explain to Bella that she needed to stay inside *this* fence after we moved, and the place I had worried that Bear might go over, in her eyes, probably wasn't a fence. I was humbled at how sacred she had kept her promise for all those years, as well as by her incredible act of trust and bravery in running to me. On the other hand, she was still peeing everywhere.

Then the dog woman next door moved out. A beautiful young Hispanic couple—both of them—were her replacements. He had rescued me when I was doing some tree trimming and had gotten a saw tangled in the limbs, though our conversation was brief—my Spanish as limited as his English. They had three little boys, all under six, who were beautiful, bright-eyed, and harmlessly ornery as sin. How their mom had the energy to deal with them was beyond my wildest imaginings.

One sunny afternoon, all was quiet in the neighborhood; I took myself out to my deck and sat down to do some relaxing by reading. A few minutes later, something fell out of the cloudless sky and landed on my book. Puzzled, I picked it up to try to figure out what it was and where it had come from. I finally deduced that it was a bone, about the size of a small chicken wing bone. I checked the sky again—no clouds for anything to hide behind, just clear Texas blue. I shrugged it off as not important and went back to reading.

And soon received another bone, apparently from the gods. What the heck? There was not a sound anywhere. I didn't see any birds, no airplane, just me sitting on the deck with no one and nothing moving. Finally, I had a possibility thought. Maybe... I got up slowly and very quietly walked over to the fence the Hispanic neighbors shared with me. I peeked through a knothole. And saw one of the boys, around age five, standing there staring at the fence, wringing his hands together. Ah ha! I now had an explanation for the flying chicken bone. So how was I going to handle it? My sense of mischief set in. In the deepest, rumbling voice I could muster, I thundered, *"IIII sawww YOuuuuuu."* The reaction was instantaneous; the handsome little prince turned and ran as fast as he could straight back to their house. And I knew it was safe now to go back to my pleasant afternoon of reading, undeterred by old bones hurled a remarkable distance by a little kid half the height of the privacy fence, and across the space of at least twenty feet. I was sure he would be trying out for the Texas Rangers in a decade or so.

Unfortunately, this family had many relatives who all gathered at their house almost every weekend. At least eight or more cars lined the street in front, and mariachi music played late into the night. I gritted my teeth and tried to enjoy the music. For hours. My tolerance ended early on Thanksgiving morning, ten months after I had moved in. I was still in bed, admiring the rainbow formed by the crystal hanging in the east window, when the commotion started. I couldn't understand why I was hearing a pig squealing, a sound familiar from my farm days when I was trying to herd them somewhere they didn't want to go—usually back into the pen they had gotten out of again.

I got up and looked out onto a once-red, rusted-out pickup truck squeezed between the houses, parked directly under my window. Four men in jeans and T-shirts were wrestling with a distressed hog in the truck bed. The squealing went on and on, as did the shouting from the men, probably trying to figure out how to hold on to the porker. I sat down on the bed wondering how I was going to like living next door to a pig again when the squealing accelerated into frantic bellows, then stopped abruptly. I went back to the window. The pig quit thrashing, and, as I watched, it crumbled, dead. The men wrestled the corpse out of the truck and into the backyard, laughing and slapping each other on the back, happy that they were well on their way to a Thanksgiving dinner of pit barbeque.

I was horrified and nauseated. I had been fortunate in never witnessing any of the killing on the farm, except for the beheaded chickens. I didn't care much for those hens who pecked, chased, and tried to claw me, even when I wasn't stealing their eggs; I was almost as afraid of the chickens as I had been of the cats.

I didn't wait to call my real estate agent, not caring that she was probably in the midst of making Thanksgiving dinner.

"Hi. Happy Thanksgiving. I want to buy a house. How soon can we go look?"

She laughed. "You just bought a house, remember?"

"No, I mean I want to buy a different house. A house where the helicopters don't fly over my garden all night, I don't get high when I go for a walk, the ground doesn't rumble for hours when the neighbors are reparing their construction equipment, and the neighbors on the other side don't butcher pigs under my window on Thanksgiving morning."

There was a moment of silence as she digested the information. "I'll call you Monday."

"OK, but I'm serious. As soon as possible. We'll have to do some incredible financing, but it can be done. I'll make it happen. Sorry about messing up your dinner."

I hung up and put a casserole in the oven. Accompanied by the wafting smells of barbecue, I shared Thanksgiving macaroni and cheese with the cats. *God, I hated the thought of moving again.*

Chapter 37
THE OLD BOY & THE GOOD GIRL

Round Rock, Texas. Fall 2004. Little/Big/Mister Bear was suddenly fifteen years old, over seventy-five, depending on which chart, in human years. *How had that happened?* My Bear was not wearing his age well, seeming to become fragile in front of my eyes. His movements were no longer lithe and easy; he moved with the stiffness of the old, especially when getting up from the floor.

Occasionally, I'd find him sitting and staring at nothing, like the elderly person that walks into a room and can't remember why. He was sleeping much more than had been his life-long habit. My energizer bunny was running out of juice. Carol confirmed that he was having some senile moments, and all those walkies had taken a toll on his hip joints.

In every other way, though, he was still my wonderful Bear. He loved to hide in plain sight and watch me acting a fool looking for him. Each morning now, he was spooned against me, his head under my chin, my first awareness of the day. When I turned on the tap in the bathroom sink, he'd still come running and try to jump up to the counter. I had to lift him up now, but he was so eager to drink out of the faucet that he didn't seem to mind. He insisted on plopping his big fat feet onto the computer keyboard when I tried to work, and he followed me from room to room, supervising anything I was doing. Any time he wasn't sleeping, he was with me, almost clinging to me.

I made a conscious effort to pay more attention to him, brushing his long coat while he obligingly stretched out so I could get to all the parts of him. His fur would fly everywhere, and every other day I would end up with a ball of hair that, when crushed tightly, was the size of a golf ball as his coat became noticeably thinner.

Then there was a repeat of the episode of a year before when he couldn't walk. Again, to the vet, again, the same results. Our walkies now decreased in length and frequency, though I would not curtail them completely. Bear would often sit down a few houses after our walk started, seeming to ask me to carry him home. It was easier than it had been; his weight had varied by only a pound or two since he had reached adulthood, but now he was losing weight. I talked with Carol, and we finally figured out that the pain was coming from the same area seen long ago in an X-ray—an osteophyte type of bone formation at the convergence of the backbone and the tail, pressing on the nerves in his back. This made sense when coupled with his inability to jump any more–the backward bend would put pressure on the backbone and tail area.

The vet recommended a once-every-three-days dose of aspirin; it made him wild and crazy. She recommended pain meds. He tore around the house, crying out guttural sounds, pressured to keep moving. I knew this reaction from medication personally, the cure being as bad as the cause. I felt so bad for my strong little Bear. The vet had nothing else to offer.

I tried a traditional acupuncturist. Unlike many vets who claim they can do acupuncture after a few veterinary school classes, traditionally-trained acupuncturists take hundreds of hours of coursework. It was a forty-five minute drive, one way. After every visit, Bear would come home relaxed and limber. But a few days later, he would be in obvious pain again. He had never been a floor cat, but now he spent most of his time there instead of in his favorite chair, a sign to me that he was hurting again.

Bear continued to have bouts of severe pain, obvious to any onlooker—limping, or trying to walk but then sinking to the floor. Eventually, we stopped acupuncture when the time in between the expensive treatments seemed to last a shorter and shorter time. I tried Reiki but saw little improvement physically though he seemed more relaxed after the treatment. Despite my knowledge of alternative remedies, and in spite of my spending hours on the Internet looking at cat vet sites, I couldn't find any help in the US, just meds available only in Canada and Australia. All I could do was to act like I was picking him up just to love on him—which I was—instead of picking him up to lessen his pain without hurting his pride.

Although my Internet searches didn't give me any help for his pain control, it had been valuable for a different reason. At last, I had a confirmed answer to Sami's death. I found a website with the proof: the symptoms, the time of potential death from the time of vaccination, everything matched *exactly* what had happened to Sami. All of it was there, in Internet living color. By accident or carelessness, the vaccinations had killed my Sami. I'd never know whether the vets didn't know and should have, or knew and continued anyway.

Bella, eight years younger than Bear, also seemed to be aging rapidly. I'd call and call for her, but she wouldn't come. I had her vet-checked again. Even with cymbals clashing behind her head, Bella was oblivious. This was the little girl who liked to wake me up to the tune of wind chimes, the one who would sit on the bed and meow and meow, singing, at different rhythms and patterns. She had done it for years before I had asked Carol about it.

"What does she want when she does that? She doesn't sound upset, but it goes on for a long time."

"Oh, she's happy; she's singing."

As soon as I heard that, I had recognized that it was true—singing her meow song to herself. Now when I called Bella, often there was no response; she was almost deaf.

I also noticed that her eyes sometimes looked cloudy, at other times transparent, as though the beautiful green color of her adult eyes was dissolving. One eye was no longer tracking right. I took her to the vet's. My suspicions were confirmed—she was also going blind.

She was still doing her periodic wild-child actions, careening around the living room, leaping up the walls, yowling at times, other times growling deep in her throat as she had the day she had been backed against the fence by the neighbor's dog. Bear watched but never interfered.

And she was still making my life miserable with her peeing. Bella had never weighed more than six pounds; how something so little could put out so much liquid was a mystery to me. The only pattern was the periodic end-of-my-patience, unproductive visits to another vet—they didn't even bother to test her urine anymore, just gave her more antibiotics, then there would be a brief remission, then the peeing again. I was beyond frustrated and realized one day that I just could not continue to deal with her. The incessant laundry, the constant carpet cleanings and deodorizing, never knowing when I would pick up a wet pillow, a soaked towel, or a stinking piece of clothing—it was overwhelming. She was especially attracted to plastic sacks and paper. Amazingly, she had never doused the sacreds: the sofa, my recliner, the bed, any of which probably would have been her death warrant. Then it happened, the last straw that broke my back. I went to bed and climbed into cold, wet, smelly sheets. Bella had violated our most sacred space.

There was only one thing I could do. No one would want to adopt her. I couldn't let her just stay outside—not almost deaf and blind. I would not leave her locked away in a bathroom. And I had to accept that there was nothing I could do to fix her—not training, not vets, not medicines, not alternative practices or energy medicine—nothing; they had all failed. Every day was a struggle.

I made the decision to call Carol and tell Bella good-bye; then I would take her to the vet for euthanasia. Eight years of cleaning up urine almost daily was way more than I had ever bargained for. I couldn't understand how she could try so hard to please me about *everything* else, yet would not, or could not, stop urinating anywhere and everywhere. But the why didn't matter any more. I sometimes just sat and cried and cried, feeling like a failure. I had tried so hard to be a good cat mom, and now I was going to get rid of her like a piece of garbage, and I loved her so much. I was devastated.

I picked up the phone and dialed. "Carol? I've got to tell Bella good..."

"She's having seizures." Her voice interrupted, emphatic and firm. Stunned, I waited for her to say more.

"I was coming home today in the car, and all at once I just knew. She has seizures, that's why I've always said there was just something not right about her brain, but I couldn't figure out what."

"Oh, that can't be. I've never seen her fall down, or black out, no frothing or extremity contractions or...."

"No, not the Grand Mal."

"Oh no!" I was stunned into silence as realization from my training at the State Hospital about seizures—the whole picture— emerged.

"You mean the complex partial seizures—the 'absence' seizures!" I felt the shock and then the surety of rightness rushing through me.

"That's why she acts so confused, why she doesn't remember, and why she flies around the room, and the staring... that explains it all!" It felt like I had been in a dark room and someone had suddenly turned a spotlight on and everything became clear and totally obvious. Why had I *never* suspected? Why had the *vets* never suspected?

"And why she keeps peeing everywhere. No wonder she was always so confused about what she had done wrong. She had no idea what we were trying to tell her because she had no idea, no memory, of what she had done," said Carol.

I was sure I was hearing my heart break at the unfairness. How many times had I punished her, confining her to a small area with the cat box, yelling in frustration, showing her I was angry with her, dragging her to vet after vet with her being poked and prodded, dealing with a different litter, a different litter box, a different location, and pills, and more pills. I wanted to curl up in a little ball because I hurt so bad that she had suffered for so long because of our collective human unknowingness. The mystery of Bella was finally solved.

We went immediately to the vet, and I told her what Carol had said. She didn't believe me, another vet who didn't believe in anything that couldn't be proven by X-ray or test tube, but she finally agreed to do a trial of a seizure medication before moving on to the death needle.

At Carol's suggestion, I found a compounding pharmacy, something I had never heard of before. They mixed the Phenobarbital prescription into a fish flavor. Dosing was no problem—Bella would smack her lips after every dropper full. If I forgot it was medicine time, I would find her sitting and staring intently at the front of the refrigerator, reminding me.

Within a week, her behavior was perfect, no puddles, no wild lunges at the walls. Her natural sweetness was now in full bloom, now that I could look at her without the pee clouding my eyes. She would even, occasionally, let me pick her up and hug her without flinging herself all around. I found a lot of reasons to pick her up. After all my raging against vets and medicine, the Phenobarbital had given me a cat that I could whole-heartedly love, without reservation or anger, after over eight years of hell. I blessed Carol every day I picked up some laundry, a plastic bag, a blanket, and found it pristine. And I would search out Bella again and tell her what a *good girl* she was. I didn't think I could ever forgive myself for not loving her as I wanted to for those first eight years.

Bella had tried my patience beyond anything I could have imagined. There had been times I felt like throwing her out into the street, followed by remorse as I remembered Carol's oft-repeated conversation that Bella really was trying to please me but couldn't understand what I wanted. As much as I had loved Sami, and as much as I loved Bear, little Bella had taken over a large chunk of my heart with her both wild and gentle ways, with the faith she had shown as she ran to me and away from the dogs that awful day, and the connection between us as I saw her trying to be friends with those who ignored her. Even at half the size of the boys, she had a heart as big as theirs. And she had connected to a place deep in my childhood heart and helped to heal it. She was *such a good girl was my sweet Bella!*

Chapter 38
BEAR'S MASTERPIECE

Cedar Park, Texas. Fall 2005. Besides just getting out and away from Pig House, part of my urgency to buy a new house was for Bear. My biggest wish was that I could give him more freedom, especially from that darn harness. I was looking for a place where that could happen.

Since leaving Alaska, I'd had the romantic dream of living in a cabin in the woods. However, practicality intruded, and I realized that living alone, miles from any town services, probably wasn't a good idea for an older, single female. It would have worked in my youth, but like Bear, I was getting stiffer the older I got.

My real estate agent showed up as promised the Monday after Thanksgiving, and we started house hunting again. It never took me long to evaluate a house, and I was always very verbal.

"Yuck, what an ugly yard."

"What's wrong with it?" she asked.

"Doesn't have any trees."

"What do you call that?" she pointed.

I sniffed my disdain at the scrawny, six-foot thing. "A bush."

"Well, you do know it's going to be next to impossible to get financing, that you're probably going to lose a lot of money... whether for a bush *or* a tree."

My agent was conventional in all things. Since becoming a cat mom, I had become less and less conventional as the years rolled by. My agent was the epitome of what I had been—conservative—but I had become more open to possibilities instead of negating everything because there might be a problem.

"I'll make it work," I promised her. "Don't forget, I was a real estate agent in Alaska, and we did more unconventional financing there than bank financing. Some people paid with gold nuggets. You find me a house, and I'll make the financing work. Somehow. I do still have a couple of small gold nuggets I panned myself."

"OK, if you say so," she said.

"It's all in the details. Now, let me feed your car some gas and you some Chinese food for your efforts."

As we headed onward, I said, "There's something else I want to tell you which is how much I really appreciate your patience and willingness to work with me, especially when you don't believe in the outcome. I know we just did this a year ago, but that house was a mistake. I really didn't like the house much, just the feeling of nostalgia in the yard. That's the first real mistake of a house I've ever bought. There were other houses I didn't love, but they were right for us for the time. I just know there's another place for us."

As we ate our rice, I threw in another reassurance. "Neither the bones—the house bones—nor the yards have been right on what we've seen so far. And I'm pretty sure my house will sell quickly since I've redecorated, and for enough to get out of it OK."

"Well, I'm glad you're so certain. There *are a few more* listed that we haven't seen, and I've got nothing else to do for the rest of the day."

"Here, how about this one? Lots of trees," she pointed out as we drove up to house number forty-five. Or maybe number fifty-seven—I'd lost count.

"That is the ugliest front door I've ever seen. I can't imagine, and don't want to, what the rest must look like. " We never got out of the car.

The next one was run-out-screaming dirty, the next a too-small bedroom and no laundry. I was Goldilocks reincarnated. My next house had to be perfect for me *and* Mr. Bear—no compromises. I was tired of moving.

Somewhere around the seventy-ninth house, she opened the front door. I walked in and, for the first time, didn't say a word. The entry led straight to the big living room with windows at the back of the house, perfectly framing tree after tree in the yard. I went straight-arrow through the house, out the back, off the deck, and counted.

"Thirty-two! Not including a few saplings and a bunch of bushes." I grinned, barely refraining from jumping up and down. We went back in, and I had nothing bad to say, except for the overpowering smell of smoke. I knew this was my house. I called my psychic and asked how much to offer. She suggested ten thousand less than the asking price, which had already been lowered.

I extended an offer for that, despite my realtor's objections. I included a rent-back so they could have the Christmas holidays in their home, and it would give me more time to sell. By February, Pig house had sold, and the kitties and I were moving into my dream-house-in-the-woods in Cedar Park, just outside Austin.

The first thing I did was to again install chicken wire on top of the privacy fence to keep the cats safe. I knew Bella *wouldn't* jump the fence, and Bear *couldn't* climb any of the trees to get to the neighbors, but I was concerned about incoming cats. The fence finished, I called Bella and Bear outside and let them go, with no restraints. They walked around and investigated, used their paws clawing at tree trunks, rolled in the dirt, and chewed the weeds. I was in heaven, watching them in this gift I had bought as much for them as for me.

Alas, the fence addition failed to keep the neighborhood's stray cats out; they simply climbed any of the multiple trees that leaned into our yard and came on over the fence like they were invited. My fearless Bear was uncomfortable with the visitors now. I could only assume that he understood that his physical vulnerability put him at a disadvantage. This meant that Bear's walkies were done only in the back yard with me keeping pace beside him as he hopped after bugs, ch-ch-ch-chattered back at the squirrels, and chewed the grass short—all without the dreaded harness. I knew that, for Bear, it was too little and too late for what he deserved. I was sad that my awareness of the many dangers of letting him wander at will had overruled the desires of my heart to let him be a cat in every sense of the word for almost his whole life. His world had been limited by my fear. Suddenly, that thought shook me—so had mine. I recalled the many times I had taken the safe road instead of the one that tugged at my heart, the things I had wanted to do, but didn't, had clung to that job I hated just for the security.

At the end of our second summer at our house in Bear's Woods, I received a flyer about a class, "Painting from the Soul." I looked at it, thought it looked interesting, but threw the circular away after my old insecurities about my artistic inabilities mocked me.

All my life I'd had moments when I imagined myself contributing wonderful things to society. I could see myself as a singer moving people to tears from the sound of my angelic voice—until I flinched at the off-key sounds I made; as a painter brushing the radiance of the sun or the coolness of water onto a canvas; as a designer cutting stained glass to simulate the way I think the sky of heaven must look, but my fingers were too clumsy. Alas, none of those had ever happened. I had trudged through my life attending to mundane details. I could do none of those wondrous things, not even on a kindergarten level. I had early on given up my dreams of being a creative artist of any kind.

Now, here was a postcard about the painting class. I considered the price, then threw *it* away also—too expensive, and I'd probably just feel frustrated at my inabilities. Then I got an email about the class. I deleted it, getting irritated.

Then I got the *fourth* notice, by email, saying only a couple of spaces were still open. I considered that it might be fun to learn something new, something I might be able to do with an actual teacher, but again decided against it. I didn't understand why I was even thinking about it, and why the announcements seemed to be sticking to me like flypaper.

The Sunday morning of the class, when I woke up I knew I must have been dreaming about being an artist. On her show one day, Oprah had talked about first getting a whisper, then a brick, and then the wall falling down—those words had awakened me. The announcement had shown up not just three, but *four* times. I needed to do something before the house came down.

I made a bargain with myself. If the class was full, that was that; otherwise, I would sign up. And how could it not be full—it started in three hours. I knew that if I got into the class, the picture would be of Bear. I kept seeing different imaginary poses as I dialed the registration number. The tail was important, that glorious flag of a tail. And his originally chartreuse eyes. By the time the phone was answered, I had turned the decision over to the fates.

"Your timing is perfect. There's one space left," said the organizer. "Someone *just* cancelled."

I got there with barely any time to spare, as the introductions were starting, still baffled at all these coincidences.

"I'm Anne, I'm a landscape artist and sell..."

"I'm Matty, and I work in clay."

"I'm Bear's mom. I don't do anything, but he insisted that I be here," I said. It sounded silly, but I really wasn't sure *why* I was there. At the end of the ten introductions, we moved on to the class.

All around the classroom, the instructor had taped large sheets of paper to the wall; acrylic paints and brushes littered long tables in the middle of the room. The instructor's directions consisted of: "Pick a station. Pick a brush and colors that appeal to you. Paint whatever your soul wants you to paint."

Not much instruction—no "hold the brush this way" or "make the strokes this way." *How much was I paying for this experience? And why, again, was I doing it at all? Because I had to.*

I did as told, beginning by mixing black and white to the approximate gray of Bear's coat. I painted quickly, covering the flimsy paper with short, urgent brush strokes, and then, somehow, Bear was on the page. He stood in the most unlikely position that I would ever have imagined using, but his green eyes were front and center, and his tail was a feathery plume, clearly visible. He was bright-eyed, just as he had been on the night of the ferret meeting, and he looked so natural standing there. *However had I done that?*

To finish—a few sparkles in the gray, I decided, so it looked like the sun was shining on the tips of his fur. The brush, seemingly without my direction, painted long streaks of green as a background around Bear while I was trying to figure out what the background should be.

I looked at the page. Of course! Bear would want to be in the grass... how silly of me to try to think that anything else would be right. The painting was done in less than fifteen minutes.

"Is it finished?" asked the instructor, making the rounds. I studied it for a minute. Bear, a white aura surrounding him, stared back at me from a field of green grasses, his green eyes rounded with happiness, ears pitched forward, with slightly crossed eyes and a smudgy nose, compliments of my ineffectiveness as an artist.

"Yes, it's finished," I told her, feeling positive that it was.

It wasn't a good painting, not in any artistic aspect, probably about second grade level. *At the most. If I was a talented child.* It was undeniably Bear though, the first recognizable thing I had ever painted other than house-tree-chimney-smoke-sun things. I knew I'd had very little to do with it. His position on the page was far more artsy and realistic than I could have imagined in my unartistic and uncreative brain, but it was indeed a painting from my soul, a reflection of something I loved dearly.

Chapter 39
LOVE YOU

Cedar Park, Texas. Fall 2007. A few months after painting his masterpiece, I noticed that Bear seemed to be evaporating. He was regal in his posture, head always held high, but his movements were done with the stiffness of the old, the space between his hips now very narrow. He was sixteen years old.

In every other way, though, he was still my wonderful Bear. He loved to annoy me by jumping onto the back of the recliner, then burying his nose in my hair and using his paws to make a rat's nest of it. Somehow, he could still make himself invisible in plain sight, materializing with a smile on his face when I blinked. He could also fold himself up to about half his size to get into a too-small box or hiding place.

He became even more clingy, following me, keeping me in his sight anytime he wasn't sleeping. He still played with his toys, still played with Funnel, but it didn't go as fast or as far across the room. I could sense that everything was more of an effort. His coat now felt thin and straggly when I brushed him.

Then he started throwing up. He had always thrown up hairballs despite hairball remedies, but this was food. His appetite dwindled. Of course, I called Carol and asked her to translate for us.

"Bear, do you know why you're throwing up? He says he needs to go to the vet. He says there is something growing inside him. I'm so sorry."

My heart sank. In all these years, Bear had only asked to go to a vet twice that I could remember, for a kidney infection, and when he had gotten poison from a toad in his eye. Intuitively, I knew this was not going to be another toad or hairball problem. The hairball was inside my throat when I hung up.

The vet did tests and pronounced that Bear was anemic. "There are three possibilities as the cause: loss of blood from surgery or injury, leukemia, or lymphoma. I'll put him on an appetite stimulant and another prescription. We'll watch him for two weeks and see if it resolves spontaneously."

I called a friend and told her what was happening. She responded by giving me a huge gift. She, too, was divorced and had recently lost one of her dogs.

"Let me come over and take some pictures of you and the cats. We who live alone take pictures of our pets, but no one takes pictures of us *with* our pets."

I hadn't thought about it before, but that was so true. Occasionally, dog owners get portraits done, but it's difficult with a cat; I'd had a portrait done with Sami when he was young, and one with Bear ten years before, and even Bear had been unhappy with the experience. The day-to-day interactions are rarely recorded for posterity because the special moments have become mundane after a few years, or we're too busy, and it's difficult to take a self-portrait of a cat and a person at arm's length.

My friend came to the house and devoted over an hour to a photo shoot of the cats with me. Finally, it was obvious that even the attention-hogging Bear had had enough. I treasure what she did for me that day; it was one of the most thoughtful gifts I could remember ever receiving. It had taken an hour, but the last picture she took was the really special one, the photo of Bear lying in a flowerpot full of catnip.

At the end of two weeks, Bear was still throwing up and eating less and less. We went back to the vet. She did a manual exam and then gave me the bad news. He had lymphoma. The nodule was the size of my little finger, situated just below his ribs on his right side. She let me feel it.

"I'm so sorry," she said. "We don't have a viable treatment, especially because of his age."

"Will he suffer much, can he die peacefully at home, or how will I know if it's time to bring him in?"

"He's not suffering at the moment, but he may later, I don't know. He might start having seizures. We can put him to sleep whenever you feel he's ready, or when you are."

During those two weeks of hoping and watching, I had tried to brace myself for the bad news. Now, as I heard the doomsday pronouncement, I took it better than I had hoped. Bear asking to go to the vet had been a very big clue that things were very bad, even though Carol had said he wasn't in pain. I took my baby home.

Bear, who had always enthusiastically eaten anything in his bowl, multiple times a day, now wasn't hungry. I tempted him with everything I could think of: canned cat food, cooked beef, baked salmon, tuna. He would walk eagerly to the bowl, put his nose down, sniff, and then walk away. The next day, I'd try a different food, flavor, or texture. And he'd walk away.

Finally, I remembered baby food—a guaranteed appetite stimulant. He investigated my finger, took a lick, and then backed away. Despite the eight kinds of cat food of every brand and flavor in the bowls strewn about the kitchen, the only thing he wanted now was low sodium chicken broth. The smell seeped out of his pores when I held him, but at least he was getting some nutrition. Every day was a day of indecision. Should I make the appointment? Should I not? How could I let him go? He wasn't ready. I wasn't ready. He was still up and about and checking on things. Was he only hanging on for me? My ability to make any rational decision seemed totally absent. I needed to call Carol again, for translation and support.

"Carol, the vet diagnosed lymphoma. I felt the tumor, and he's not eating."

She checked in with him. "No, he's not well, very weak, but no pain. He wants to eat, but when he smells food he gets nauseous."

"Is he ready to leave?"

There was a slight hesitation, then, "Soon. He says he has good-byes to say yet. He wants to go outside more."

"I'll take him out. Is there anything else he wants?"

Another hesitation. "No, he's OK. He's just disconnecting, saying goodbye, and slowly releasing."

"Tell him how very much he has meant to me, how much he has added to my life, how happy I am that he was with me all these years."

"He knows."

"How will I know when he's ready? I want the decision to be his." I swallowed and swallowed, forcing my voice out, trying to keep the tears away.

"You'll know," she assured me, implying she thought I had much more sensitivity and confidence than I felt.

"Tell him there is one thing I'd like to complain about. He is the *stubbornest* animal I've ever run into!"

"Back at you, he says." She chuckled, and so did I, through my tears.

Carol had been privy to, if not directly involved in, many of the "discussions" between Bear and me when he wanted to do something I didn't want him to do, such as going over the fence. And then there had been that big kitchen table battle so long ago. Sometimes Carol had been our referee, sometimes just an audience when I vented my urge to strangle him.

"Please tell him I love him. He's been a wonderful companion to me. I remember so well when he came to me." I switched and talked directly to him.

"And you and Sami loved each other so. I hope you will find Sami, and tell him I still love him, too.'"

"He says he will. He says you were an *excellent* cat mom!"

"I'm glad. Bear, tell me when its time, when you need to leave, and the doctor will help you. Thank you for finding me and being in my life. I'll never—not ever—forget you, I promise, and I'm sure you, and Sami, and Bella, and I will all be together again some day."

"He loves you. He says again you've been a great mom to them. I've told you many times that all of your cats have *really* loved you. When I tune in to them, I just feel it all over."

Carol had translated our preliminary goodbyes. I was satisfied that I had been able to tell him everything—twice over—that had to be said, and yet if we talked for years I couldn't tell him enough how much I loved him.

We disconnected, but I continued to hold stubborn old Bear close in my arms, breathing in his scent, with a bit of chicken broth aroma clinging to his fur. He was light in my arms, no longer The Tank, but he still fit me like a jigsaw puzzle piece. I looked into his eyes—clear, with no hint of confusion or pain at the moment, just looking back at me lovingly.

"Not today," I told him. "Not today, Bear."

Nor the next day. I held him in my arms like a baby. He looked into my eyes again, pulled himself upward, and licked my nose, his paw cradling my cheek. I thought of all the things that had happened between that first paw pat from Princess, so many years ago, and now.

A few days later, I got the pictures that my friend had taken. How could my Big Bear be so *little*? Just as shocking were the pictures of Bella. I had been so focused on Bear, that I hadn't noticed how scrawny my sweet Bella had gotten, how big her feet seemed to have grown in comparison to her body, how vacant her eyes were beginning to look. *Oh god, please, not her, too.* I couldn't even think of it. I kept swallowing to get my heart out of my throat, and clutched Bear even tighter. *How could I let them go?*

Chapter 40
THE GREATEST GIFT

Cedar Park, Texas. December 28, 2007. Bear would celebrate his seventeenth birthday some time in April if we had guessed his birthday accurately when he came to me. It was already December, but that last trip to the vet had erased my hopes of being able to give him another tuna cake with cream cheese frosting for his next birthday.

I selfishly just couldn't face going into the New Year of 2008 with Bear clinging to life and withering away in front of me like a melting snowman while each day I had to make a decision as to "when." Had the vet been able to assure me that he would go quietly, I would have let him die naturally at home even though I was exhausted from worrying about and caring for him. But she said she could not assure me of that as sometimes at the end there might be pain. I argued back and forth with myself, I dithered, I procrastinated, then finally took out the calendar and called the vet.

"I think it's time to say good-bye. Do you have something still open this week?" I silently begged for a no—then it wouldn't be my decision.

"Tomorrow is the last day we're open until after January 1st. I have a 4:00 appointment with your vet if you want it."

I didn't want it. But I told her yes. It seemed symbolic that his passing should be on one of the last appointments on one of the last days of the year, closure of the year and of his life. That night I slept with Bear in my arms, and he allowed it.

The next day, I got the carrier ready. He seemed interested in what was going on, checking everything out. Then I picked him up and talked to him. "I'm so sorry, my Bear-Cat. We have to go see the vet today. Let's take a look around outside, shall we?" I set him back down on the ground and opened the back door, an invitation to go outside. He walked across the deck, then laid down at the end of it, a sign of how weak he had become. I gathered him up in my arms and took him for a walk.

"Oh, look over here, love, this is the tree with the shaggy bark, the one you like to sharpen your claws on. Here's where you found the tiny red-brown frog that matched the leaf it was sitting on that very first day we moved here, remember? Back here, under these little trees, this is where I've made a home for you, right here where you used to come and lie in the shade on hot summer days."

We visited all the spots, in and out, that had been his favorites. Then I looked at my watch. It was time.

Bear offered no protest as I put him in the carrier after wiping him down with Rescue Remedy. He was quiet in the carrier on the way to the vet for this last time. I glanced at him frequently; he was alert but relaxed. I stuck my finger through the openings in the wire door as I drove, and he nuzzled my finger with his nose.

We had to wait only a few minutes before they put us in the exam room. I opened the carrier and Bear strolled out, then meandered around the room, sniffing everything, tail straight up and slowly waving. He pushed the lace curtain on the door aside and looked back out into the waiting room, showing he was interested in what was going on.

My heart sank. *This was not the right decision!* It couldn't be. He wasn't ready. *I wasn't ready. I could not do this today!* I couldn't do it any day, not ever, I'd take him home and... before I could grab him and bolt, the vet came into the exam room.

I picked Bear up and put him on the table. He stretched out on his side, put his head down, and gave a sigh. He made no attempt to reach out to the vet he liked so much, made no effort to greet her, to smell her and get a pat. He was still, as though any movement was more than he could accomplish. She petted him lovingly throughout the examination and looked deeply into his wide-open eyes.

"Yes. He's ready to leave now." I heard only conviction and finality in her voice.

The tech came in, shaved Bear's paw, then the vet gave him the shot. Bear offered no protest, as though he had used his last bit of energy satisfying his curiosity about the room. I encircled him with my arms, not feeling any movement of any muscle as he quietly slipped away, going one last time over the fence. This time, I knew I would never see him again, that no amount of running frantically through the neighborhood would ever bring him back home to me.

I wondered where he had gone, if Sami had been there to greet him. I wondered if and how Bear might make contact with me. I couldn't believe that he wouldn't, not with the strong bond we'd had. Would I notice? Sami had never come back as far as

I knew, unless my suspicions about the Sami-Bella connection were true. I hoped I would feel Bear in the night sometimes and be reassured that he was all right.

The vet handed me some tissues, wrapped him up in the towel and laid him in the box I had brought. For the second time in my life, I carried a body empty of life out of a vet's office.

It was a revelation to me, the way the "dead" body felt. The transformation was like putting a new, stiff, and starchy shirt into the washer and a few minutes later getting back a limp thing that bore no resemblance to what I had started out with.

I felt relief that it was over, as well as great loss. Once I had made the decision that today was the day we would end our journey, his actual death was more bearable than the thought of it had been all those weeks when I was trying to make the right decision of when to let him go, but it still felt terrible—*I still felt terrible.*

After driving home, I carried him into the house and placed the box gently on the living room floor so Bella would be able to smell him and understand that Bear, as she knew him, was gone. She came quietly over, sniffed, crept closer, sniffed again, then suddenly bolted. She ran over to her favorite chair, tucked herself into a small ball, put her head down, and closed her eyes. I wanted to do the same.

Leaving Bear's pelt there on the floor—that's the way I thought of it now—just a pelt, I went out to finish preparing the grave. No avocado trees for Bear, he would rest under the saplings at the back of the lot. I'd had a friend dig the hole weeks before. Now my Bear would fill that yawning mouth. I lined the grave with a black plastic yard bag, placed a towel on top of it, sprinkled in the offerings of his favorite food that he hadn't been able to eat for weeks. I knew he would be really hungry. I clipped off some green grass, the long stringy kind he liked to chew on. Catnip, of course, he loved catnip, it always made him crazy for a few minutes, and he and Sami would mock fight, then he would fall sound asleep. Though he didn't play with it much anymore, he couldn't leave without Funnel. I mentally went through the list. I put in his collar and tags, but not the halter, not the pink lead—those I would throw away in the next week's garbage.

My copious tears were watering the grave as I did the preparation, and I had to stop several times, take deep breaths, and blink my eyes. I added sprinkles of water to the sprinkle of tears on the ground where Bear would lay. He loved to drink, would stand at his bowl and lap until he got tired, then sit and lap some more. I sometimes wondered why he didn't burst. I didn't want him to be thirsty. Water is very good for cats. He was going over The Rainbow Bridge. I was sure there would be water in the stream. But just in case, I wanted him to have enough.

Then everything was packed in and ready for his journey, one without me, where there would be no harness and lead. If he hadn't already, he would fly over the fence one last time with nothing to hold him back. Returning to the house, I sprayed myself with several doses of Rescue Remedy in the hope that I could stop the tears. It worked within a minute, and I was feeling calmer, calm enough to pick up that gray and white fuzzy body one last time. I was more wistful than upset as I used both arms to pick up his towel-shrouded form and cuddle him, one last time, against me.

I went out the back screen door onto the deck. The sun was shining in that half-hearted way of a warm December day that would end swiftly in less than an hour. As I started toward the far end of the deck, I saw something out of the corner of my eye off to my right, at the top of the side steps. I turned my head slightly, glancing downward, expecting, as I had in the past, that I would see the neighbor's young black and white cat who was fascinated by Bear, though I always scooped Bear up when Fred came into the yard.

There *was* a cat, but it was not the neighbor's tuxedo As I stood there with Bear's limp body in my arms, almost an hour after his death, I found myself staring at Bear at his most striking. He was beautiful! He *glowed*—not in any surrealistic way, just a healthy cat standing in the sunshine, looking *exactly* as he had in the picture he insisted I paint of him. He had the same pose, facing me head on. He had the same bright expression in his eyes as in that painting, the same as the night he'd rushed into the kitchen, trying to get me to follow him out into the moonlight to meet his new ferret friend. His eyes were huge and yes!—chartreuse green again—not Mr. Bear's old golden eyes, but Little Bear's. They were round with excitement now. His tail went straight up to the sky, the hairs electrified with brilliance, waving in the slight breeze and sparkling in the sunshine. He was simply radiating wonder and happiness, more real, more solid, more *Bear*, than the scruffy body I held in my arms. This was Bear in his prime, young, and vibrant, and expectantly waiting to go walkies. I just stood there, so astonished I couldn't make my brain work enough to move toward him.

The picture seared itself into my memory. Then, in the time it took me to inhale sharply, he was gone. No puff of smoke, no foggy aura, no gentle fading, he was simply... gone. Nothing left, just empty space. I was totally unnerved and disbelieving. I stood there, hugging my not-Bear. I finally synchronized my brain and my mouth, calling out—"Bear? *BEARRR!*" But I was too late.

All that was left now was the empty shell in my arms. Bear had disappeared over his last fence, and this time, I knew I wouldn't find him again no matter how hard I looked or how much I wished for it. I just stood for a few minutes, trying to comprehend the incomprehensible.

Finally, I stopped staring at the spot where he had been. I took his wrapped body out into the yard and placed his remains in the grave, then shoveled dirt, leaves, and rocks over the amazingly tiny body. What he had left behind was so small, not like my Mr. Bear at all. I was both crying and smiling. Covering the grave, placing the rocks snugly together to keep any critters out, covering it with brown leaves, I said goodbye. Again.

I hurried to call Carol, to tell her that Bear was gone. I also wanted to tell her of my apparition, my visitation—whatever I should call it, still totally believing and totally disbelieving. Unlike some communicators, she didn't usually work with animals who had crossed over, but I needed reassurance that *I* hadn't crossed the bend while Bear was crossing that last fence. Thankfully, she answered right away.

"Carol, Bear's gone, but you'll never believe what I think just happened. I think I saw him after he was dead. I've never heard of this! I've heard of some paw prints or the outline of a body on a bed, a toy moving by itself—but, but... *Carol!* He was as solid and whole and real as my own hand. I swear, I'm *not* crazy or hallucinating, you know I don't drink or take drugs! He was just so solid! If I had dropped his corpse, I could have reached out and touched *him*." The words rushed out of my mouth; I so needed to get confirmation.

"It's rare, but I *have* heard of it before, but only a few times. It takes an incredible amount of energy for them to be able to materialize like that. You know I've told you many times in our conversations that when I talk to your cats, every time, I can feel how very much they love you. I talk to many pets. Some feel affection for their owners, a lot of them love their caretakers, some could care less if their caretakers disappeared, but yours—yours *adore* you."

I thanked her for reminding me again—she had said that to me, many times, and a part of me had always disbelieved it, but now, with Bear's reappearance, I had no doubt—I really *had* been a good cat-mom.

"I loved him so much, I was totally unprepared for that to happen, especially after Sami who I never saw any sign of again. Well, unless he came back as Bella. I think of Bear as my soul kitty. There was an extra bond with him. I loved them all, in different ways, but he just wormed his way in that very first day when he stood at the neighbor's door and called to me to come back and get him."

"He gave you a big gift," she said, her voice gentle.

"Yes. Leave it to Bear." I snuffled, and blew my nose. "I told you he was the most stubborn cat on the planet, and he said his good-bye on his own terms."

For the next few days, I lived the words "sorrow lay heavy on my heart"—and on my arms, and in my throat. I would be OK for a little while, then I would turn, see his favorite chair, remember he wouldn't be there, and I'd want to collapse to my knees with the pain. I would hear a strange sound and come alert, thinking Bear was playing tricks, doing something he wasn't supposed to because he thought I was preoccupied so he could get away with it. I would be lost in a project, surface back to reality, and immediately feel the pain of loss in my chest even though he had not been in my thoughts a fraction of a second before.

The only thing that eased the pain, that could separate me from this heavy feeling of loss, was another dose of Rescue Remedy that seemed to place a temporary glass shield between me and the emotional pain. I was so glad Bear had shown me how helpful it was.

A week or so later, I got a sympathy card from a friend. The verse was lovely, *"There is no death, only a change of worlds."* Chief Seattle.

With that, I realized just how great this last gift of Bear's really was. He wasn't "dead"—he had just changed worlds. Whether one called it "Heaven" or "Nirvana" or "over the Rainbow Bridge," the one certainty I now knew was that Chief Seattle was a very wise man, because Bear had shown me so.

It comforts me to believe Bear had finished a job he had accepted when he chose to become my cat, my love, my teacher, my guardian. I remembered how Penny had said he had appeared in the neighbor's yard, been there for a couple of days, had been taken away by someone, and then returned to the same place. I think that he must have been trying to find me all along; he had just been one building off course. Knowing that his job with me was now over, he had to hurry on to his next big assignment, just as he had always hurried over the fence to his next adventure.

I've never definitively felt, saw, heard, or experienced Bear again except in the one-way communications with all of the cats that I often practice before I go to sleep at night. I send them my love, and believe sometimes I hear them answering by purring back at me. And each night I promise them again that I will love them always and forever.

Chapter 41
CHILD OF MY HEART

Cedar Park, Texas. May 2008. Once I was no longer totally focused on Bear—his comfort, his care, his feeding, his "needing"—I turned my attention to Bella. When I looked into her eyes, I could see that there was little focus when she looked back at me. She had become very tentative in her movements, searching with a paw in front of her before taking a step. Her hearing had deteriorated to almost nothing. When I wanted her attention I had to reach out and touch, carefully, so as not to startle her. She no longer ran around, no longer showed any interest in even Red Thang.

I was very frustrated. Her body was OK, but all her senses were shutting down. She no longer sang to herself, and my sky-high girl now stayed on the bed, the couch, or the floor. I waited for the feeling that it was time for her to go. She still didn't like to be held, but now she sat beside me for long hours, the only thing that seemed to give her comfort. When the peeing started again, after a two-year absence, I knew the seizure meds which had made such a difference to our quality of living were no longer helping—I was sure she had a brain tumor, and it had grown—it was the only thing that would account for all this shutting down.

We all—myself, the vets—had failed this girl, had failed to understand she was having seizures and not just being uncooperative. Carol had been saying for Bella's whole life with me that she just didn't understand what she was doing wrong. As it had been explained to me at the State Hospital, a person in the middle of the petit mal seizure may wander aimlessly, pick at threads, stare at nothing, but they have no knowledge of what they are doing at the time they are doing it, nor any memory of that time afterward. In retrospect, I was sure the flying at the walls, the screaming, and the peeing were indications of her seizures.

My heart had hurt for her for years. Sunny, who loved cats, had ignored her, the other cats left her alone, visitors barely acknowledged this sweet-natured girl who just wanted to be liked. In my mind, Bear was worth a big deal being made over him. But so was Bella.

Watching her, a shell of my former joyous girl, finally became too painful. Bear had been gone for over a year now, and she had deteriorated until now she was a shell of her former funny, inquisitive, sweet little kitty self. There was little I could do to comfort her now. All I could do was let her go to find her big brother Bear who had watched over her since she came to us (or, I would always wonder, was it possible that "she" would be reunited, or reintegrated with Sami?) It had taken more than a year for Bear to accept her fully, to begin playing and hanging out with her, but it had happened, and after that they were usually together, though never with the closeness that "the boys" had had.

Once again, I carried a cat to the vet, held her in my arms as we waited, and then carried the remains home. I felt she would like it that her bones would be next to Bear's. I hoped that somehow it would comfort her.

I went out to the back fence area and removed the leaves and the rocks that had never once been disturbed since Bear's burial and dug into the earth where I had buried him. Then I stopped, puzzled, and checked the location again.

I *had* to be in the right place—next to that sapling tree, with all those rocks in a pile, right where I had buried him over a year before. But the grave was empty and revealed no trace of that other burial. The towel I had wrapped him in, the black plastic trash bag I had lined the grave with—all were gone, though this was obviously that grave I had buried him in. The warnings about the eons of time needed to dissolve plastic bags rang in my ears, but Bear's plastic bag had definitely disappeared, not a trace left. How could that be? I kept digging, enlarging the hole until I could have buried three cats in it, and still *there was nothing left in it, nothing except one small bone, the size of the flying chicken bones. Every other trace, every bone, hide, hair, toys, even his hard plastic funnel— everything—was gone. How had they dissolved so fast? Or had Bear taken them all with him when he jumped the final fence?* I was baffled.

There was only empty space left in the grave—plenty of room to put in one leftover bone, one dainty kitty and her Red Thang, and the usual blessings—and a very large chunk of my heart. I placed her body where Bear had been, covered her up with another towel and refuse bag to keep the water away—she hated to be wet even more than Bear.

I finally could release her from her long ago promise. "Fly free, Bella, go over the fence and find your big brother Bear so you can watch out for each other." I stood up and imagined I guided her on her way, hoping she could hear the love song in my release as she started her last journey.

Chapter 42
THE FOREVER PROMISE

Central Texas. 2016. Sami, Bella, and especially Bear were the catalysts for huge changes in my understanding and perceptions about everything from expressing gratitude to the idea of life and death itself. They totally changed my attitudes and understanding of animals, of healing, of spirituality, of the connectedness of all things. It was because of the cats that Sunny and Amy came into my life to lead me into the world of alternative healing and the energy of life. Because of all of them, I delved deeply into the mysteries of cat behavior and cat care-taking.

Bear also gave me the greatest revelation—confirmation that there is indeed life after earthly death—and he came back to show me it is beautiful and exciting. There are still mysteries I must unravel, but I have seen the magic and the possibilities. My cats supported me, loved me, and lived with me through the mayhem of a terrorist attack, a mold claim, multiple homes, illnesses, and crazy renters.

Every day my memories of my beloveds keep them alive for me. When I pick up a string from the carpet, or wrap a gift with ribbon, Sami is with me. When I hear the tinkle of wind chimes, I smile, sure Bella is playing with them. Any time I see a privacy fence or the picture of a ferret, it brings again to me the sensation of Bear's excitement as he flew to freedom, and the joy in his communion with his ferret friend. As I amble about on a lonely walk, I look for the leaves, the bugs, and the caterpillars that Bear loved to find on our walkies—I notice them now.

I had heard the stories many times of the earthly visitations of humans and animals who have "crossed over." I had both believed and disbelieved, hopeful that it was true, but doubting that it could be. Bear's lesson to me was, in my mind and soul, confirmation that the spirit does not cease to exist after earthly death. Over the years, I had learned to read his emotions well, and with every piece of hair on his fuzzy body he was telling me at that last visit that everything is OK, there is no reason to be afraid. I know wherever he is, he's happy. I will not be complete again until the day all my kits, past and those now present, are gathered around me, and then I will be in heaven, real or proverbial.

For always, Sami will be my first child, the awakener of my heart and my knowledge of the word motherhood; Bella the direct connection to my own childhood and a rosebud of innocence in my heart. And Bear... *ah, my Bear*. Bear was, is, and will always be both a child of my heart and a part of the very essence of what I understand as my soul.

I had avoided checking in with the Rainbow Bridge kitties through my communicators. I had thought about it, but each time it just didn't feel right. After years of waiting, finally, while writing the final chapters of this book, I made a call.

"Carol, I've never asked before, and I know you don't usually like to work with the Rainbow Bridge kitties, but would you try to check up on them?"

Usually, her communications began almost instantaneously. This time, however, she was quiet for a bit before reporting, "I can't bring in Sami, but Bear is here. Bella is with him."

I would still wonder, always, if Sami and Bella had somehow become one. I hoped so, and hoped that some way Sami and Bear were together forever.

"How are they doing?"

She was again silent for a few more seconds, then said, "He's watching out for Bella, and they are both fine."

I felt a burden of doubt fall off my shoulders. "I'm so glad. One thing more. Tell Bear thanks for his help with his book. And ask him, please... is he happy with it? It's almost finished, and I've worked very hard on preparing his messages to send out to everyone. Oh, and tell him I will need his help telling people about it."

There was another short silence, then she said, "He's not saying anything that I can hear. But I can see his face... and he has a *big* grin on it."

THE END

=^.-.^= =^.-.^= =^.-.^=

PURRFECT THOUGHTS

=^,-,^=

How it is that animals understand things I do not know, but it is certain that they do understand. Perhaps there is a language which is not made of words and everything in the world understands it. Perhaps there is a soul hidden in everything and it can always speak, without even making a sound, to another soul.—Frances Hodgson Burnett

=^,-,^=

The whole problem with the world is that fools and fanatics are always so certain of themselves, and wiser people so full of doubts.—Bertrand Russell

=^,-,^=

"Lots of people talk to animals... Not very many listen though... that's the problem." — Benjamin Hoff, *The Tao of Pooh*

=^,-,^=

"I have lived with several Zen masters -- all of them cats."—Eckhart Tolle, *The Power of Now: A Guide to Spiritual Enlightenment.*

=^,-,^=

"My cat reached out to my soul and gave it whiskers"-- Deanna Chesnut, *Purrs & Promises*

THE ANIMAL COMMUNICATORS OF PURRS & PROMISES

(In order of appearance)

VAL HEART, *The Real Dr. Doolittle* at www.valheart.com, phone 1-210-860-7713, San Antonio, Texas, USA. Val was the first to open the door to Animal Communication for me with her lecture and through personal consults with Sami and Bear. She is founder of the *Heart System* for solving pet problems, hosts the *Animal Talk Coaching Club* and *The Real Dr. Doolittle Podcast Show*, and is an energy healer for pets and people.

JERI RYAN, PH.D., www.assisianimals.org, phone 1-510-532-5800, California, USA. Jeri is a psychotherapist and founder and director of *Assisi International Animal Institute, Inc.*, and an internationally known Animal Communicator. She was my awesome first teacher, gives workshops world-wide and does private consultations.

CAROL WRIGHT, email: wrightcaw@gmail.com, California, USA. Carol has interpreted for me and my animals for over a decade, helping with emotional, behavioral and physical issues. She was featured in *Communicating With Animals: The Spiritual Connection Between People and Animals* by Arthur Myers © 1997.

LETA WORTHINGTON, www.herbsandanimals.com, Santa Fe, New Mexico, USA. Leta sold me herbs for my Sami 25 years ago. She is an Animal Communicator, herbal healer, and gives consults and workshops. Her book, *Learn How to Talk To Animals, A Practical Guide for a Magical Journey*, can be found on Amazon.com

CARLA MEESKE, www.spirithealer.com, email carla@spirithealer.com, Phoenix, Arizona, USA. Animal Communicator and shaman available for personal consults, classes, and retreats. (Not featured in *Purrs & Promises*.)

GENERAL INFORMATION & IMPORTANT LINKS

For more about Deanna, her cats, and her forthcoming books, search: www.dchesnut.com and for Deanna's All-Things-Cat Care blog go to www.purrfecttalker.net.

To learn more about the intuitive language of animal communication, search at your local library or on-line for *Animal Communication Interspecies Communication, and Telepathic Communication.*

For more information, explanations, stories, books, interviews, teleclasses, and a comprehensive listing of Animal Communicators who give classes and/or do consults, see the directory on the website for Penelope Smith, attributed as the grandmother of animal communication: www.animaltalk.net.

Watch animal communication at work, and view Anna Breytenbach's profound video *Communicating with Spirit, the Black Leopard* at www.animalspirit.org/media-articles.

For more about Flower Essences, search: Rescue Remedy, Nelson Bach USA, available at health and natural food stores. There are other Flower Essence companies including companies that do not use alcohol base as their preservatives. Search words: Flower Essences.

The RAINBOW BRIDGE—grief support group for humans grieving the loss of pets and other animals, www.rainbowsbridge.com

A FINAL MEEEOOWWWW
—OUR PLEA—

THE INTERNET brings us face to face with the cruelty, savagery, neglect, abuse, carelessness, and atrocities on how humans are treating the animal species. My greatest respect and admiration go out to those who devote their lives, or parts of their lives for volunteering to help save, or make life easier for the animals of the planet.

In order to do my part, I have written this book with the intention to assist all animal caretakers, rescuers, and others in their relationships with animals. Fifty percent of all proceeds from sales of this book will be donated to an animal charity, set up in an irrevocable trust for perpetuity.

If you can help, Sami, Bear, Bella and I ask, on behalf of all animals, that you consider ways to do so.

1. DONATE. Brother, if you can spare a dime, or a dollar, please do so. That dollar can buy enough cat food to spare a life for another day. Shelters always appreciate donations of food, litter, rags, cleaning products, toys, and beds.
2. VOLUNTEER even for just a few hours. Rescue organizations and shelters always need volunteers for everything from office work, to dog walking, to reading to cats and dogs, and help with adoption events.
3. ELDERLY ASSISTANCE. The elderly often are unable to continue with care for their animals without help. Check Meals on Wheels or organizations for the elderly, churches, and neighbors for how to help feed, clean cat boxes, take the dogs for a walk, so they can keep their beloved animals with them.

4. EDUCATE
    a. Check with teachers, Scout leaders, Sunday school teachers to do special events teaching children how to respect, handle and treat animals for their protection and education.
    b. Read, research, and educate yourself to help others about training cats and making your house safe from any destruction by your companion animals. Every bad behavior has a solution; it is the caretaker's responsibility to educate themselves in order to teach the animal as to what is acceptable. Ask the experts or check the Internet or your library for help. There are hundreds of sites that offer advice on cat and dog health and training. For cats: www.purrfecttalker.net
    c. Learn all about Flower Essences and Animal Communication to aid in training.
5. ADVOCATE for cessation of abuse and ill treatment of animals by by-passing attendance at zoos, "shows", and other entertainments that use animals for entertainment purpose. If there are zoos and aquatic shows, look behind the curtain—research their treatment of the animals in their care.
6. SPAY & NEUTER. Inform friends and acquaintances of these facts: An estimated 70 MILLION animals are homeless in this county and 35 MILLION are euthanized for lack of a home. Stop the slaughter by making sure companion animals are neutered and spayed so that if they become homeless they won't contribute. There are often low cost opportunities available through charity and rescue organizations in many communities.
7. IDENTIFY your animals with a low cost chip implant, then update the registration if you move. Always keep a collar (break away collars only for cats) with ID—get tags made at vet offices or, at the very least, black marker a phone number on the collar itself.
8. DECLAW—NEVER! Don't kid yourself—this is an AMPUTATION of the equivalent from the tips of your fingers and toes to your first knuckle. Imagine yourself waking up and finding that every thing you use to walk, stretch, exercise, cover your feces, and even feed yourself causes extreme pain forever—Veterans with amputations say the pain never goes completely away. And if it hurts to scratch in a litter box, why would a cat continue to do that when there is a nice soft carpet? There are many, many ways to teach your cats not to scratch and not to damage furniture or people, including information on my blog site: www.purrfecttalker.net. For more info on declaw: www.declaw.lisaviolet.com
9. INSIDE/OUTSIDE. I cringe when people assure me their cats are safe outside. Some day, they may leave with the help of the sadistic cat hater in the

neighborhood, by the car that hits them as they chase a butterfly over the fence, by poison from the snake or the neighbors' yard, the raptor from the sky, and infection from a cat bite, or an attack by coyotes or loose dogs, or the kids with arrows and BB guns. For the price of an emergency vet visit, there are many plans for cat enclosures, cat fences, and beautiful "catios" on the internet that keep your yard neat and your cats outside but safe.

10. RELINQUISH THEM if you must, for circumstances beyond your control, but never on Craig's list, or to the first person that comes by. Arrange to relinquish them through charities, contact rescue organizations, check for breed specific rescue organizations, talk to your neighbors. If you are relinquishing a pet to someone, always ask a fee to keep the hoarders, the cat-nappers looking for animals to sell for research, and people out for "amusement" by torturing or maiming to keep them safe.

11. MOVING One of the most often used reasons for getting rid of companion animals is, "I'm moving and there's a no-pet policy." PLEASE, consider carefully. There are lots of places to live, and many DO allow pets with a pet deposit—a deposit that might initially seem prohibitive. But consider your responsibility to this animal who depends on you, and then consider this:

    You found a perfect apartment for about the same rent you have been paying—say $1000/month. You must pay a pet deposit of $500 and you say that is too expensive. If you stay at that apartment for a year, then the pet deposit—which is often fully or partially refunded--- would actually be the equivalent of adding $42 per month to your rent, a lot less than paying for cable, or even a single family meal at a restaurant.

12. RESPECT ALL LIFE. Keep all promises. Show mercy. Report suspected neglect, abuse, hoarding, animals left in hot cars, dog fighting, puppy mills and bad breeders.

    NOTE: THE FBIA has reclassified animal abuse as a felony. This will begin in 2016 and it means that the worst cat abuse cases will be prosecuted the same as murder, burglary, and arson.

=^.-.^=

Thanks for Reading!

SAMI   BEAR   BELLA

Made in the USA
San Bernardino, CA
14 October 2016